MW00812594

HOUSING, CLASS AND GENDER IN MODERN BRITISH WRITING, 1880–2012

Domestic interiors and housing environments have historically been portrayed as a framing device for the representation of individuals and social groups. Drawing together a wide and eclectic collection of well-known, and less familiar, works by writers including Charles Booth, Octavia Hill, James Joyce, Pat O'Mara, Rose Macaulay, Patrick Hamilton, Sam Selvon, Sarah Waters, Lynsey Hanley and Andrea Levy, the author reflects upon and challenges various myths and truisms of 'home' through an analysis of four distinct British settings: slums, boarding houses, working-class childhood homes and housing estates. Her exploration of works of social investigation, fiction and life writing leads to an intricate stock of housing tales that are inherited, shifting and always revealing about the culture of our times. This book seeks to demonstrate how depictions of domestic space – in literature, history and other cultural forms – tell powerful and unexpected stories of class, gender, social belonging and exclusion.

EMILY CUMING is Research Fellow in the School of English at the University of Leeds.

HOUSING, CLASS AND GENDER IN MODERN BRITISH WRITING, 1880–2012

EMILY CUMING

University of Leeds

CAMBRIDGE
UNIVERSITY PRESS

CAMBRIDGE
UNIVERSITY PRESS

One Liberty Plaza, 20th Floor, New York NY 10006, USA

Cambridge University Press is part of the University of Cambridge.

It furthers the University's mission by disseminating knowledge in the pursuit of
education, learning, and research at the highest international levels of excellence.

www.cambridge.org
Information on this title: www.cambridge.org/9781107150188

© Emily Cuming 2016

First published 2016

Printed in the United States of America by Sheridan Books, Inc.

A catalogue record for this publication is available from the British Library.

Library of Congress Cataloging-in-Publication Data
Names: Cuming, Emily, author.
Title: Housing, class and gender in modern British writing, 1880–2012 / Emily Cuming.
Description: New York : Cambridge University Press, 2016.
Identifiers: LCCN 2016011214 | ISBN 9781107150188 (Hardback)
Subjects: LCSH: English literature–20th century–History and criticism. | Home in literature. |
Dwellings in literature. | Gender identity in literature. | Identity (Psychology) in literature. | Social
classes in literature. | BISAC: LITERARY CRITICISM / European / English, Irish, Scottish, Welsh.
Classification: LCC PR478.H64 C86 2016 | DDC 820.9/355–dc23 LC record available at
https://lccn.loc.gov/2016011214

ISBN 978-1-107-15018-8 Hardback

For my parents
Geneviève and Michael

Contents

Figures

Acknowledgements

I am very grateful to my editor at Cambridge University Press, Ray Ryan, for his encouraging support for this book from an early stage; also to Rachel Cox and Joshua Penney for their help with the preparation of the manuscript. Many thanks also to Tony Crowley, Nicholas Reeves and Paul Young, who generously took the time to read entire drafts of the manuscript, and to the two anonymous Cambridge University Press readers whose incisive and detailed comments were invaluable.

An earlier version of parts of Chapter 1 appeared as '"Home is home be it never so homely": Reading Mid-Victorian Slum Interiors', *Journal of Victorian Culture* 18:3 (2013), 368–86, copyright © Leeds Trinity and All Saints College, reprinted by permission of Taylor and Francis Limited, www.tandfonline.com, on behalf of Leeds Trinity and All Saints College; and an earlier version of sections of Chapter 4 appeared as 'Private Lives, Social Housing: Female Coming-of-Age Stories on the British Council Estate', *Contemporary Women's Writing* 7:3 (2013), 328–45, reprinted by permission of Oxford University Press. Thanks are due to Nuffield College Library and Morley College Gallery, which kindly provided images which appear in this book, and to Bloodaxe Books for permission to reproduce a line from Bernardine Evaristo, *Lara*, new ed. (Tarset: Bloodaxe, 2009).

I am indebted to Terry Eagleton, who supervised my PhD thesis on Irish life writing in 2002–06 and whose work has profoundly influenced me. My thanks also to colleagues, friends and teachers who have inspired and supported me in a multitude of ways: Pamela Bickley, Jane Chin Davidson, Stephanie Hare, Gail Hershatter, Ken Hirschkop, Hao Huang, Grace Laurencin, Christine Llewelyn, Becky Munford, Dion Scott-Kakures, Liane Tanguay, Nicole Thiara, Sheila Walker and Paul Young. I would also like to pay special tribute to the Humanities Major students at Scripps College, who took my 'Interiors' and 'Writing Culture' courses between 2011–13, for their brilliant contributions and enthusiasm.

I am very grateful to the School of English at the University of Leeds for providing me with a Postdoctoral Fellowship which enabled me to complete this work and to my colleagues for their support. In particular, thanks to Bridget Bennett, Richard Brown, Sam Durrant, Tracy Hargreaves, John McLeod, Katy Mullin, Francis O'Gorman, Jane Rickard, Jane Taylor and John Whale. Many thanks also to the members of the editorial board of *Key Words* for warmly welcoming me into the ranks.

Thank you to my friends Laura Kennedy, Esther Norman, Caroline Parry and Becky Reeves; and to friends in the US, Fazia Aitel, Teresa Delfín, Susan Kim, Lisa Roy and Laura, again, who helped to make bringing up young children a long way from home and family so much fun. I am very grateful for the love and support of my family, particularly to my brother Robert as well as to the extended Bonnavaud, Cuming and Crowley families. This book is dedicated to my parents, for everything, with much love. Thank you to my children Joseph and Louise, for the happiness and delight they have brought and the new meaning they give to everything. Lastly, my deep thanks and love go to Tony for his partnership and support over many years. As well as pointing in me in the direction of many a fascinating etymology, he has tirelessly read and commented on countless drafts of this work, inspired me with his lucidity, rigour and commitment as a writer, and encouraged me to find my own writing voice and to see this book through to the end.

Introduction

Home. I searched but could not find myself.
–Bernardine Evaristo, *Lara*, new ed.
(Tarset: Bloodaxe, 2009), p. 123

i Moving away from home

This is a book about the representations of the relations between housing, interiors and forms of self and collective identity. It addresses how accounts which frame individuals within domestic space articulate intricate stories of class, gender, social belonging and exclusion. More broadly, this study aims to reflect upon and challenge various domestic myths and truisms through an analysis of particular residential settings that have often been deemed marginal or peripheral to dominant images of home. Thus against idealised or abstract notions of home, my book analyses and historicises representations of four distinct British domestic settings in literature and non-fiction from the nineteenth century to the present: slums, boarding houses, mid-century working-class childhood homes and council housing estates. But rather than seeking simply to add more marginalised residential forms to the academic record, this book shows how attention to these contexts and locations might present significant alternative ways of reading and thinking about the meanings of housing environments and culture more generally. For as I will argue, domestic spaces that do not form part of a hegemonic narrative of home not only force a reconsideration of lofty pronouncements about dwelling and being, but are also key sites through which to re-evaluate conventional ways of linking interiors, housing and identity.

This study therefore aims to shift attention away from an insistence on the general importance of home and many of the assumptions that this ubiquitous term implies. For in popular and academic discourse, home is often posited as a rooted place of belonging, a transcendent signifier which cuts across cultures and identities, or a privileged location through

I

which models of selfhood are found or forged. Invocations of home can all too often be predicated upon narrow models of housing: the self-contained home of one family, as opposed to multiple occupancy; home ownership rather than renting; the house as a site of leisure or the expression of personality rather than a workplace. In addition, imaginings and analyses of home are frequently governed by an ideological framework which posits an implicit or explicit association between place of residence and a sense of self. So while studies of home have radically expanded in recent years to encompass non-normative domestic spaces (including attention to the institutional domesticity of asylums, prisons and missionary settlements), traditional and even conservative ideas surrounding the function of the dwelling continue to hold sway. In other words, the locations of the domestic within studies of home have shifted, but the underlying tenets which privilege forms of bourgeois interiority often remain in place.

My concern is with a multifaceted and often problematic idea that exists in cultural descriptions of domestic space, specifically the notion that there is a steadfast and evident correspondence between self-identity and the interior – or between home ownership and self-possession. The analysis in this book therefore constitutes an attempt to move the focus away from discussions of the interior that are (consciously or not) based on a tenacious conception of bourgeois interiority. For that very notion, in which the individual's real self is to be found 'at home', is founded on a spatial model which privileges the idea that essential truths lie at the heart – or hearth – of some kind of interior. It follows that while this book is concerned with a variety of dwellings, it challenges the long-standing ideological tenet that truth lies 'within' and argues that there is much more at stake than narratives of self-identity in descriptions of living spaces.

Throughout this work, my intention is to extend the range of housing environments that are deemed to be significant or of cultural and aesthetic value and to reframe approaches to the interior more generally. By moving away from home and 'insidedness' as a locus for the private individual surrounded by a repository of signifying objects, I emphasise the significance of the social interior and, more broadly, the sociality of domestic space. This is achieved through a consideration of three connected topics: the idea of housing in relation to more expansive concepts of interiority (including collective networks of relations which extend beyond those of the nuclear family); the interior as a part of a wider public world in its constitution and function; and the social and ideological nature of the particular narratives and forms through which cultural images of domestic space are represented.

My emphasis on private homes as forms of social space is based on the recognition that the domestic interior, as a material object and discursive construct, is fundamentally shaped by economic and class relations. For as the sociologist Paul Harrison puts it: 'A house is not merely a physical entity. It is the product of social relations, of builder and buyer, of landlord and tenant, of successive generations of inhabitants and owners with particular incomes. The occupants are an inseparable part of the story'.[1] In this respect, the term 'housing' can serve as an important supplement to conventional ways of imagining home and interiors. For while 'home' and 'interior' are firmly rooted in literary and cultural discourse, 'housing' is a word which is more frequently encountered in the disciplines of the social sciences and often has political associations in public discourse. But as several recent studies have shown, the idea of housing can provide suggestive and profitable ways of thinking about the role of domesticity in cultural texts.[2] In this regard, Matthew Taunton notes that 'housing is one of the key mechanisms by which economic relations are transformed into lived experience and cultural practice'.[3]

Moreover, as a collective noun, the word 'housing' itself underscores the way in which home is as much about social relations as it is about the self, emphasising the sense of people living cheek by jowl rather than in detached seclusion. Indeed, the term is commonly used in social or political discourse to denote *other* people's places of residence; we talk about 'housing allocation', a group's 'housing needs' or, indeed, a 'housing crisis'. Housing, unlike the idea of home, is thus not primarily bound up with notions of self-identity, affect and comfortable seclusion. A distinct practicality underscores the word because as the historian John Turner writes, 'housing' in English can function as a noun or a verb (the gerund, 'housing', specifically denotes the act of putting people into homes).[4] Thus at a semantic level, 'housing' highlights a social process and signals complex issues of agency and power within the very language used to describe where people live. The sense of transition and movement in the word

---

[1] Paul Harrison, *Inside the Inner City: Life Under the Cutting Edge* (London: Penguin, 1985), p. 192.
[2] See, for example, Peter King's 'The Room to Panic: An Example of Film Criticism and Housing Research', *Housing, Theory and Society* 21:1 (2004), 27–35, and Matthew Taunton, *Fictions of the City: Class, Culture and Mass Housing in London and Paris* (Basingstoke: Palgrave Macmillan, 2009).
[3] Taunton, *Fictions of the City*, p. 2.
[4] John F. C. Turner, 'Housing as a Verb', in John F. C. Turner and Robert Fichter (eds.), *Freedom to Build: Dweller Control of the Housing Process* (New York: Collier Macmillan, 1972), p. 151.

further establishes the way in which for many people, domesticity has been and is about flux rather than rootedness: from the dislocations of migrancy, to the trauma of eviction, to the insecurity of tenancy in a private rental market. Summoning images of bureaucracy and welfare rather than private life and homeliness, 'housing' does not have the cultural capital of the word 'property' or the rich symbolism of 'home'.[5] But this is not necessarily to its detriment. To use housing as a lens through which to read the domestic in literary and social documents can perhaps offer a more historically based and materialist perspective which profitably strips back some of the veneer of that talismanic word and idea 'home'. Housing, in this sense, might function rhetorically as a counter to home and its ideological accoutrements of belonging, identity, the nuclear family, nostalgia and the imagination.

An attention to housing thus necessarily brings with it a closer consideration of the economic and class relations of domestic space – aspects that are often excluded from invocations of home. For the history of housing reform and planning in Britain, from nineteenth-century Victorian liberalism to the neoliberal discourse of home ownership, is explicitly a story about money, the British class system and the social attitudes that accompany it. The protracted reports into slum dwellings in Victorian Britain, for example, are underpinned by nineteenth-century constructions of the 'deserving' and 'undeserving' poor. And in the late twentieth century, Margaret Thatcher's notorious Right to Buy policy, allowing council tenants to purchase their own homes, was a key element in the attack on a fundamental form of working-class life and served to propagate the neoliberal doctrine of property ownership as a form of social mobility. Since the 2008 crash, housing, homes and their relationship to ideas of class, social mobility, well-being and forms of migration have been at the forefront of social and political debates. Indeed the issue of housing is arguably one of the key domestic political issues of our times; as Ben Chu puts it: 'Britain has a nightmare, and its name is housing'.[6] The singular noun phrase, 'housing crisis', nevertheless elides a plethora of interlinked complications related to shelter in twenty-first-century Britain: the shortage of social housing caused by a failure to build a sufficient number of new homes; the deregulation of the rental market sector; house price inflation;

---

[5] Anna Minton notes that housing 'is not a sexy subject. ... "Property", on the other hand, has spawned supplements filled to bursting and countless television programmes'; *Ground Control: Fear and Happiness in the Twenty-First-Century City* (London: Penguin, 2009), p. 113.

[6] Ben Chu, *The Independent*, 9 February 2014, www.independent.co.uk/property/house-and-home/property/britain-is-suffering-from-a-housing-crisis–who-is-to-blame-and-how-can-we-fix-it-9113329.html.

a lack of affordable homes (particularly in London and the South East); cuts to welfare benefits and their impact upon the affordability of social rents; the effects of poverty and poor housing on physical and mental health. The problem, as James Meek notes in his searing analysis of the housing question(s), is 'Where will we live?'[7] As the title of his essay implies, the crisis is collective, if not immediately for those who currently reap the benefits of consecutive housing 'bubbles', then certainly for future generations. Housing questions are therefore always a product of their time – ones which develop according to variations in social policy and political agendas as well as changing fashions and tastes.

The historical range of this book, which broadly moves from mid-Victorian liberalism to post-Thatcherite neoliberalism, is crucial in providing a critical framework which establishes the historicity of particular discourses of interiors and housing in British cultural and social life. Through case studies of housing environments that exist and form part of a cultural imaginary, this book encompasses key historical moments which include Victorian reformism and philanthropy, the restructuring of Britain after two world wars, the arrival of the *Empire Windrush*, the Butler Education Act and the Right to Buy policy. It is not my aim, however, to provide a comprehensive overview of writings on interiors and housing over a period which encompasses such profound social change, and this book does not set out to provide an exhaustive historical narrative.[8] A broad historical scope is nevertheless key to this study's intention to examine a number of significant historical and cultural developments in forms of domestic ideology.

ii   Traces and imprints: The ideology and iconography of the bourgeois interior

In order to mount an analysis which examines apparently deviant or non-normative forms of domestic dwelling spaces, it is useful to set out briefly the constitution of the dominant model from which these 'other' dwellings

---

[7] James Meek, 'Where Will We Live?', *London Review of Books* 36:1 (2014), www.lrb.co.uk/v36/n01/james-meek/where-will-we-live.

[8] Existing analyses of literary representations of working-class domestic space include Carolyn Steedman, 'What a Rag Rug Means', in Inga Bryden and Janet Floyd (eds.), *Domestic Space: Reading the Nineteenth-Century Interior* (Manchester: Manchester University Press, 1999), pp. 18–39; Philippa Tristam, 'Dorothea's Cottages: The Houses of the Poor', in *Living Space in Fact and Fiction* (London: Routledge, 1989), pp. 66–115; and Nicola Wilson, *Home in Working-Class British Writing* (Farnham: Ashgate, 2015), which was published as this book went to press.

might be seen to depart. As a number of important critical studies have documented, the regulative and hegemonic ideology of domesticity was institutionalised in the Victorian period.[9] Rather than summarising this well-traversed terrain, I will examine one important aspect of the so-called Victorian 'cult of domesticity' – namely, the ideology and 'symbolic power' of the interior.[10] For critics have shown that in the nineteenth-century, revelations of selfhood – or interiority – were often crucially located at home, along with the concomitant idea that the self could be exhibited and 'read' as a form of domestic display. But I argue that the after-effects of this particular ideological construction have perhaps been far more long-lasting than other aspects of Victorian domesticity. For although the modernist rejection of the Victorian interior – of its apparently stifling, fussy, ornamental finishes – was deemed to be revolutionary in terms of style, it perhaps differed rather less in terms of the content of the domestic imaginary itself. In other words, interiority may have looked different across the course of the twentieth century, as elaborate mouldings and cornices became firmly *démodé*, yet the idea of the interior as signifying individuality and privacy, and the belief that we are bound up with our rooms in necessarily meaningful ways, have never quite gone out of fashion.

The notion that interior domestic space reflects and expresses the life of its occupant is an enduring cultural trope, as evinced by its recurrence in the pages of the British novel. Classic examples are the revelation of Mr Darcy's true nature through the perfectly proportioned rooms at Pemberley; Miss Havisham's decaying dressing room in Satis House; and the enduring traces of Rebecca's presence that suffuse the spaces of Manderley. In these instances, the dwelling place, with its panoply of signifying objects, is constructed as a projection and an extension of the proprietor or inhabitant: interior space is literally 'full of character'. These literary examples support the theory that posits a link between ideas of privacy, individualism, domestic space and the 'rise of the novel'. Chiara Briganti and Kathy Mezei, for example, have traced a literary tradition in

---

[9] See, for example, Leonore Davidoff and Catherine Hall, *Family Fortunes: Men and Women of the English Middle Class, 1780–1850* (Chicago: University of Chicago Press, 1987); Anne McClintock, *Imperial Leather: Race, Gender and Sexuality in the Colonial Contest* (New York: Routledge, 1995); Jane Hamlett, *Material Relations: Domestic Interiors and Middle-Class Families in England, 1850–1910* (Manchester: Manchester University Press, 2010).

[10] See Pierre Bourdieu's discussion of the 'performative discourse' of symbolic power as 'the power to make things with words' in 'Social Space and Symbolic Power', *Sociological Theory* 7:1 (1989), 14–25 (23).

which 'novels *and* houses furnish a dwelling place – a spatial construct – that invites the exploration and expression of private and intimate relations and thoughts'.[11] The correlation between the words 'interior' (a spatial setting) and the recorded use of 'interiority' (denoting 'inwardness' or 'inner character or nature') in 1701 also seems to bolster the idea that a cultural shift towards privatisation, reflected and produced in the modern form of the novel, aligned images of interiors with individual identity.[12] Briganti and Mezei reaffirm this association by pointing to the coalescence of terms used to describe literature and domestic architecture ('structure, aspect, outlook, character, interior, content … liminal, threshold, entry point, style, perspective').[13] Indeed, according to Diana Fuss, this process of 'interiorization' gathered pace in the Victorian period: 'The interior, defined in the early modern period as a public space, becomes in the nineteenth century a locus of privacy, a home theatre for the production of a new inward-looking subject'.[14]

The idea of domestic space as a crucial framing device for the modern individual is also key to the writings of two of the most commonly cited theorists of the interior: Walter Benjamin and Gaston Bachelard.[15] Bachelard's phenomenological study *The Poetics of Space* presents an image of dwelling in its most eulogised and lyrical form. The house, according to Bachelard, is a space of origination, unity and permanence: 'Without it, man would be a dispersed being. … It is body and soul. It is the human being's first world. Before he is "cast into the world," as claimed by certain hasty metaphysics, man is laid in the cradle of the house'.[16] According to this account, the conception of the house lies outside history, functioning

[11] Chiara Briganti and Kathy Mezei, 'Reading the House: A Literary Perspective', *Signs* 27:3 (2002), 839. For other studies that posit a connection between the increasing privatisation of bourgeois identity and the centrality of representations of domestic space and houses in literature and art, see: Tristam, *Living Space*; Charles Rice, 'Rethinking Histories of the Interior', *The Journal of Architecture* 9:3 (2004) 275–87; Victoria Rosner, *Modernism and the Architecture of Private Life* (New York: Columbia University Press, 2008).

[12] Charlotte Grant provides a useful history of the changing senses of the term 'interior' in 'Reading the House of Fiction: From Object to Interior, 1720–1920', *Home Cultures* 2:3 (2005), 233–50.

[13] Chiara Briganti and Kathy Mezei (eds.), *The Domestic Space Reader* (Toronto: University of Toronto Press, 2012), p. 321.

[14] Diana Fuss, *The Sense of an Interior: Four Writers and the Rooms That Shaped Them* (New York: Routledge, 2004), p. 9.

[15] See Walter Benjamin, 'Louis-Philippe or the Interior', *Charles Baudelaire: A Lyric Poet in the Era of High Capitalism*, Harry Zohn (trans.), (London: Verso, 1983), pp. 167–69; Walter Benjamin, 'I [The Interior, The Trace]', in Rolf Tiedemann (ed.), *The Arcades Project*, Howard Eiland and Kevin McLaughlin (trans.), (Cambridge: Belknap, 2002), pp. 212–27; Gaston Bachelard, *The Poetics of Space*, Maria Jolas (trans.), (Boston: Beacon, 1994).

[16] Bachelard, *Poetics*, p. 7.

as a prelapsarian site which pre-exists the moment that the individual is
'cast into the world' and thereby becomes a social being. Through the
analogy of the home as a type of 'cradle' or 'womb', Bachelard insists upon
the existence of an intimate, timeless and universal connection between
self and home:

> But over and beyond our memories, the house we were born in is physically
> inscribed in us. It is a group of organic habits. After twenty years, in spite of
> all the other anonymous stairways, we would recapture the reflexes of the
> 'first stairway,' we would not stumble on that rather high step. The house's
> entire being would open up, faithful to our own being. We would push the
> door that creaks with the same gesture, we would find our way in the dark
> to the distant attic. The feel of the tiniest latch has remained in our hands.[17]

Needless to say, there have been many challenges to Bachelard's evocation
of home as a cloistered, nurturing place of wonder, intimacy and protection.[18] Yet despite the evident problems with Bachelard's class-blind,
universalising and often sentimental theorisation of home, many critical
essays and studies of home return to this particular work. I would suggest
that it is perhaps the tone and style of *The Poetics of Space*, encapsulated by
the passage above, which accounts for its tenacious presence within discourses of home across academic disciplines. For the idea that home and
self are innately and timelessly bound together coheres around a seductive
and compelling form of rhetoric: one which uses the language of univer-
sality to conceal its social and historical specificity. Indeed Bachelard's
Poetics does not just describe the apparent allure of home, it enacts it.

Benjamin also conceived of the 'age-old – perhaps eternal' image of the
dwelling as a protective space for the individual, evoking the idea of the
'maternal womb' and the 'shell' as original forms of human abode.[19] But
for the nineteenth-century bourgeois citizen, Benjamin argued, the need
for 'dwelling in its most extreme form' had become a type of addiction,
buffering the bourgeois citizen against the shocks and estrangement of
modernity.[20] Thus in the section or convolute of *The Arcades Project*
entitled 'The Interior, The Trace', the domestic interior is presented as a
space in which an array of objects is designed to produce an effect of
privacy and security. For Benjamin, the interior serves as the location in

---

[17] Bachelard, *Poetics*, pp. 14–15.
[18] See, for example, the introduction and essays contained in Gerry Smyth and Jo Croft (eds.), *Our House: The Representation of Domestic Space in Modern Culture* (Amsterdam: Rodopi, 2006), and King's 'The Room to Panic'.
[19] Benjamin, 'I [The Interior, The Trace]', p. 220.
[20] Benjamin, 'I [The Interior, The Trace]', p. 220.

which the bourgeoisie is comforted and estranged by an assortment of fetishised commodities and objects. For as Benjamin noted, 'the private citizen who in the office took reality into account, required of the interior that it should support him in his illusions'.[21] Thus whereas for Bachelard the original house is somehow 'physically inscribed' within the individual for all time, Benjamin emphasises the reverse: the domestic interior as a type of canvas on which can be found the traces of human inhabitation. Indeed, the 'fit' operates in such a way that the individual is integrated – almost rendered into an object – within domestic space. In this way, he observes that the nineteenth century

> conceived the residence as a receptacle for the person, and it encased him with all his appurtenances so deeply in the dwelling's interior that one might be reminded of the inside of a compass case, where the instrument with all its accessories lies embedded in deep, usually violet folds of velvet. What didn't the nineteenth century invent some sort of casing for! Pocket watches, slippers, egg cups, thermometers, playing cards – and, in lieu of cases, there were jackets, carpets, wrappers, and covers.[22]

Epitomised by the decorative fabric 'plush' (which Benjamin describes as 'the material in which traces are left especially easily'), the classic bourgeois dwelling serves to encase and record human imprints in a strange, lingering display of private life.[23]

More recently, Diana Fuss' fascinating and moving exploration of interiority in the context of the rooms inhabited by four writers and thinkers – Emily Dickinson, Sigmund Freud, Helen Keller and Marcel Proust – brings together the model of reciprocity between self and interior and tropes of the mould, imprint and trace. Her aim in *The Sense of an Interior: Four Writers and the Rooms That Shaped Them* (2004) is to investigate precisely the 'houses that sheltered and shaped the imagination of writers' or how spaces 'mold the interior lives of the writers who inhabit them'.[24] But while ascribing to rooms a type of animate quality or agency, Fuss' methodology is also underpinned by the idea, posited by Benjamin, that the individual leaves his or her 'trace' or 'imprint' within the domestic interior: that rooms, in other words, are a sensitive medium that express something meaningful about the lives of the individuals who reside within them. The cultural mythology of the writer's room thereby functions as the epitome of the posited alliance between interior space, the individual subject and creativity. Fuss' approach is certainly illuminating as a way

---

[21] Benjamin, 'The Interior', p. 167.   [22] Benjamin, 'I [The Interior, The Trace]', pp. 220–21.
[23] Benjamin, 'I [The Interior, The Trace]', p. 222.   [24] Fuss, *Sense of an Interior*, pp. 1, 4.

of understanding these specific writers and individuals within their object-world environments. But the method itself is premised on and therefore reiterates the link between an intimate, sensory alliance between individuals and interiors which is, as I have argued, a specific aspect of bourgeois ideology.

The poetics of the bourgeois interior is relevant and illuminating with regard to particular socio-economic spaces, or the rooms of certain individuals at particular points in history. And yet like all ideologies, its effect has been to produce a type of naturalised imaginary of home. Drawing on comments by Karl Marx on ideology, Stuart Hall notes that

> ideology works because it appears to ground itself in the mere surface appearance of things. In doing so, it represses any recognition of the contingency of the historical conditions on which all social relations depend. It represents them, instead, as outside of history: unchangeable, inevitable and natural.[25]

This historicising function of ideology might explain why students in the classroom nod in recognition at Bachelard's evocations of garrets and cellars, lavender-scented wardrobes and small caskets (features with which they may well be entirely unfamiliar in reality). This and the fact that a significant trend in popular culture, embodied in countless property programmes and real estate pitches, conveys the standard assumption that self-identity is reinforced and expressed through the image of the home. It appears, as Julia Prewitt Brown argues, that while the former property-owning gentry, or 'ruling class', may now have been dispersed into more free-flowing forms of global capitalism, the 'mythology of bourgeois domesticity is with us still'.[26] From Victorian liberalism, which promoted the idea of home as a site for the formation of character, to neoliberal notions that home ownership is a form of citizenship and full subjecthood, it is clear that a wide range of discursive practices have provided precisely a stock of images, motifs and premises to furnish the apparently natural idea that the 'real self' is to be found indoors. Thus it is clear that the ideology of home is iterated not only in the particular values ascribed to descriptions or representations of models of domestic life or interiors, but in the very discourse which expresses, in Hall's turn of phrase, 'a recognition of the things we already knew': namely, that domestic residence is central to the formation and display of self-identity.[27]

[25] Stuart Hall, 'The Rediscovery of "Ideology": Return of the Repressed in Media Studies', in Michael Gurevitch et al. (eds.), *Culture, Society and the Media* (London: Methuen, 1982), p. 76.
[26] Julia Prewitt Brown, *The Bourgeois Interior* (Charlottesville: University of Virginia Press, 2008), p. 6.
[27] Hall, 'The Rediscovery of "Ideology"', p. 75.

This contingency is exposed to some extent by contrasting the theoretical approach to the home found in Bachelard, Benjamin and Fuss to that of the American cultural theorist bell hooks. In a powerful passage from *Where We Stand: Class Matters*, hooks draws upon a memory of her own childhood home:

> Our first house, a rental home, had three bedrooms. It was a concrete block house that had been built as a dwelling for working men who came briefly to this secluded site to search the ground for oil. There were few windows. Dark and cool like a cave, it was a house without memory or history. We did not leave our imprint there. The concrete was too solid to be moved by the details of a couple with three small children and more on the way, trying to create their first home. . . . We tried to give this house memories, but it refused to contain them.[28]

The primacy and symbolism of the 'first house' is immediately qualified here by the fact that it is an impermanent rental property, designed for male Kentucky oil drillers rather than a place of family ownership. Instead of memorable nooks and crannies, hooks notes merely its forgettable shape and materials; in her description, the home seems cave-like in a literal rather than a metaphysical sense. Crucially, hooks refuses to read this house as a setting or canvas that bears the traces of the occupant family, insisting 'we did not leave our imprint there'. The domestic interior of her childhood did not cosset or reinforce any sense of self. In fact, she recalls in all too literal terms how the unforgiving concrete interior could knock a child out if they fell out of bed. 'I fell once', she remarks caustically, adding: 'That's my imprint: the memory that will not let me forget this house even though we did not live there long'.[29] Thus in material and figurative terms, hooks' description resists and undermines conventional notions that posit the idea of the domestic interior as a space that necessarily reflects, or is in some sense fashioned by, its occupant.

But although hooks insists that this rudimentary shelter was a poor and ineffective memory site for her family's history, her description of the home is nevertheless revealing in its own way. It has important things to say, for example, about the relations between place of residence and work, the idea of the dwelling as a site of temporary accommodation in specific social contexts, and the ways in which class and social exclusion are given spatial form. In this particular context, the approach to the interior – indeed, the very idea of interiority – has to be reconfigured since this

[28] bell hooks, *Where We Stand: Class Matters* (New York: Routledge, 2000), pp. 10–11.
[29] hooks, *Where We Stand*, p. 11.

narrative of dwelling does not conform to familiar images of the memory space of a childhood home.

hooks' approach informs my own consideration of representations of interiors and housing space within a British cultural context, particularly in relation to my concern with the social implications of the domestic beyond the culturally dominant middle-class home or the enduring formulation of the bourgeois interior. Thus in the chapters that follow, I show how domestic interiors and housing environments can be interpreted as telling particular stories about the people who live in them, but how they also need to be understood as paradoxical and often opaque sites which are determined by economic specificities and social circumstance. Indeed, as will become clear, many of the texts demand an approach which recognises the way in which domestic scenes are often about *mis*representation and *not* telling.

iii   From the bourgeois interior to social housing

The discussion of the sociality of the interior necessarily requires some consideration of the idea of public and private spheres as they relate to housing. My work draws on feminist approaches to domestic space which have transformed knowledge in this area. Indeed, the putative divide between public and private realms – including the idea of the domestic interior as a private space, set apart from an external social world and existing only on the fringes of modernity – has been effectively challenged over the past decades. Feminist scholarship has clearly demonstrated the way in which, far from being a feminised zone or a separate sphere of seclusion, the domestic interior and the home are illuminating sites for understanding historical change and the condi-tions of modern life for women as well as men. Private life, recent studies have revealed, can paradoxically be conceived as a social and material affair, imagined in collective ways in different historical periods, demanding a body of workers and a host of devices and resources in order to furnish, service and maintain it. The spaces of home, according to this understanding, are always shaped by the world beyond its architectural borders and are, in and of themselves, sites of social production and exchange.

In their respective accounts of the Georgian home and the nineteenth-century urban apartment in Paris and London, for example, Amanda Vickery and Sharon Marcus provide illuminating readings of domestic space that challenge the common equation of private homes with private lives, showing instead how houses and apartment blocks were historically sites of commercial exchange, encounters, sociability and work.[30] Likewise, in her analysis of the nineteenth-century novel, Monica Cohen depicts eighteenth- and nineteenth-century homes which, regardless of class and geography, were the base for 'an army of virtual strangers – extended relations, surrogate relations, servants, servants' relations and a host of others who, in regularly crossing any given home's threshold, can be said to have comprised the home as well as set the tone for the kind of sociability that transpired there'.[31] My own analysis will show how, in contradistinction to the ideological representation of selfhood that accompanies familiar literary and cultural domestic spaces (the parlours of realist novels, the ubiquitous British country house, modernism's metaphysical rooms), these 'other' interiors require us to think about domesticity as a space in which forms of self-identity may be forged not in a room of one's own, but in close, difficult and sometimes enabling proximity with the other bodies of family members, neighbours and strangers.

Analysis of forms of interiority in nonhegemonic domestic spaces requires a different approach and method – one that takes into account the home as a place of labour and transience that is at times utterly inimical to any sense of identity. For example, the role of objects in domestic space, as markers of self and ownership, has been a privileged mode of enquiry in domestic studies. But the very description of the furnishings and arrangement of a room without its occupant, and the implication that it is meaningfully related to the personal identity of the absent individual who resides in it, itself enacts the ideology of bourgeois interiority. Seeking to identify the role of objects in working-class interiors, however, requires a more intricate methodology – one that takes into account the very different significance of material articles in a worker's dwelling, for example, or that is self-reflexive about the ideological connotations of the very act of looking for objects in other people's homes and the ascription of value judgements based on this survey. In some accounts of nineteenth-century working-class homes or transient dwellings, the absence of objects itself has to be interpreted carefully (in the context of a pawning economy, for

---

[30] Amanda Vickery, *Behind Closed Doors: At Home in Georgian England* (Yale: Yale University Press, 2009); Sharon Marcus, *Apartment Stories: City and Home in Nineteenth-Century Paris and London* (Berkeley: University of California Press, 1999).
[31] Monica Cohen, *Professional Domesticity in the Victorian Novel: Women, Work and Home* (Cambridge: Cambridge University Press, 1998), p. 48. See also George K. Behlmer, *Friends of the Family: The English Home and Its Guardians, 1850–1940* (Stanford: Stanford University Press, 1998).

example).[32] For this reason, my aim is to show that it is not necessarily through a consideration of material objects in the home or interior décor that the dynamics of class are revealed. This reflects another way in which this work is less concerned with the domestic materiality of the dwelling place than it is with a more socially oriented methodology of putting people back into homes that are always-already inhabited, tenanted, leased, crowded or worked in. Ultimately, my analysis attempts to reconfigure the ways in which subjects and objects are interlinked, offering new coordinates for thinking about domestic possessions – and forms of dispossession.

Furthermore, while it can be argued that domestic space is a locus of historical and social relations, it is also clear that the discursive modes and visual methods linking domestic space to the individual, or to a sense of interiority, have a history. Throughout my work, I emphasise how housing and interiors can be approached as social spaces not only by dint of their content – as spaces in which social relations take place or as a location of labour and economic exchange – but also in terms of form: how they are seen, perceived and framed by the onlooker or narrator. Indeed, the idea of interiority or inwardness as the repository of truth is specifically complicated by the social and class dynamics that underlie historical representations of the homes of the working class or groups that are socially excluded. The chapters thus trace a number of the predominant cultural discourses and tropes by which the relations of selves and living spaces have been configured since the Victorian period: from anthropomorphic models which compare buildings to bodies and vice versa, to the sense of the strangely familiar trope of the 'uncanny', to recurring depictions of individuals gazing out (or in) through the window-eyes of the home.

In fact, the very idea of the interior paradoxically depends on the sense of an exterior viewpoint – a point articulated by the editors of a recent collection on nineteenth-century interiors which sets out to explore 'the ways in which someone's domestic space is constructed for them by somebody else'.[33] For this reason, my work is concerned not just with locations but also with the social and discursive contexts from which these spaces are narrated: the sanitary report; the ethnographic encounter; the novel's method of free indirect discourse; the retrospective mode of the autobiographer. For as critics

---

[32] As Robert Roberts notes in his important account of working-class Salford, 'position in our Edwardian community was judged not only by what one possessed but also by what one pawned'; *The Classic Slum: Salford Life in the First Quarter of the Century* (London: Penguin, 1990), p. 25.

[33] Inga Bryden and Janet Floyd, 'Introduction', in Bryden and Floyd (eds.), *Domestic Space*, p. 13.

from Raymond Williams to Doreen Massey note, the specific modes of seeing of the narrator and observer are informed by and reveal class and social relations.[34] It is possible to argue, therefore, that the ideology of the bourgeois interior is not just present in the material contents of what Bachelard and Benjamin describe – the drawers, bibelots and boxes – but also in the narrative form and authorial stance that shape such observations. It is the aim of this book to question any static idea of the interior as a representative 'still life', paying close attention instead to the networks and processes that underlie representations of particular domestic spaces and their inhabitants. My book's interiors are spaces that are, in turn, dramatically unveiled, surreptitiously peered into, looked out from, broken into, surveyed, retrospectively recreated, desired and imagined through another person's eyes.

The recognition that viewpoints are sites of power and knowledge, and the questioning of the constitution of public and private realms, have been fundamental to feminist analysis and cultural studies approaches that take class as their focus.[35] But feminist and class-based approaches have not always been viewed as natural or even compatible allies. In a pioneering study of domesticity, for example, Leonore Davidoff and Catherine Hall rightly maintain that studies of class have often overlooked 'the family, the private, the home, the place to which women have been conceptually relegated' for the more 'public' world of work, production and the state.[36] In literary and cultural studies more generally, the usefulness of the category of class as a descriptive and analytical tool has been called into question in recent decades. Indeed, in some versions of this critique, class has been superseded, in a marketplace of identity politics, by the categories of race, ethnicity, sexuality and gender.

The narrative of the decline of class as an analytical tool, however, runs counter to current scholarly work in which class is not in competition but rather in formative alliance with other modes of identity. Feminist scholars from Carolyn Steedman to bell hooks have effectively shown the intricate ways in which the categories of class, gender and racial identity work together

---

[34] Raymond Williams, *The Country and the City* (Oxford: Oxford University Press, 1973), pp. 120–26; Doreen Massey, *Space, Place, and Gender* (Minneapolis: University of Minnesota Press, 1994), p. 3.

[35] The literature on this subject is vast, but representative examples include Gillian Rose, *Feminism & Geography: The Limits of Geographical Knowledge* (Minneapolis: University of Minnesota Press, 1993), and Elizabeth Wilson, 'The Rhetoric of Urban Space', *New Left Review* 209 (1995), 146–60.

[36] Davidoff and Hall, *Family Fortunes*, p. 29.

to illuminate social relations of power and inequality.[37] Furthermore, in their lucid account of the relations between class and gender in an increasingly neoliberal society, Valerie Walkerdine, Helen Lucey and June Melody point out the revival of interest in the category of class among academic women from working-class backgrounds for whom 'class is lived as an identity designation and not simply as an economic relation to the means of production'.[38] Indeed, there are many ways in which specific Marxist and feminist accounts traverse the same ground and intersect, not least in the ways they have sought, with varying degrees of emphasis, to complicate and interrogate the boundaries between public and private worlds, interiors and exteriors, and the separation of the personal from the political.

My own approach is rooted in the understanding that the category of class is not a blunt theoretical instrument, but rather one that facilitates an interpretative approach which enriches the analysis of social phenomena such as housing and the idea of the interior. Thinking about class specifically enables a consideration of how constructions of privacy – both in the sense of selfhood and dwelling – operate within an irredeemably social context. For as Raymond Williams points out, in the nineteenth century the word 'class' was no longer restricted to the idea of social divisions (the working class, the upper classes) but developed to indicate social relations between classes (*class prejudice, class legislation, class consciousness, class conflict, class war*).[39] Thus in place of the earlier and more rigid term 'rank', the word 'class' registers precisely 'the changed social structure, and the changed social feelings' of the post Industrial Revolution period.[40] It is a word whose multiaccentual meaning is the result of social conflict and change – and one that has lost none of its clout in the twenty-first century. For while there is significant variation in the understanding and deployment of the term, the invocation of class still has the power to cut through liberal politesse, as well as neoliberal talk of 'classlessness', to act as a reminder of the persistent social inequities in relation to educational opportunity, community resources and access to forms of power.

Class is sometimes at the very forefront of the texts surveyed in this book, while at other times it recedes into the background or is displaced by other forces and identities that are, in certain contexts and circumstances, of more

[37] hooks, *Where We Stand*; Valerie Walkerdine, Helen Lucey and June Melody, *Growing Up Girl: Psycho-Social Explorations of Gender and Class* (Basingstoke: Palgrave, 2001).
[38] Walkerdine, Lucey and Melody, *Growing Up Girl*, p. 13.
[39] Raymond Williams, *Culture & Society: 1780–1950* (New York: Columbia University Press, 1983), p. xv. (Emphasis in the original.)
[40] Williams, *Culture*, p. xv.

pressing significance. This dual role, as an active and latent force, is representative of the function of class in lived experience; it is written into the landscape – for example, in the differential architecture of high-rises, terraces, bungalows, villas – and can be strangely invisible, while still not losing its power to shape behaviour, perception and access to certain kinds of opportunity. Indeed, as Pierre Bourdieu notes, class operates within a multivalent economy which involves economic, cultural, symbolic, social and educational capital.[41] Thus housing tenure itself is often directly related to income (although gender and particularly race may play integral roles in terms of access to property), and since the nineteenth century, as Alison Ravetz has shown, housing policy has arguably been 'strictly related to social class'.[42] But while housing and interiors may be obvious markers of class, my readings will indicate that they are not as rigid or quantifiable as Bourdieu's analysis would sometimes propose. Domestic spaces, as a recurring thread throughout this book will suggest, do not tell the whole story.

If class is often interpreted in forms of external display, it is crucially also about interiority, profundity and embodiment. As the feminist scholar Annette Kuhn remarks: 'Class is something beneath your clothes, under your skin, in your reflexes, in your psyche, at the very core of your being'.[43] In other words, class is perceived and experienced in ways that are internal and external, material and abstract, spoken and unspoken – all of which makes it an enduringly compelling area of interpretation, decoding and analysis. Indeed, as Marxist critics have shown, relations of class are most effectively unravelled at the level of form (including narrative structure, tone, viewpoint, use of genre, textual silences and the 'political unconscious' of the text) rather than in a text's manifest content. It is for this reason that a literary approach to the relations of class in a range of texts helps to move peripheral moments to the centre and makes manifest the historical development of tropes, narrative modes, and that telling cultural form, the cliché, across a diverse array of writing.

iv Housing types, housing tales

Marked by deep-rooted associations of class and gender, the British cultural landscape is full of housing stories. There is thus a powerful

[41] Pierre Bourdieu, *Distinction: A Social Critique of the Judgement of Taste*, Richard Nice (trans.), (London: Routledge & Kegan Paul, 1984).

[42] Alison Ravetz, 'A View from the Interior', in Judy Attfield and Pat Kirkham (eds.), *A View from the Interior: Women & Design*, 2nd edn. (London: Kirkham, 1995), p. 188.

[43] Annette Kuhn, *Family Secrets: Acts of Memory and Imagination*, new edn. (London: Verso, 2002), p. 117.

argument to be made that class is inscribed into the very housing landscape of Britain; as Lynsey Hanley puts it, that 'we are divided not only by income and occupation, but by the types of homes in which we live'.[44] But the discursive and narrative forms commonly attached to particular types of residence can also bear different degrees of symbolic capital. For as Fuss notes in *The Sense of an Interior*, architectural historians have tended to emphasise the more 'literal' aspects of domestic space, such as décor and function, while literary critics have tended to see interiors as 'pure figuration', to the extent that houses are always 'metaphors for something else'.[45] Working-class and lower-middle-class domestic spaces have been particularly subject to this kind of separation of the material and the symbolic in that they are more often approached in terms of historical and anthropological evidence, rather than as aesthetic and literary locations. As noted earlier, however, a focus on these less celebrated spaces helps to reconceive dominant assumptions about space and identity through the interpretative prism of social class and gender, while also raising questions about ideas of the interior, self-identity and how these complex relations are framed and reconfigured. For the living spaces of economically marginalised groups are, like all interiors, both real and imagined, physical places of shelter and symbolic sites of belonging or exclusion. As will become clear throughout this work, there is an important aesthetic mode to be found in cultural representations of even the bleakest of houses.

My focus on housing in this book does not constitute an attempt to read what are predominantly working-class places of residence in narrowly material terms. In fact, this book argues that there *is* a poetics or aesthetics of (all) housing, but that it can be richly expressive of the complex social worlds individuals inhabit rather than solely indicative of 'character' or 'personality'. Housing environments and interiors have provided a compelling visual and conceptual backdrop or frame for cultural narratives of self-development and social formation. Furthermore, as recent cinematic documentaries, controversial television series and oral histories testify, housing stories are anything but mundane. Indeed, while the term 'housing' may evoke unaesthetic connotations of bureaucracy and planning regulations, it is clear, from nineteenth-century exposés of housing conditions to twenty-first-century art installations, that the tales told about housing environments and their residents can be moving, plot-driven,

---

[44] Lynsey Hanley, *Estates: An Intimate History* (London: Granta, 2008), p. 18.
[45] Fuss, *Sense of an Interior*, p. 3.

strange and even epic in scope. In addition, like all good stories, fictional and non-fictional housing narratives are populated by a cast of familiar characters and uninvited guests: the lodger in the room at the top, the landlady, the homeworker, the social investigator, the woman at the window, the reader in the dark.

While bringing together a varied selection of texts based in different geographical settings risks losing the detail that a focus on a particular locale or region might produce, I have adopted this approach precisely in order to trace broader patterns and alliances in cultural representations of interiors and housing. The housing environments in this book are – aptly for an account which tries to shift the discussion away from a focus on individualism – often 'characters' and 'types' in themselves. For in exactly the same way that the British country house setting invokes tropes and associations that are historically rooted and imaginative recreations, slums, boarding houses, mid-century working-class homes and council estates are significant sites of imaginative and cultural narration. Each chapter of this work therefore explores the domestic interior and representations of identity in the context of a particular housing type which also functions in social discourse as a metonym, trope or byword for particular social and cultural issues.

The book's eclectic approach, bringing together works of fiction, non-fiction, memoir and visual culture from the Victorian period to the present, is partly intended to show the pervasiveness of housing stories across genres and forms. But it also aims to show how housing – as a discursive formation which is embedded in concrete, lived experience, as well as an intimate part of personal and collective imaginaries – moves easily between the historically unstable categories of fictional and non-fictional writing. As I will show, many of the non-fictional writings under examination, from Victorian social exploration to postwar sociological ethnography, are literary, enigmatic and, indeed, often imaginative works. It follows that while I address a range of texts that occupy or cross different genres, my readings are rooted in principles of literary analysis, including close attention to form, narrative, and literary and visual tropes. The consideration of non-fictional writing in particular is integral to this book's critical tenet that the interior is partly constructed from the outside, by observers and social commentors, and that subjectivities (especially of marginalised social groups) are often situated, constrained and have to work against these framing discursive devices.

More broadly, producing readings of sociological material and non-fiction reinforces my point that the cultural discourse about housing, including its myths, clichés and stereotypes, has a powerful social presence and effect. For housing never ceases to be an emotive topic which taps into individual and social anxieties and desires. It is by now axiomatic that the homes of the middle and upper classes, from seventeenth-century Dutch interiors to *Downton Abbey*, are in part the cultural product of a kind of collective imagining (a wide-reaching exploration of the subject in a recent edited collection was significantly entitled *Imagined Interiors*).[46] But this book tries to apply the useful phrase of the 'imagined interior' to domestic spaces that are not part of the dominant social order; to explore how these housing types are also bound up in complex and problematic ways with subject-formation; and to demonstrate the way in which these writings provide distinctive genres and modes of imagining people in domestic places.

v   Outline of chapters

Chapter 1 addresses the idea of the 'slum' interior as it appears in mainly non-fictional and autobiographical accounts from the Victorian period to the early twentieth century. Housing was a dominant concern in this period and manifested itself in eulogies of ideal homes and a demonisation of the domestic 'other' as well as in slum clearances, important legislation passed in the areas of housing and sanitary reform, and the evolution of model dwellings. Moving from accounts of slum living conditions produced by Victorian social investigators, a discursive mode which had become dominant by the 1880s, to autobiographical writing from the first few decades of the twentieth century by writers who look back to their late-Victorian and Edwardian childhoods, my first chapter juxtaposes the view of the slum as seen from the point of view of 'outsider' and 'insider'. It challenges a binary view of such accounts by showing how social investigators, such as Henry Mayhew, interpreted the slum in such a way as to reconfigure received notions concerning domestic space and selfhood, while later autobiographers produced their own genre of traditional domestic interiority framed around ideas of privacy, cleanliness, literacy and autonomy.

In Chapter 2, I discuss how a consideration of boarding and lodging houses as places of dwelling tests the normalising assumption that the place of home can be counted on as a reliable haven in a moving world.

---

[46] See Jeremy Aynsley and Charlotte Grant (eds.), *Imagined Interiors: Representing the Domestic Interior Since the Renaissance* (London: V&A, 2006).

I explore how the inner worlds of boarding houses and lodging houses, as places which allowed for the mixing of classes, genders and races, encapsulate social shifts in Britain as seen through the prism, not of the family, but of the makeshift social groups forced by economic circumstance to share a common domestic space. Like the slum terraces and tenements that appeared to function in material and symbolic terms as the spatial 'other' to the middle-class bourgeois homestead, the seemingly atypical domesticity of the boarding and lodging house often led them to be cast as illegitimate, illicit and even potentially dangerous spaces. But as places of temporary accommodation which brought together disparate individuals in often straitened circumstances, the boarding house served as a dynamic stage set – with all the implications of theatricality and performance – for intriguing intersubjective encounters. This chapter charts particular shifts in the boarding-house tale that reflect wider changes in a structure of feeling about the family, home and hospitality towards the 'stranger'.

Chapter 3 focuses on representations of subjectivity and domestic space in both the autobiographies and autobiographical novels produced by writers who form part of the 'Butler generation' – a group that entered the grammar school system following the 1944 Education Act. In this chapter, I trace a tradition of autobiographical writing which eschews gritty realism or nostalgic idealism in its portrayal of childhood and the working-class home, displaying instead a preference for Gothic modes which represent and transform domestic spaces, such as the urban terraced house, into an unhomely and unsettling site of memory and imagination. I explore how these writers use the aesthetic mode of the uncanny – the *unheimlich* – to articulate the deep ambivalence produced by social mobility and their sense of a dislocation from childhood homes, or the idea of home itself, through the processes of higher education. My readings of the narratives of 'scholarship boys' and 'scholarship girls' pay particular attention to the gendered and spatial implications of the experience of social mobility.

Chapter 4 turns to examine postwar housing estates – a central part of the residential fabric of Britain, but one that is variously overlooked or reductively portrayed in popular cultural representations. This chapter addresses the difficulty, expressed in the literature, of finding a narrative of self and community in a landscape that seems to militate against individuality and collectivity. This chapter further focusses on the gendered nature of the social housing estate and its implications for the way that narratives of development are plotted. This chapter provides a deliberate counterpart – in terms of the material and theoretical approach – to the 'Slums' chapter with which my study began. For although I again address the way in which domestic interiors are constructed through the investigative lens of outside observers, I shift focus in order to explore autobiography, literary work and films that represent the estate as a significant and nuanced cultural setting from the inside out.

CHAPTER I

Slums
Reading and writing the dwellings of the urban poor

Introduction

Noting at the turn of the century that his description of the poorest London streets might well have applied to Liverpool, Manchester and even New York, Charles Booth asserted that in impoverished urban areas 'everywhere the same conditions repeat themselves'.[1] The journalist George Sims made a similar point with less brevity, and in doing so displayed the paradoxical tendency among many Victorian investigators of poor urban districts to explicate at great length what was apparently a familiar sight:

> The Mint and the Borough present scenes awful enough in all conscience to be worthy of earnest study; but scene after scene is the same. Rags, dirt, filth, wretchedness, the same figures, the same faces, the same old story of one room unfit for habitation yet inhabited by eight or nine people, the same complaint of a ruinous rent absorbing three-fourths of the toiler's weekly wage, the same shameful neglect by the owner of the property of all sanitary precautions, rotten floors, oozing walls, broken windows, crazy staircases, tileless roofs . . . these are the things which confront us, whether we turn to the right or to the left, whether we linger in the Mint or seek fresh fields in the slums that lie round Holborn. . . .

'The story of one slum', Sims went on to assert, 'is the story of another'.[2]

This chapter seeks to challenge the view that there is one 'story' to be told about those deprived areas of urban housing which were conceived through the trope of the slum. It does so by tracing a number of distinct forms and approaches that various writers, differently positioned, employed in their approach to the housing of people living in poverty.

[1] Charles Booth, *Life and Labour of the People in London*, 2nd edn. (London: Macmillan and Co., 1902), First Series, vol. II, p. 44.
[2] George Sims, *How the Poor Live; and, Horrible London* (London: Chatto & Windus, 1889), pp. 45–46.

As with descriptions of all housing environments, the Victorian slum was frequently framed around ideas of interiors and exteriors, insiders and outsiders. But this takes on an added layer of complexity in the context of a body of writing which was centrally concerned with one group's exposure and publicisation of the dwellings and lives of others. Throughout these sections, I show how slum writing as a genre is more varied and less fixed than its caricature suggests. Portrayals of individuals within slum homes were presented in different ways and for a variety of purposes across the Victorian period and into the twentieth century, with long-lasting effects on the discursive practices and images by which the lived experience of poverty and social exclusion has been – and continues to be – depicted.

This chapter encompasses a broad historical span in order to show the diverse range and tone of the writing, but also because accounts by tenement dwellers are necessarily written retrospectively (late-Victorian and Edwardian childhoods were produced and published in the 1920s and 1930s). My focus throughout is on representations of this housing environment as it appears in non-fictional writing (journalism, social exploration, housing reports, memoir) rather than in the Victorian realist novel. This choice is based partly on a need to delimit the frame of reference, but it also serves to emphasise the way in which writing about the homes of the poor in the nineteenth century can be seen as constituting a broader social narrative. By focusing on representations of slum interiors and slum housing as they are evoked in non-fictional writings, my analysis is concerned with works that significantly traverse – or slip – between factual reportage and imaginative license. For like the bourgeois interior, the slum interior is a distinctive setting across a range of written modes; as such, it is equally both a historical site as well as the product of a collective act of imagination.

The use of the word 'slum' itself requires a degree of interrogation and explanation. Its first citation is in a dictionary of slang – James Hardy Vaux's *Vocabulary of the Flash Language* (1812) – where it refers to a 'room' as well as a criminal 'racket' or 'rig' (the two senses of the term are conjoined in Vaux's reference to 'lodging-slum', a word which denotes the practice of stripping a rented furnished room of its 'valuables', such as plates and linen).[3] The term develops to signify a district characterised by overcrowding and squalid conditions, and by the 1860s the *OED* records

---

[3] See under 'Slum' and 'Lodging-Slum', in James Hardy Vaux, *Memoirs of James Hardy Vaux*, 2nd edn. (London: Hunt and Clarke, 1827).

how it is deployed as an attributive (thus, 'slum-area', 'slum-dweller', 'slum-people', 'slum-bred', 'slum-sister'). In a similar manner, the word gives rise to creative semantic hybrids: 'slumland', 'slumite', 'slumdom', 'slumopolis', 'slummery', 'slumminess' and 'slummy'.[4] With regard to the latter of these terms, 'slummy' functions as an adjective and a noun, which serves to entrench the idea that the person and the quality of the place are interrelated.

The derogatory use of the word 'slum' was deployed liberally throughout nineteenth-century writing by those who charted, surveyed and demonised the existence and associated practices of impoverished districts marked by crowded tenements. But it is important to note that the history of the word does not point to a complete colonisation of the term by journalists, reformers and inspectors; one memoirist, as we shall see, claims 'slummy' with apparent affection and a sense of ownership. The word 'slum' therefore has a dual sense, referring to a particular setting which is widely thought to have a distinctive historical provenance, but also to an imaginative and speculative location in negative but also possibly more positive ways (for example, in its slang roots and appropriation as a category of identity by particular inhabitants). Throughout, I use the word in this complex sense without quotation marks or 'scare quotes'. While I recognise and am sensitive to the pejorative connotations of the term, I also believe that the distinct historicity of the word – as well as the way in which it signifies a material and symbolic landscape – makes it an important critical term.

i A tale of two interiors?

As noted in the Introduction, the dominant ideology of the middle-class home as 'characterful', in the sense of displaying the personality of its occupants, was firmly rooted in Victorian cultural forms. In painting, for example, the European Biedermeier style of portraiture, which expressed the new way individuals regarded 'their interiors as reflections of themselves, controlling what went into them', was an important influence on the development of an aesthetic in Victorian painting whereby individuals formed a part of the domestic arrangement.[5] In the context of print culture,

---

[4] Those not listed in the *OED* include 'slumdom' (the title of a chapter in John Law [Margaret Harkness], *In Darkest London, Captain Lobe* (London: Bellamy Library, 1891)), while 'slumites' appears in Sims, *How the Poor Live*, p. 44.

[5] Frances Borzello, *At Home: The Domestic Interior in Art* (New York: Thames & Hudson, 2006), p. 81.

Deborah Cohen cites the Victorian journalistic 'at home' feature, which gained in popularity throughout the nineteenth century, as an example of the increasing coupling of people and homes. In this new format, writers and politicians were interviewed in their own houses among their private possessions, a method firmly based on the assumption – taken for granted in similar 'at home' features today – 'that the domestic interior expressed its inhabitant's inner self.[6] In the Victorian novel, of course, décor, room furnishings and objects as indicative of personality fill the pages of Charles Dickens' novels; from Miss Havisham's stop-clocked wedding scene or the *nouveau riche* Veneerings' gaudy furnishings to the deep-set Christian values of the respectable working class manifest within the confines of the Peggottys' snug boathouse. Indeed nineteenth-century literature, according to Philippa Tristam, emerges as the cultural chronicle to the way in which 'living space itself develops individual character'.[7] This is an important point to emphasise in relation to accounts of the domestic taste of the Victorian middle classes: that the idea of the bourgeois interior is partly an elaborate construct of literature, painting and rhetoric. Indeed, as one critic puts it, 'the middle-class Victorian home must surely rate as one of the most consciously contrived creations of domestic space in history'.[8]

It is within this context that the apparent 'other' – or perhaps necessary counterpart – to this 'creation' of ideal domesticity can be seen to emerge in the representative image of the slum interior. These textual vignettes and visual images of the homes of the very poor produced an inverse, but equally prevalent, alignment of identity and homes. Indeed, the very phrase 'slum interior' seems almost oxymoronic since the idea of the interior, and all that it signifies, is so deeply associated with bourgeois mores. Thus when one of the many urban investigators to chart the households of the slums first uses the term 'interior' to describe a ruined East End home, he places the term gingerly within quotation marks as if to highlight the irony of the phrase.[9] The costermonger's spartan dwelling, it is implied, can only ever be a deviant 'bad' copy of the shared meanings of the conventional Victorian home.

---

[6] Deborah Cohen, *Household Gods: The British and Their Possessions* (New Haven: Yale University Press, 2006), p. 123.
[7] Tristam, *Living Space*, p. 23.
[8] Moira Donald, 'Tranquil Havens? Critiquing the Idea of Home as the Middle-Class Sanctuary', in Bryden and Floyd (eds.), *Domestic Space*, p. 106.
[9] Sims, *How the Poor Live*, p. 58; he does the same with the term 'domestic interior' (p. 131).

As a form of domestic other, the slum interior was often depicted as a space defined by lack in material as well as figurative ways. The cliché of the impoverished interior ('the damp cellar with an empty grate, one chipped teacup and a pile of rags', as Ruth Livesey puts it) was all the more striking at a time when decorative objects, trinkets, coverings and furniture were in many ways the defining elements of the ideal Victorian home.[10] As Thad Logan notes of the middle- and upper-middle-class Victorian parlour, 'it is the accumulation and display of many such objects that sets Victorian interiors apart from those of the eighteenth and twentieth centuries'.[11] The bourgeois eye of various social investigators who surveyed the homes of the poor was thus frequently directed at the lack of room furnishings in the most destitute of living environments. These observers never failed to express surprise and alarm when faced with evidence of broken furniture in the slum dwellings, at the lack of tableware or indeed at the complete absence of objects of any kind. As Steven Marcus points out, one of the earliest systematic surveyors of slum homes, Friedrich Engels, seemed particularly struck by the fact that what he finds in some of the Manchester slum dwellings is precisely '*absolutely nothing*'.[12] Thus Marcus comments that throughout Engels' descriptions, 'these nests or dens are virtual emptinesses, whose evacuated spaces are the counterpart of the densely packed humanity with which such absences are filled'.[13] Acknowledging the powerful ideological effects of such descriptions of empty interiors, Marcus goes on to remark crucially that 'it is quite impossible to know whether this is an image or a reality; that is its point'.[14] As Marcus' comment implies, like their apparent opposite – the bourgeois interior itself – representations of the homes of the poor are a curious and ambiguous amalgam of evidence and ideology.[15] Certainly, many of the illustrations which accompanied slum reports, for example the wood engravings produced by John Brown and Frederick Barnard which featured in Godwin and Sims' accounts, accentuated precisely an overriding sense of emptiness. In these bleak images, a visual effect of the bareness

[10] Ruth Livesey, 'Reading for Character: Women Social Reformers and Narratives of the Urban Poor in Late Victorian and Edwardian London', *Journal of Victorian Culture* 9 (2004), 56.
[11] Thad Logan, *The Victorian Parlour* (Cambridge: Cambridge University Press, 2001), p. 7.
[12] Friedrich Engels, quoted in Steven Marcus, 'Reading the Illegible', in H. J. Dyos and Michael Wolff (eds.), *The Victorian City: Images and Reality*, vol. I (London: Routledge Kegan & Paul, 1973), p. 269.
[13] Marcus, 'Reading the Illegible', p. 269.　　[14] Marcus, 'Reading the Illegible', p. 269.
[15] Indeed, a 1993 archaeological excavation of the privies of the impoverished East London Limehouse district, for example, revealed a surprising amount of household possessions and domestic objects. See Alastair Owens et al., 'Fragments of the Modern City: Material Culture and the Rhythms of Everyday Life in Victorian London', *Journal of Victorian Culture* 15:2 (2010), 212–25.

of rooms is in notable contrast to the verbal excess and detail which came to characterise the writing of social exploration. For the most part, illustrators such as Brown and Barnard settled on a semiotic code that figured a stark empty interior – often with a solitary inhabitant – as a visual shorthand for urban destitution.

The paradoxical nature of the slum interior is underlined by the fact that while the slum environment was frequently portrayed as an unfathomable maze-like network of courts or a dark underworld of poverty and criminality, these representations themselves were very much part of *public* discourse. Throughout the Victorian period, images of the slums existing in British cities such as London, Liverpool, Manchester and Glasgow were disseminated through social and sanitary reports as well as journalistic exposés and appeared as a memorable setting and backdrop within the Victorian novel – that most domestic of literary forms. This way of seeing and narrating the homes of the very poor arguably turned the slum interior into a rather familiar and easily recognisable image for a middle-class readership, again binding the two interiors in unexpected ways. Images of slum life as they occurred in the novel as well as in the writing of the 'social investigators' – from George Godwin to Jack London – performed a type of familiarisation that served to render the insalubrious world of urban poverty into a form of narrative and visual order. Moreover, the strong narrative impetus of these writings had the effect of drawing attention to the putative readership of the work. Like sensationalist literature or the detective story, slum writing was a thoroughly domestic genre designed for the middle-class reader who sits, as Henry Mayhew phrases it, 'beside your snug sea-coal fire, in your cosy easy chair'.[16] Indeed, it has now become a critical commonplace to point out that these reports into the courts and alleys of the Victorian industrial city could offer a type of domestic colonial adventure: a 'book of travel' for a 'stay-at-home public' (although there is as yet little work on the significance of a working-class readership of slum exposés).[17] So while the ideal and the slum interior may well have been held up as opposites, they were dialectically connected in a way that provided a mutual reinforcement of domestic ideology. Despite the stark outward contrasts drawn in the representations of these different interiors, the two were underpinned by an ideological framework which equated rooms with character, personality and morality.

[16] Henry Mayhew, 'Home Is Home, Be It Never So Homely', in Viscount Ingestre (ed.), *Meliora, or Better Times to Come* (London: Frank Cass, 1971), p. 264.
[17] Sims, *How the Poor Live*, p. 1.

ii   Domestic evidence: Henry Mayhew's interiors

The idea of the slum is thus very much a social construct – a description of a particular environment which is frequently a hybrid composite of journalism and storytelling, revealing as much about the social mores of the observer as it does about its human subjects. As Carol L. Bernstein puts it, the heterogeneous genre of 'slum sketches' feature narrators who are often 'substituting their words for the inarticulateness of the slum-dwellers'.[18] Indeed, the very attempt to 'read' the lives of the working class and urban poor through their place of residence has been viewed by some cultural historians as a disciplinary and ideological project in and of itself. Mary Poovey, for example, presents Edwin Chadwick's *The Sanitary Condition of the Labouring People* (1842), a Poor Law report which surveyed the conditions of working-class housing in British cities, including Glasgow, Manchester, Liverpool and Bradford, as reflecting his own middle-class estimation of the importance of place of residence. According to Poovey, far from merely surveying the domestic conditions of workers' homes, the report performed a 'strong moralizing – and ideally, regulative – component'.[19] Poovey suggests further that these reports distorted and overvalued the importance of home for working men and had the underlying aim of concealing – and curtailing – working-class men's engagement in public life and political activity. She writes that 'both working-class societies and respectable domesticity, in other words, tended to link the individualized identity of the working man to his family *instead of* to any all-male association'.[20] The idea that the lives of the working classes were distorted by observing them through a domestic lens is echoed by Priti Joshi's assessment of Chadwick's *Report*, who argues that 'the effect of speaking of the poor almost exclusively in their homes was to place undue attention on their behavior, habits, lifestyle, and morals'.[21] And the idea that a more authentic portrayal of working-class life might be located in the public spaces of the street, rather than in an apparently inauthentic 'home' under surveillance, would persist in forms of social discourse well into the twentieth century.

---

[18] Carol L. Bernstein, *The Celebration of Scandal: Toward the Sublime in Victorian Urban Fiction* (University Park: Pennsylvania State University Press, 1991), p. 7.
[19] Mary Poovey, *Making a Social Body: British Cultural Formation, 1830–1864* (Chicago: Chicago University Press, 1995), p. 119.
[20] Poovey, *Social Body*, p. 125.
[21] Priti Joshi, 'The Dual Work of "Wastes" in Chadwick's *Sanitary Report*', University of California, Santa Cruz, http://omf.ucsc.edu/london-1865/victorian-city/sanitary-report.html.

Yet the need to recognise the cultural and literary construction of the slum for the consumption of a middle-class readership also has to be carefully circumscribed – indeed it could be argued that there has been a disproportionate critical shift towards this viewpoint. In this account, the slum interior – in all its inverted, oppositional form – becomes nothing but the projection of bourgeois anxiety about the urban poor, apparently rendering little actual material or historical evidence of the lived experience of those who inhabited these urban districts. From this standpoint, the slum interior, symbolising everything that the middle-class home is not, becomes a space through which 'to tell other people's stories: to tell some kind of story of the bourgeois self'.[22] And yet, paradoxically, it may well be a capitulation to the persuasive rhetoric of scores of Victorian surveys if the idea of the slum interior is approached in merely negative terms as signifying nothing but the inverse of ideal homeliness.

Although his work predates the heyday of slum writing (from the 1880s on), one writer whose accounts contradict this tendency, as well as disrupting the Foucauldian reading of depictions of the homes of the poor as state disciplinary devices, is the journalist and social investigator Henry Mayhew. In his investigative 'letters' to the *Morning Chronicle*, for example, which appeared in 1849–50 (and provided much of the basis for his well-known *London Labour and the London Poor* published over a decade later), Mayhew wrote about what he perceived to be a veritable profusion of meaningful evidence or signs to be found in the interiors of workers' residences. It may thus be unfashionable to herald Mayhew's aim of uncovering various home truths from his enquiry into the living and working conditions of working-class and impoverished households, a concept with which Poovey and Joshi take issue for good reason; yet it is important to register how the dwelling place for Mayhew seemed not to be a meaningless, aberrant void – but was instead a type of puzzle requiring interpretation.[23]

In this regard, it is crucial to bear in mind that Mayhew's interest in observing the dwellings of the poor was motivated by economic enquiry: specifically, he stated that his intention was to determine the London

---

[22] Steedman, 'What a Rag Rug Means', p. 29.
[23] A recent bicentennial roundtable on Mayhew's work suggests that he is 'one of the most commonly misread Victorian social explorers' and invites a reconsideration of his writing; Sarah Roddy, Julie-Marie Strange and Bertrand Taithe, 'Henry Mayhew at 200 – The "Other" Victorian Bicentenary', *Journal of Victorian Culture* 19:4 (2014), 488. Important re-evaluations in this edition include John Seed, 'Did the Subaltern Speak? Mayhew and the Coster-Girl', 536–49 and Carolyn Steedman, 'Mayhew: On Reading, About Writing', 550–61.

workers' weekly income, the cause of their 'inadequate return' and then to 'ascertain, by positive inspection, the condition of their homes – to learn, by close communion with them, the real or fancied wrongs of their lot'.[24] In order to get at certain social and economic truths (rather than liberal moral certainties), specifically in relation to the workers' low wages, 'the workpeople themselves must be sought out, and seen privately at their own homes'.[25] So while domesticity was not his purported focus, a portrayal of house interiors was inevitable because many of the subjects of his inquiry – the tailors, needlewomen and pieceworkers – worked primarily in the home. This indirect recognition of domestic interiors as places of labour is furthermore an important rejoinder – even today – to general accounts or images of home that uncritically assume its leisured, private nature.

What is immediately striking in Mayhew's reports is that unlike other slum 'travellers', he does not struggle to comprehend or articulate the domestic scene he encounters. There is far less of a sense that the domestic interior of the poor is an affront to either the eyes, senses or intellect. These are on the whole not abject spaces; on the contrary, Mayhew, the collector, oral historian and taxonomist seems to make the point that these miniature domestic case studies offer up a veritable profusion of signs. In a suggestive comparison, Enid Gauldie thus describes Mayhew as 'one of the best observers of interiors, bringing to the squalid slums of London the kind of eye for detail with which Vermeer painted the gleaming tiled rooms of Flemish merchants'.[26] Despite the manifest contrast of the settings, Mayhew's vignettes, like the Dutch interiors, depict home scenes as detailed canvases that are replete with clues about, for example, the domestic economy of the households, the inhabitants' family history and national identities, and the strategies they used to disguise their poverty (from hidden pawn tickets in a drawer to a woman's chipped crockery that has been carefully turned to the wall). On occasion – and like a Vermeer painting in form rather than content – Mayhew's interiors seem imbued with secrecy, a sense of privacy and things left unsaid. But at other times the interiors defy principles of realist composition and harmony to display a type of proto-surrealist domesticity: a toymaker's bedroom crammed with the tools and parts to make penny mousetraps, or the doll part maker's opening of a box containing 190 glass eyes which seem disarmingly

---

[24] Mayhew, Letter I, 19 October 1849, in *The Morning Chronicle Survey of Labour and the Poor: The Metropolitan Districts*, vol. I (Horsham: Caliban Books, 1981), pp. 40–41.

[25] Mayhew, Letter IX, 16 November 1849, *Morning Chronicle*, vol. I, p. 169.

[26] Enid Gauldie, *Cruel Habitations: A History of Working-Class Housing, 1780–1918* (New York: Barnes & Noble, 1974), p. 96.

to return the investigator's gaze.[27] In an intriguing encounter with the manufacturer of a 'speaking doll' in High Holborn, the doll-maker provides Mayhew with a mythical account of invention – a slum court version of the Pygmalion myth. He recalls how

> I determined to try and manufacture a speaking doll, I persevered day by day, thinking of it when doing other things, and completed it in three months. I often dreamed of it, but never got a hint of the speaking doll in my sleep, though I have in other discoveries. When I heard my first speaking doll call me 'papa' . . . I said in a sort of enthusiasm . . . 'I've got her at last.' . . . Many doll-makers have dissected my speaking doll to get at my secret. . . . I laugh – I don't care a fig. I have the fame and the secret, and will keep them.[28]

In defiance of the typical depiction of the destitute worker's passivity in investigative reports, the doll-maker makes a bold claim to originality, invention and secrecy. Invoking the crucial trope of dissection – that emblematic methodology of getting to the centre of things – he points out that this penetrative method still *fails* to disclose the secret of his doll's power to speak. The interior, the doll-maker intriguingly suggests, offers no guarantee of revelation.

Mayhew's interpretative stance, whereby he surveys these domestic scenes and ascribes significance to them, clearly bears the hallmarks of the paternalist, middle-class imperative of speaking for and about the poor. But this charge can be qualified by noting two distinguishing features of his approach. First, Mayhew's accounts are substantially made up of 'verbatim' oral testimony given by the workers themselves, a crucial point that has been sometimes strangely overlooked or underplayed by historians and critics. Additionally, Mayhew's survey also presents workers and subjects talking in intricate ways *about* the objects on which they are working, demonstrating a marked self-reflexivity about their labour, their domestic situation and their exchanges with Mayhew which deserves far more attention. Second, his attempt to expose the homes of the poor to a public readership should be interpreted within the context of Mayhew's belief that secrecy and opacity were precisely the elements upon which sweated labour and exploitative landlordism depended. It is therefore important to evaluate Mayhew's investigative methods in a context in which privacy (in the specific sense of something hidden from view)

---

[27] See Letter XXXVII, 21 February 1850, *Morning Chronicle*, vol. III, pp. 210–17, and Letter XXXIX, 28 February 1850, *Morning Chronicle*, vol. III, pp. 239–42.
[28] Speaking doll-maker, quoted in Mayhew, Letter XXXIX, pp. 242–43.

was the hallmark of the political economy within which these homeworkers operated and which enabled landlords to reap vast profits from hazard-
ous residences.

Taking opacity or a lack of transparency as a political issue, Mayhew
often comes across as an early example of the urban detective, trying to
deduce a social or class-inflected narrative of the inhabitants from the
traces or 'clues' of their interiors, furnishings and clothing.[29] In what will
become the literary detective's trademark, Mayhew often senses that
appearances in the domestic interior are misleading – rather than self-
evidently abject – and require further interpretation. For example, in one
home, he details a female waistcoat-maker's interior which is 'scrupulously
clean and neat. The old brass fender was as bright as gold, and worn with
continued rubbing. The grate, in which there was barely a handful of coals,
had been newly black-leaded, and there was not a cinder littering the
hearth'.[30] In a characteristic move, he questions the surface detail, going on
to reveal that the display of cleanliness was 'partly the effect of habits
acquired in domestic service, and partly the result of a struggle to hide her
extreme poverty from this world'.[31] Even in his reports into the 'nests of
Irish', Mayhew reads the interior differently from so much pernicious
commentary on this social group, noting their framed pictures and displayed religious iconography as well as 'household care and neatness that
I had little expected to have seen'.[32]

As Livesey argues, many social investigators frequently portrayed the
slum interior as a strange display that defied comprehension. And she
suggestively observes that within these descriptions,

> one thing is 'possibly' another, things that only make sense as a whole –
> chairs, floor cloths – are in 'pieces'. . . . the bourgeois reading subject is
> placed into a disorientating world where familiar objects become uncanny,
> where plants, flowerpots and chairs become the liveliest inhabitants of
> 'homes' which are symbols of public destitution.[33]

---

[29] See for example Mayhew's reading of the soldier-trouser-maker's sublet rooms which contain an
anomalous grand piano; Letter VII, 9 November 1849, *Morning Chronicle*, vol. I, pp. 135–41.

[30] Mayhew, Letter VI, 6 November 1849, *Morning Chronicle*, vol. I, p. 121.

[31] Mayhew, Letter VI, p. 121.

[32] Henry Mayhew, *London Labour and the London Poor* (1865) (London: Penguin, 1985), p. 58. See also
Richard Kirkland's discussion of the Irish-populated St Giles 'Rookery' for an interesting account of
this social landscape as 'a world of its own possessing its particular codes, rules, and shibboleths –
and a place that engaged economically with the wider city'; 'Reading the Rookery: The Social
Meaning of an Irish Slum in Nineteenth-Century London', *New Hibernia Review* 16:1 (2012),
16–30.

[33] Livesey, 'Reading for Character', p. 58.

But for Mayhew, the detection of the uncanny relations between inhabitants and their furnishings has inescapably economic implications. The empty interiors are paradoxically loaded with, not emptied of, meaning. For one thing, Mayhew was keen to point out the grim irony attending the fact that domestic bareness, for example, came at a scandalously high price because inhabitants often paid an extortionate weekly rent to landlords for their 'waterless, drainless, floorless, and almost roofless tenements'.[34] Thus the bare slum interior – an enduring textual and visual signifier of abject poverty – in Mayhew's report becomes meaningful in relation to the aesthetic or visual code of accumulation and Victorian materialism: that 'urban carnival of objects and signs' animating the pages of so much Victorian writing.[35] Mayhew's depictions of crowded slum interiors, filled by the presence of multiple household members and coworkers but devoid of personal belongings, are arguably not merely a sensationalist discursive device but graphic accounts of the unsettling interdependence of body and commodity in capitalist conditions of production.

Where objects in the home are described, in Mayhew's survey, they do not necessarily function as 'décor'. Instead, they have an important social significance. For in his account, objects often serve to reflect the disorienting role of the commodity detached from its intended place in the shop display or the bourgeois home. The examples of darkly ironic presentations of people and commodities in the *Morning Chronicle* letters are seemingly endless, but they are striking in detail: a father, mother and child who form a family unit through their compound labour, fabricating the parts of a toy doll; the destitute tailor-maker's wife who has pawned her own underclothing; the 'slop-workers' who cover themselves at night with the sleeves of the coat they are preparing; or the drawer-maker who has never possessed and has no need for a chest of drawers into which he might put belongings. The objects here are part of a political economy and circulate between worker and market accordingly. For the homeworker, within these stark vignettes of what Marx terms 'alienated labour', is literally pauperised by the work that he or she undertakes; the object or commodity is produced at the expense of the worker's body. As Marx writes, using the rhetoric of paradoxical opposition that animates so much of the writing of social exploration: 'The worker places his life in the object; but now [his life] no longer belongs to him, but to the object.

---

[34] Mayhew, Letter I, p. 41.   [35] Bernstein, *The Celebration of Scandal*, p. 29.

The greater his activity, therefore, the fewer objects the worker possesses. What the product of his labour is, he is not.'[36]

The issue of sparse furnishings is thus more complex and suggestive than it first appears, for rather than signalling the slum's remoteness from the world of consumer capitalism, the object-less dwellings are in fact precisely the sites of production of many of the commodities which fill up the bourgeois interior itself. It could therefore be argued that the objects in the slum home are inherently *more* meaningful than the classically decorative furnishings of the celebrated bourgeois parlour. The slum, revealing the human labour and components that make up the commodity, is thus the manufactory and truthful counterpart to the Parisian Arcades, envisaged by Walter Benjamin as the architectural display of the nineteenth-century commodity, or indeed to the Crystal Palace's imagined national interior.

Looking closely at the significance ascribed to the role – or apparent absence – of objects in the slum interior thus requires different ways of thinking about domestic materialities. It necessitates a closer consideration of the function of objects within domestic space: who is in possession of them (a point of crucial importance in the context of the home as a site of the manufacture and production of goods); the transactional and often temporary nature of domestic items (in the context of pawning as a means of economic survival); and a consideration of the bodily labour of workers involved in the production of material goods that furnish the domestic interiors of middle-class households.

iii   Excessive forms: Containing the body of the slum

Mayhew's accounts of urban dwellings are distinguished by an effort to individualise the voices of the working people in London who were living in impoverished housing conditions and by a systematic attempt to reveal the correlation between low and insecure wages and poverty. Nevertheless, his forensic approach, which demonstrated sensitivity to the difference and variations in the conditions of economic hardship, was arguably superseded by a strand of writing about urban slums which became more concerned with recording the homogeneous, abject quality of the slum environment than the lives of its residents. To a large extent, Mayhew's careful interpretative approach, which suggested that the interiors of the

---

[36] Karl Marx, *Economic and Philosophical Manuscripts* (1844), in Karl Marx, *Early Writings*, Rodney Livingstone and Gregor Benton (trans.), (London: Penguin, 1992), p. 324.

poor were complex imbrications of signs, images and narrative accounts, gave way to a vein of social exploration in which the slum becomes an immersive, sensory and haptic experience for the observer of the scene and the reader of the report.

If Mayhew was attentive to the significant and telling differences in the categories of workers and their homes, many later investigators produced volumes of reports devoted to describing the homes of the poor in terms that announced, in somewhat ironic fashion, the overriding *sameness* of tenement or slum. The apparent homogeneity of conditions is reflected (and arguably produced) by the similarity in detail and tenor of many of the accounts by writers such as James Greenwood, Andrew Mearns and Sims: a preoccupation with registering scales of dirtiness, shock at levels of overcrowding and a repetition of characteristic adjectives ('rotten', 'greasy', 'black', 'oozing', 'crazy').

The defining aspect of such representations is the detail given to the homogeneity of 'dirt' itself, which functions as the opposite of the idea of the 'proper' (derived from 'propre', the French sense of 'clean') home. If the bourgeois home was increasingly associated with the maintenance of sanitation and hygiene, involving the suppression of not only forms of filth but also of the visibility of the instruments and hands that dealt with it, then it finds its apparent other in the bleak spaces of the slum interiors with their 'heavy incubus of accumulated dirt'.[37] Mearns, for example, writing in 1883, stated simply of one London home: 'Walls and ceiling are black with the accretions of filth which have gathered upon them through long years of neglect. It is exuding through cracks in the boards overhead; it is running down the walls; it is everywhere.'[38] The significance of this figuration of dirt, as Alain Corbin and others have powerfully demonstrated, is to establish distinctions and inviolable degrees of accept-ability.[39] The social investigators thus commonly see filth as being manifest not only tangibly, but also figuratively, as expressed in their frequent representation of the profane language of the poor in their homes. Thus in his famous exposé of the habits of homeless men who shared an institutionalised domestic space, 'A Night in a Workhouse', Greenwood seems as scandalised by the men's 'abominable' anecdotes, their 'deluge of

---

[37] Octavia Hill, *Homes of the London Poor* (New York: State Charities Aid Association, 1875), p. 6.

[38] Andrew Mearns, *The Bitter Cry of Outcast London: An Enquiry Into the Condition of the Abject Poor* (London: James Clarke & Co., 1883), p. 8.

[39] Alain Corbin, *The Foul and the Fragrant: Odor and the French Social Imagination* (Leamington Spa: Berg, 1986).

foul words' and a song capped with a 'bestial chorus', as by the scenes of apparent 'Bedlam' he witnesses in the men's shelter.[40]

Indeed the reports frequently exhibit a self-reflexiveness about language and representation and there is often a struggle between excess (of words, of the sheer 'filthiness' or horror of the scene that is witnessed) and the lack of an adequate means of truthful or proper representation. The writers evince at times a valiant attempt to overrepresent – hence a litany of repetitive, hyperbolic verbosity – alongside a discourse proclaiming the ineffability of the housing conditions. In *How the Poor Live*, for example, Sims claims that 'some of the terrible sights which we have seen we have too much respect for the reader's feelings to reproduce', while in *The Bitter Cry of Outcast London*, Mearns, in a familiar rhetorical mode of shock and enticement, promises: 'This is bad, but it is not the worst'.[41] It follows from this that if the domestic interior more generally is always partly an 'imagined' space, as critics have recently argued, the decaying slum home is one which also requires an act of creative embellishment, although of a far less idealising kind.

The idea of rhetorical excess – and a demand placed on the reader to *imagine* the condition to which the reporter is witness – is particularly salient with regard to the issue of smell. For smell is always described as having a dominant sensory effect on the outsider and yet one which the writer cannot evoke with the immediacy it demands through text (nor can it be rendered through pictorial illustration).[42] The emphasis on the sensory affront of smell has to be seen in the context of the design of the middle-class Victorian house in this period, with its emphasis on the compartmentalisation of household activities; for example, the separation of kitchens, bedrooms and bathrooms from the everyday living spaces of the parlour.[43] The recognition of the overpowering odour of the slum, predictably enough, signalled precisely a lack of such boundaries. But it is

---

[40] James Greenwood, 'A Night in a Workhouse', in Peter Keating (ed.), *Into Unknown England 1866–1913: Selections from the Social Explorers* (London: Fontana, 1976), pp. 40, 45. Hugh Shimmin, the Liverpool-based social explorer, is frequently affronted by 'foul speech' and 'disgusting language' in the slums, especially among the women he observes. See, for example, John K. Walton and Alastair Wilcox, *Low Life and Moral Improvement in Mid-Victorian England: Liverpool Through the Journalism of Hugh Shimmin* (Leicester: Leicester University Press, 1991), pp. 43, 50.

[41] Sims, *How the Poor Live*, p. 69; Mearns, *Bitter Cry*, p. 20.

[42] For the way the sanitary reformers struggled to classify and thus explain the smells that overwhelmed them, see David Trotter, 'The New Historicism and the Psychopathology of Everyday Modern Life', in William A. Cohen and Ryan Johnson (eds.), *Filth: Dirt, Disgust, and Modern Life* (Minneapolis: University of Minnesota Press, 2005), pp. 30–48.

[43] For a discussion of the design and arrangement of the middle-class home, see Hamlett, *Material Relations*, pp. 40–60.

also important to note that the confluence of smells arising from the housing's bad drainage and ventilation, the communal latrine, the mingling of bodies and the keeping of animals also signalled the multifarious activities and uses of the domestic space in the slum home. And thus a significant aspect of the 'bad smell' of tenement houses is its revelation of labour and production in the home. Mearns, to give one example, comments:

> Here you are choked as you enter by the air laden with particles of the superfluous fur pulled from the skins of rabbits, rats, dogs and other animals in their preparation for the furrier. Here the smell of paste and of drying match-boxes, mingling with other sickly odours, overpowers you; or it may be the fragrance of stale fish or vegetables, not sold on the previous day, and kept in the room overnight.[44]

In this regard, the anxiety about the merged boundaries of home and work space crystallise in recurrent images of the atmosphere of the slum home (and of the visitor) polluted by the by-products of outsourced labour.

The supposed capacity of the slum to breach its unstable boundaries is reiterated through descriptions of the physical houses themselves – structures which are repeatedly described as broken down and dangerously toppling. In one characteristic example, the housing reformer Thomas Beames records how

> the houses inclined considerably over the pavement with their ragged crumbling fronts – the first story particularly seemed to overhang the ground-floor, as though it had been originally built so; the roofs with their broken tiles, the plaster with which some of the houses were covered peeling off and the crazy doors by which you entered speaking of years of neglect.[45]

Against the dominant image of the solid storeyed bourgeois house, the recurrent emphasis on the ramshackle and irregular shapes of these urban dwellings can be seen to be characterised in an almost carnivalesque idiom. In this regard, Peter Stallybrass and Allon White's system of categories may be usefully applied to the way in which the housing structures of the poor, rather than descriptions of their bodily selves, are sometimes deployed in Victorian social writing to convey an effect of degradation. As in Stallybrass and White's account of the lower-ordered body, which is characterised by its multiple openings and orifices, 'mobile, split, multiple . . . never

---

[44] Mearns, *Bitter Cry*, p. 10.
[45] Thomas Beames, *The Rookeries of London: Past, Present, and Prospective* (London: Thomas Bosworth, 1852), p. 103.

closed off from either its social or ecosystemic context', slum structures function as a type of architectural 'other' to the solid Victorian house and home.[46]

This is particularly manifest in descriptions of water and wetness (and the associated tropes of stagnation, residuum and blockage) that pervade many descriptions of poor urban dwellings and their accompanying illustrations. Sims, for example, records walking across floor boards in a dilapidated London home, an act which produced 'a slushing noise of a plank spread across a mud puddle in a brickfield'.[47] All that is solid, in these analyses of architecture and structure, seems to be on the point of dissolution; Canning Town itself, in Godwin's aptly named *Town Swamps and Social Bridges* (1859), was said to be sinking below the Thames' high water mark.[48] This is starkly manifest in Mayhew's famous description of Jacob's Island, 'the Venice of Drains' – an area of slum housing marooned by a pestilent sewer, immortalised as the site of Bill Sikes' self-hanging in *Oliver Twist* – which provides an archetypal description of the unnatural elements and industrial pollutants that constituted the slum environment.

In relation to the 'decaying' subdivided slum house, regular water supply and the associated issue of sanitary drainage was a particular problem for those homes that had not been built with the intention of servicing multiple households. But in the writing of social investigation, the idea of the leaky, sodden interior clearly takes on a symbolic meaning, emphasising the idea of slum housing as a threat to the sealed, sober properties of the model, moral Victorian house. But even the element of wetness is given a characteristic stamp in these writings, for it often characterises not movement but precisely the idea of residuum or stagnation. For Hector Gavin, an earlier sanitary reformer writing in 1848, this manifests itself in descriptions that constantly focus on the way in which the solidity of streets and houses metamorphose into a horror of liquid and decomposing forms. Just two pages of his notebooks detailing Bethnal Green streets furnish the following descriptions: a 'soil permeated by cesspools', a 'putrescent mass', 'a stagnant pool of most offensive and filthy slime', 'yards ... little dissimilar to the stagnant gutter, or ditch itself', 'muddy and slimy pools', 'stagnant pools of foetid, and putrid mud with their green scum', 'pool of foetid slime', a 'kind of thickened, black, slimy,

[46] Peter Stallybrass and Allon White, *The Politics and Poetics of Transgression* (New York: Cornell University Press, 1986), p. 22.

[47] Sims, *How the Poor Live*, p. 12.

[48] George Godwin, *Town Swamps and Social Bridges* (London: Routledge, Warnes & Routledge, 1859), p. 58.

and putrescent mud'.[49] Pleasant-Place Street, he notes, is 'nothing more or less than an elongated lake or canal; only, in place of water, we have a black, slimy, muddy compost of clay and putrescent animal and vegetable remains'.[50] There are, in fact, few descriptions of domestic interiors (and no people) in Gavin's slimy landscape, where the centre constantly gives way to inorganic breakdowns into what he terms 'effluvia'.

In the characteristic manner in which metaphors gain momentum in the writings of slum commentators of the period, by the time of Jack London's turn-of-the-century exploration of the East End of London, the watery analogy had become axiomatic. Published just after Joseph Conrad's *Heart of Darkness* (1899), London's *The People of the Abyss* (1903) likens the urban investigator's pioneering exploration of the under-belly of the city to a sea voyage. As London prepares to 'plunge' himself into the abyss of poverty, he comments:

> And as far as I could see were the solid walls of brick, the slimy pavements, and the screaming streets; and for the first time in my life the fear of the crowd smote me. It was like the fear of the sea; and the miserable multi-tudes, street upon street, seemed so many waves of a vast and malodorous sea, lapping about me and threatening to well up and over me.[51]

The idea of slum housing being characterised by tropes of disintegration, pulpiness and forms of fluidity lends itself to the wider nineteenth-century discourse of degeneration.[52] It is underpinned by the fact that many of these dwelling types consisted of subdivided houses that had formerly belonged to single families and were associated with the process of 'town decay' as the wealthier classes moved from the cities to the outlying suburbs. Beames, who was interested in tracing the historical genealogy of slum quarters in London, for example, remarks on the process by which, as he puts it, 'the hotel of the peer may become the hovel of the pauper' and how easily poorly built houses 'degenerate into Rookeries'.[53] The crumbling interiors of formerly grand houses in some of the 'dingiest streets of the Metropolis' thus seemed to bear witness to profound social shifts. Many of these ancient houses, Beames notes, still contain

[49] Hector Gavin, *Sanitary Ramblings: Being Sketches and Illustrations of Bethnal Green* (London: John Churchill, 1848), pp. 10–11.
[50] Gavin, *Sanitary Ramblings*, p. 11.
[51] Jack London, *The People of the Abyss* (London: Macmillan & Co., 1903), p. 8.
[52] Judith Walkowitz discusses how Lamarckian and Spencerian evolutionary thought was applied to the slums and their inhabitants in *City of Dreadful Delight: Narratives of Sexual Danger in Late-Victorian Britain* (Chicago: University of Chicago Press, 1992), pp. 35–36.
[53] Beames, *Rookeries*, pp. 44, 69.

rooms of which are lofty, the walls panelled, the ceilings beautifully ornamented, (although the gilding which encrusted the ornaments is worn off,) the chimney-pieces models for the sculptor. In many rooms there still remain the grotesque carvings for which a former age was so celebrated.[54]

'In a literal sense', the housing historian John Burnett writes in the twentieth century, 'much tenement housing was residual – what had been left over and abandoned after the needs of the more prosperous had been satisfied in newer, more salubrious, districts'.[55] The literally residual nature of this housing is interesting in light of the recurrent 'flotsam' imagery that the explorers use to describe the tenants of these places; even Burnett himself uses the metaphor to describe the status of those unable to 'filter up' out of their position: 'the poor could not exercise any real choice, and, like flotsam, they constantly eddied back and forth but ended up in the same places'.[56] Indeed, the trope endures in housing discourse today, specifically in the technical use of the term 'residualisation' by housing analysts and activists to refer to the spiralling process by which undesirable properties shelter the most disadvantaged tenants.

From dirt, to smell, to wetness and the possibility of degeneration, the sensory landscape of the urban slum presented a setting which compelled social investigators to narrate, make sense of and attempt to contain it. Unsurprisingly, the very need to maintain a firmly demarcated distance from the overpowering and encroaching senses of the environment is present at the level of form. One method, noted by Poovey in her work on Victorian sanitary reform, was the deployment of the trope of the social body and its associations of health and organic wholeness which informed the work of some of the early reports. Arguing that 'the image of the social body was one of the two principal images used to depict society in the 1830s', she addresses the way in which Chadwick's door-to-door sanitary report 'cast the city (and society more generally) as a giant body that required a physician's care'.[57] In this way, preventative measures could be applied to the 'residual' slums – so often portrayed as a site of unnatural stagnation and blockage.

> It was the task of trained observers, especially medical men knowledgeable about sanitary reform, to identify those symptoms for what they were so that government officials could intervene before congested lungs bred epidemic fevers. In the city, signs of disease took the form of clogged drains

---

[54] Beames, *Rookeries*, p. 16.
[55] John Burnett, *A Social History of Housing: 1815–1970* (London: Methuen, 1980), p. 65.
[56] Burnett, *Social History*, p. 67.   [57] Poovey, *Social Body*, p. 37.

and overcrowded tenements; these problems also forecast social disorder, because, in an analysis that conflated physical with moral 'debility', environmental factors were thought capable of eroding self-discipline and moral rectitude: insalubrious living conditions, in short, could breed prostitution, trade unionism, and revolutionary politics.[58]

The identification and dissection of ailing parts of the social body through urban surveys lent themselves to a form Poovey terms 'anatomical realism'. This approach was underpinned by the working principle that 'far from residing on the surface where it was obvious to the eye, then, the truth of the body was assumed to hide in its interior'.[59] In such a way, the slum home needed to be cut open and exposed in order to remedy its ailments.

Poovey provides a striking example of this dissective approach by pointing to illustrations from George Godwin's *London Shadows: A Glance at the 'Homes' of the Thousands* (1854), which expose interior living conditions for the curious reader. Poovey notes the 'influence of anatomy upon this kind of social survey . . . in the engravings that depict working-class houses with their external walls peeled back to reveal sparsely furnished interiors, babies crawling on damp-stained floors, and overcrowded beds'.[60] The relationship between the sectional view of the house and dissection is further implicit since there is a long history of the house being likened to a body in the form of 'anthropomorphic analogy'.[61] This notion of stripping back or laying bare the body of the house further connects to the social explorers' stated goal: that 'truth will be given in stark nakedness'.[62] By anthropomorphising the slum dwelling through visual and textual metaphors, these writers continue the practice of making intimate connections between the dwelling, the bodies it contained and the house itself as a type of body which they can dissect, peer into and diagnose. As I argue later in this chapter, the discourse linking body, room and behaviour evolves throughout the nineteenth-century writings of such reformers as Charles Booth and Octavia Hill – often in the guise of a debate as to whether the insalubrious home might be responsible for the inhabitants' bad character or whether their immoral and unsanitary ways leave their imprint on the homes.[63]

---

[58] Poovey, *Social Body*, p. 41.   [59] Poovey, *Social Body*, p. 79.   [60] Poovey, *Social Body*, p. 83.
[61] Anthony Vidler surveys the architecture–body analogy in 'Architecture Dismembered' in *The Architectural Uncanny: Essays in the Modern Unhomely* (Massachusetts: Massachusetts Institute of Technology Press, 1992), pp. 69–82.
[62] Mayhew, Letter II, 23 October 1849, *Morning Chronicle*, vol. I, p. 52.
[63] Shimmin, for example, states: 'The character of the inmates is clearly indicated to some extent by the exterior, yet in these matters it is not always safe to judge by appearances; therefore enter house Number One' (Walton and Wilcox, *Low Life*, p. 109); while Booth makes a note concerning

On the One-pair Floor.

Fig. 5.—On the Ground Floor.

Figure 1 – Sectional view of a slum interior. Woodcut by John Brown, from George Godwin, *London Shadows: A Glance at the 'Homes' of the Thousands* (London: George Routledge & Co, 1854). Photo courtesy of Nuffield College Library.

However, it is important to note that as a form of representation, the revelation of inhabitants and rooms in their 'Rembrandtish gloom', as presented in Brown's wood-engraved images, does not serve simply to shock the viewer in its exposure of destitution because it is also underpinned by an undercurrent of voyeuristic pleasure.[64] For the sectional view was a more general popular mode of representing the Victorian household

one of his 'Purple' streets that '[t]here is a low, vicious look about the people which seems to stamp itself upon the houses', *Life and Labour*, First Series, vol. II, p. 188.
[64] George Godwin, *London Shadows: A Glance at the 'Homes' of the Thousands* (London: George Routledge & Co., 1854), p. 19.

and finds its most domestic and familiar expression in the doll's house (itself a 'quintessential trinket of the nineteenth-century home') as well as in cross-sectional depictions of apartment buildings which reveal the lives within.[65] As a representative mode in the context of slum writing, the doll's house serves to domesticate and miniaturise these destitute interiors, allowing for an apparently omniscient view into the dwellings of the so-called outcast poor. In this sense, it is an artefact that emblematises the allure – as well as the limits – of the idea of the interior. As Susan Stewart beautifully puts it, 'occupying a space within an enclosed space, the dollhouse's aptest analogy is the locket or the secret recesses of the heart: center within center, within within within'.[66] The doll's house perspective thus provides 'the promise of an infinitely profound interiority' but one which has very little to do with the relationship between the actual occupant of the home and the dwelling.[67] It is the ideology of 'interiority' as a visual mode and form which is at play here, enticing the viewer with the promise of some kind of meaningful revelation.

In *London Shadows*, Godwin self-reflexively draws attention to the forensic nature of the act of peering into the homes of the poor. Directly addressing the bourgeois reader located in comfortable domestic surroundings, Godwin writes:

> There are fifteen houses in this narrow place. Let us take one at random, and look into the interior. We have, Asmodeus-like, removed the front wall from the top to the bottom, that our readers may examine without fear, and at their leisure, the extraordinary and distressing scene it presents. Let us schedule its contents. . . .[68]

Godwin's reassurance to his reader that his method will enable them to look into these interiors 'without fear' and 'at their leisure' renders explicit the desire of some of these writers to present the horrors of poverty within a controlled, safe and domestic frame. Indeed, the etchings are striking for their pared-down quality; rather than abject suffering or visual evidence of the oft-mentioned overcrowding, they often portray families engaged in quiet industriousness.

Godwin's reference to Asmodeus merits further comment: a devilish cupid figure who appears in a French novel by Alain-René Lesage,

---

[65] Didier Maleuvre, *Museum Memories: History, Technology, Art* (Stanford: Stanford University Press, 1999), p. 134.

[66] Susan Stewart, *On Longing: Narratives of the Miniature, the Gigantic, the Souvenir, the Collection*, new edn. (Durham: Duke University Press, 1993), p. 61.

[67] Stewart, *On Longing*, p. 61.   [68] Godwin, *London Shadows*, p. 17.

Figure 2 – Frontispiece by W. McConnell, from James Hain Friswell, *Houses With the Fronts Off* (London: James Blackwood, 1854).

Le Diable Boiteux (1707), Asmodeus was said to have removed the roofs from the houses of a village during a night flight to reveal the secrets of the inhabitants' private lives. In a notable instance of intertextuality, another writer from this period, James Hain Friswell, refers in his investigation of the homes and dwelling places of the poor to the same Asmodeus, who 'for his especial amusement lifted off any roof he wished to pry under, to let him see what the inhabitants were at'.[69] Friswell states that he will take inspiration from this figure and 'determines for some little time to play the devil' in the pages that follow by removing the front walls in order to glimpse the private lives within.[70] The title of his work, *Houses with the Fronts Off*, reinforces the idea of dismemberment and the forensic gaze into the interiors of the poor. In addition, the book – a hybrid form of social reportage and Gothic creative fiction – enacts the familiar house-as-body trope,

---

[69] James Hain Friswell, *Houses with the Fronts Off* (London: James Blackwood, 1854), p. ix.
[70] Friswell, *Houses*, p. x.

for Friswell's device is to render each chapter through the device of a particular house that speaks through an array of individuated and colloquial first person voices. The 'character' of the first chapter, for example, is the abandoned and destitute 'House in Chancery' who complains of having 'rheumatism in my cellars, lumbago in all my back rooms, and vertigo in my attics'.[71] The ironically named 'No. 5, Paradise Place', meanwhile, articulates the tenement building's familiar litany of ruin: 'My roof is not waterproof; ... my drains, to say the least of them, are bad; I have a cess-pool in my cellar; my stairs are broken, and I have not a banister on the staircase.'[72] Friswell's ventriloquist narrative reiterates the sense that interiors can speak for themselves – a belief firmly entrenched in the ideology of the bourgeois interior and yet one which was clearly not as stable or self-evident as it appeared.

iv   Slum housing, character and improvement: Charles Booth and Octavia Hill

Alongside the discursive genre that presented poor interiors as a disorienting spectacle in need of order and visual control was a strand of writing that argued for a reformist approach. Following the door-to-door format of Chadwick's *Report* and Gavin's *Sanitary Ramblings*, sections of Charles Booth's sweeping *Life and Labour of the People in London* (1886–1903), compiled by a group of investigators that included Clara Collet and Beatrice Webb, provided an inventory of the conditions of some of London's poorest quarters. Booth's methodology in the 'London Street by Street' section is structured by a type of progress towards the domestic interior, whereby the reporters move inward from street, to house, and finally to the tenants' rooms. The reports are predicated to a large extent on a binary model: either the note-takers confirm the way in which the 'bad' appearance of a house contains a 'low' person or they express their surprise that the outward signs of deviancy are not borne out by what they find inside the home. The logic works both ways as it so often does with interiors; when the house/person assessment does not correlate exactly (a 'bad' looking house harbouring people with 'neat' habits, for example), the discrepancy itself serves to reinforce the underlying supposition that structural and moral dilapidation go hand in hand. The exception, in other words, proves the rule.

---

[71] Friswell, *Houses*, p. 5   [72] Friswell, *Houses*, p. 13.

Scouring the blackest streets (Booth's colour code moved from the 'lowest' streets which were black and dark blue to the more affluent hues of red and yellow), Booth's investigators invoke familiar tropes of instability in their surveys of impoverished households. In the notorious Shelton Street (which had actually been demolished since the initial publication of the report), Booth notes that the 'houses looked ready to fall, many of them being out of the perpendicular'.[73] Like the houses themselves, the inhabitants of the poorest dwellings are often characterised by a lack of fixity. The quality of 'shiftiness' – a keyword that recurs throughout the pages of the notebook – again equates slum households with images of flux and movement in contrast with architectural tropes of Victorian steadiness and structure. Just as houses in urban exploration are shown to be unstable, excessive and grotesquely protruding, the bodies of this notably immigrant population are typified as disruptively mobile and resistant to staying in one place. 'Shiftiness' is used with particular emphasis to describe the families of Irish Roman Catholics, an immigrant group repeatedly vilified throughout the pages of the notebooks; one family, in a typical summation, is said to be 'living in dirt, fond of drink, alike shiftless, shifty and shifting'.[74]

The reports from within the interiors of the houses only serve to affirm the model which posits a stable alliance between the appearance of a dwelling and its occupants. For example:

> At *No.* 34 there are eight rooms, and during the eleven years of the missionary's visits never can he remember finding a family in any one of them that could be called decent in person, room, or behaviour. Dirt, drink, and swearing prevailed with all.
>
> The north side of Shelton Street contained houses and people of similar character.[75]

The triad of 'person, room, or behaviour' is firmly established, and rests on the bourgeois principle that the interior is reflective of the person and of their moral conduct. As Livesey has argued, Victorian social reformers, particularly in the 1880s and 1890s, were preoccupied with the 'need to read and write the characters of the poor – to deduce an interior self from external description, and transcribe this for a readership'.[76] And as she goes on to observe, the narrative modes of naturalism in the novel – and

---

[73] Booth, *Life and Labour*, First Series, vol. II, p. 48.
[74] Booth, *Life and Labour*, First Series, vol. II, p. 51.
[75] Booth, *Life and Labour*, First Series, vol. II, p. 60.   [76] Livesey, 'Reading for Character', p. 45.

particularly its forensic attention to the reading of social signs – were crucial to late Victorian and Edwardian urban reform literature; in both modes, Livesey argues, 'character was reified: it was an object, a property legible through detailed description and determining individual destiny'.[77] Booth's notebooks thus constantly depend upon the assumed alliance and interchangeability of room and person, as exemplified by the following observations: 'the grate fireless, and the children without shoes and stockings'; 'the room and its occupants alike dirty and offensive to sight and smell'; 'the room poorly furnished and [the tenants] poorly clothed and fed'; 'the houses have at times a furtive secret look, but the evil character of the black streets is rather to be seen on the faces of the people – men, women, and children are all stamped with it'; 'the people who dwell here look as poverty-stricken as the houses'.[78]

As might be expected, Booth often remarks that the housing conditions imprint themselves on the moral character and gait of the inhabitants, with the strong implication that 'the trouble at bottom is "bad property rather than bad people"'.[79] Anticipating what is now a commonplace concerning the relationship of housing condition and behaviour, he claims that there is an irrevocable causal relation between the state of the home and moral character. Once character is warped by its surroundings, he seems to imply, the individual is corrupted by a taint that they then literally embody. Thus, he argues, 'when the people move [house] they carry their low standard of housing and crowding into districts where there need be no pressure of population'.[80] The idea of the threat of contamination naturally seemed to extend to the note-takers themselves; one of Booth's reporters comments of a slum house in Shelton St, said to be infested by 'vermin', that a 'visitor in these rooms was fortunate indeed if he carried nothing of the kind away with him'.[81]

At certain points, the idea that the condition of the home imprints itself on the body of the inhabitant is rendered in a more literal way. Where work is performed in the home, some of the tenants are presented as being effectively crippled by this domestic mode of production. In one case, a widowed loom-weaver's body has almost moulded itself to her work tools; 'Sitting to her loom had so cramped her that she was bowed together and

[77] Livesey, 'Reading for Character', p. 60.
[78] Booth, *Life and Labour*, First Series, vol. II, pp. 58, 67, 68, 82, 120.
[79] Charles Booth, *Life and Labour of the People in London*, 2nd edn. (London: Macmillan and Co., 1902), Third Series, vol. I, p. 189.
[80] Booth, *Life and Labour*, Third Series, vol. I, p. 190.
[81] Booth, *Life and Labour*, First Series, vol. II, p. 47.

could not lift herself up.'[82] But on occasion, interdependence between body and housing structure is strikingly reversed in passages where the bad 'character' of the tenant marks the house itself. In streets situated off the Holloway Road in North London, for example, inhabited by a motley group of labourers, costermongers and 'some thieves', Booth notes:

> The houses have 'loafer' stamped upon their walls, the bricks blackened and shiny where they have been leant against, the mortar picked or kicked away by idle hands and feet.[83]

And in Headley Street, backing onto a railway line, Booth again makes note of the way in which the houses are literally altered by the mixed population of workers and 'loafers' in this light blue – coded street.

> Many of the doors stand always open – the surface of the bricks round about the entrance of each house is black and polished by rubbing arms and shoulders, and the mortar has crumbled away from between the bricks or been picked out by idle fingers.[84]

Another trope deployed by Booth makes the body-house-sign continuum explicit. This is found in instances where the houses themselves seem to advertise their 'character' (in the sense of morality or respectability) as well as the physical labour performed within their walls through actual signs posted in the windows. Booth's reporters often read social significance into these advertisements, where, for example, 'mangling is done here' signals the 'small custom' of the domestic worker, whilst 'lodgings for a respectable single man' is a sign which indicates 'a low level in the social scale'.[85] In this respect, George Acorn, whose memoir will be addressed in detail later, recounts a seemingly apocryphal story concerning local interest in the livelihood of one Mrs Dartmouth, who lived in the East End neighbourhood.

> The query was how Mrs. Dartmouth kept three rooms nicely furnished . . ., herself, and a gouty husband who had never been known to work. I doubt if we should have known even by this time had not a shortage in business forced her to give up one of her rooms, and to hang a card in the front window. It was startlingly crude, this piece of cardboard with the words –
>
> 'DEAD BODIES WASHED HERE'
>
> written across it.
>
> *That* was how three rooms and a gouty husband had been maintained![86]

[82] Booth, *Life and Labour*, First Series, vol. II, p. 68.
[83] Booth, *Life and Labour*, Third Series, vol. I, p. 141.
[84] Booth, *Life and Labour*, First Series, vol. II, p. 146.
[85] Booth, *Life and Labour*, First Series, vol. II, p. 182.
[86] George Acorn, *One of the Multitude* (New York: Dodd, Mead and Company, 1912), pp. 83–84.

In Acorn's story, Mrs Dartmouth exhibits the outward signs of respectability (relative cleanliness, an apparent surplus of rooms from which she is able to accrue income, nice furnishings), but these are ironically achieved precisely through the abject practice of tending to deceased bodies secretly within the interior. The sign in the window that she is eventually compelled to display reveals the economic means by which she purchases this outward respectability, thereby simultaneously sullying it. As Anne McClintock has noted, part of the efficacy of the display of cleanliness is based on concealing the actual labour that produces it.[87]

As with Mayhew's work, at certain points Booth helps to convey a more nuanced domestic semiotic, or materialist epistemology, which works to destabilise conventional associations of self and objects. For example, the usual equation of the bareness of a room with poverty, and a plethora of objects with domestic well-being, is complicated by an attention to the prevalence of 'ready furnished' rooms for rent, a phenomenon that signalled short-term lets for the more 'shifting' immigrant population (who did not possess their own furniture). Likewise, the presence of Roman Catholic Irish inhabitants is sometimes associated with the manifestation of a clutter of pictures and icons (rather than domestic bareness); Booth notes of a house tenanted by Irish costermongers that one family would 'only open their door wide enough to afford a glimpse of wall covered with pictures and shut it again'.[88] But the overall effect of these house visitations in Booth's work is to render what Livesey identifies as the presentation of a 'vacant still life'.[89] In other words, this is a textual form which operates by establishing a recognisable set piece which confirms the reporters' viewpoint momentarily before they move on to have expectations confirmed again, or, less commonly, overturned. By this device, things seem to occur paradoxically in the moment and for all time; Booth's observational pursuit is, in this way, markedly different from Mayhew's more diachronic reading of what are effectively the root causes of the correlations between work, low wages, poverty, class and inadequate housing.

The association of the person or family with their house and interior (particularly with regard to the cleanliness and order of this inner space) was also key to the writings of the social reformer Octavia Hill, who played a key role in the development of forms of social housing. This conviction is at the core of her famous pronouncement: 'You cannot deal

[87] McClintock, *Imperial Leather*, pp. 161–62.   [88] Booth, *Life and Labour*, First Series, vol. II, p. 50.
[89] Livesey, 'Reading for Character', p. 57.

with the people and their houses separately. The principle on which the whole work rests, is that the inhabitants and their surroundings must be improved together'.[90] The very logic of her reforming endeavour was based on the environmental determinism that had preoccupied earlier sanitary reformers, such as Chadwick. In Hill's work, however, in a practical inversion, it was envisaged that the benevolence and good, clean habits of Hill's designated female rent collectors, landladies and housing reformers would rub off on the renegade tenants. For in the setting of the poorest London courts, Hill used the principles of domesticity as a conversion tool to raise the residents from moral waywardness to 'civil- ised', rent-paying citizens. House management literally acquired evangel- ical overtones in Hill's essays, where the missionary principles of reform and enlightenment were transmitted in ordinances of good housekeeping. Hill writes:

> I think no one who has not experienced it can fully realize the almost awed sense of joy with which one enters upon such a possession as that above described, conscious of having the power to set it, even partially, in order. Hopes, indeed, there are which one dares scarcely hope; but at once one has power to say, 'Break out a window there in that dark corner; let God's light and air in;' or, 'Trap that foul drain, and shut the poisonous miasma out;' and one has moral power to say, by deeds which speak louder than words, 'Where God gives me authority, this, which you in your own hearts know to be wrong, shall not go on.'[91]

The result is that throughout Hill's essays, the domestic motif of 'setting the house in order' is seamlessly aligned to the idea of 'ordering' the individual. 'Order' is a revealing word because it suggests the discipline and surveillance that Hill so insistently proscribes, but also implies the inculcation of hegemony, whereby the tenement dwellers' own self- regulation becomes the ultimate design. Like the most effective forms of ideology, Hill's operations are directed towards her tenant-pupils' self- governance. Thus taking the relations of rooms and selves as naturally given, Hill's charismatic advocacy of room refurbishment assumes the wholescale conversion and enlightenment of the individual:

> As soon as I entered into possession [of the court rooms], each family had an opportunity offered of doing better: those who would not pay, or who led clearly immoral lives, were ejected. The rooms they vacated were cleansed; the tenants who showed signs of improvement moved into them, and thus, in turn, an opportunity was obtained for having each room

[90] Hill, *Homes*, pp. 47–48. [91] Hill, *Homes*, p. 17.

distempered and painted. The drains were put in order, a large slate cistern was fixed, the wash-house was cleared of its lumber, and thrown open on stated days to each tenant in turn. The roof, the plaster, the woodwork were repaired; the staircase-walls were distempered; new grates were fixed; the layers of paper and rag (black with age) were torn from the windows, and glass was put in.[92]

The implied reformation of the degraded lower classes is given vivid visual detail in accounts of the actual practice of setting unemployed tenants to work in the process of 'restoring and purifying the houses'.[93] This serves as a particularly expedient metaphor, in which the standard model dwelling will regulate – and literally domesticate – deviant selves into 'model' citizens. In sermon-like tones, Hill poses herself a set of questions and solutions, with a utopian, declamatory style that strikingly pre-empts some of the aesthetic principles, schematic design and tenets of mass housing articulated by Le Corbusier in the next century:

> You may say, perhaps, 'This is very well as far as you and your small knot of tenants are concerned, but how does it help us to deal with the vast masses of poor in our great towns?' I reply, 'Are not the great masses made up of many small knots? Are not the great towns divisable into smaller districts? . . . And why should there not be some way of registering such supervision, so that . . . the whole metropolis might be mapped out, all the blocks fitting in like little bits of mosaic to form one connected whole?'[94]

While Hill's discourse is based on an appeal to modernisation, standard-isation and the forward march of reform and progress, it also nostalgically invokes feudal forms of land holding and hierarchical tenancy. Ravetz attempts to defend Hill from the label of 'political reactionary', arguing that while she was no progressive, her methods, which centred on the importance of 'user control', align her with aspects of modern anarchist thought in relation to housing. In addition, she claims, Hill engendered a distinctly 'feminine' version of housing reform: 'She herself likened her work to housekeeping. She was involved with people's most intimate encounters with dustbins, drains, floorboards, clothes-lines and window-panes.'[95] Yet there is something archetypally conventional and deeply conservative in the pastoral aspect of Hill's vision of *noblesse oblige* and her self-representation as a type of 'country proprietor with a moderate number of well-ordered tenants'.[96] Just as in pastoral landscape painting, in which the point of view of the scene is that of the proprietor and surveyor,

---

[92] Hill, *Homes*, p. 17.   [93] Hill, *Homes*, p. 40.   [94] Hill, *Homes*, pp. 27–28.
[95] Ravetz, 'A View from the Interior', p. 191.   [96] Hill, *Homes*, p. 26.

Hill adopts the privileged perspective of the omniscient supervisor of these courts. She makes it clear that any element that does not fit this philanthropic housing scene is to be castigated and then ejected, for the incipient threat to orderly housing always comes in the form of those neighbours who simply will not conform to these standards. The physical dirt can be whitewashed, she appears to argue, but bad behaviour and language among the tenants has a pernicious, contaminating effect.

The rehabilitation of the slum interior and its residents, marked by the literal and symbolic 'whitewashing' of the previously unruly home, would have markedly long-lasting effects. While Hill was an advocate for collective forms of social housing, the ideological model on which her reforms were based valorised the nuclear family household and the self-regulating individual. In the next section, I will develop this analysis by tracing the way in which autobiographical depictions of childhood are framed around a similar narrative trajectory which leads from a social network of slum life to the writer's representation of selfhood, marked by forms of domesticity, literacy and privacy.

v The writer's room: Privacy, literacy and autonomy in George Acorn's *One of the Multitude*

The first part of this chapter surveyed some of the discursive techniques and ways of seeing of Victorian social investigators, whose work has received considerable – and, to some minds, a disproportionate – degree of critical attention. Cultural historians have increasingly tended to be critical of modes of urban voyeurism and moralism that apparently ascribe little agency or voice to their historical subjects. An alternative to such accounts are first-person narratives of 'slum life', although these are evidently more difficult to locate than the voluminous works produced by the social explorers. While important first-person testimony relating to the experience of destitute urban life was available in an early form in Mayhew's mid-Victorian oral histories, it is not until the beginning of the twentieth century that individuals who lived in slums began to publish their own autobiographical accounts.

As a genre, autobiography offers a particularly suggestive medium through which to address the idea of the domestic interior and subjectivity, as it is a mode in which the childhood home is frequently explicitly linked to the writer's sense of origins and roots. It is equally important to attend to the figurative nature of home in many working-class autobiographies, particularly given the emphasis in studies of working-class culture and childhood on material or historical insights that such texts provide. For as Jonathan Rose notes in the preamble to his important study of working-class reading habits and literary imagination, *The Intellectual Life of the British Working Classes*, there has been a tendency among social historians to address 'the grittier or material aspects of working-class life – diet, housing, workplace culture, trade unions, radical politics, crime, and family structure' at the expense of an engagement with working-class cultural activity.[97] Following this trajectory, my analysis suggests that the aesthetic and creative ways in which home is established in texts about working-class childhoods in impoverished urban districts are just as important as their potential to provide historical detail.

Working-class life writing is usually examined in literary studies as a collective body of work, and individual texts are often grouped together according to common themes, concerns and tropes.[98] In contrast to this 'collective' approach, I focus in this section on just three specific works by writers for whom the slums self-reflexively represent a defining aspect of their life story. My approach reflects the fact that these particular texts, which are governed by a strong sense of individualism, are more striking for their idiosyncratic nature than any collective 'ethnographic' similarity. Indeed the memoirs under consideration conform to one of the most conventional of life writing forms – namely, the story of the development of the writer (the *Künstlerroman*). Like all forms of life writing, in other words, these memoirs display the paradoxical properties of being self-reflexively 'individual' and generic at the same time. In addition, it is not my intention to present these works as authentic 'insider' accounts that refute decades of social survey that often sensationalised and dehumanised the lives of the very poor. For in these first-person accounts, the slum often figures, once again, as an evocative and melodramatic setting – one in which the degradations of poverty are expounded in graphic detail and domestic violence is rife. But there is a crucial difference in that these details now furnish the backdrop for individualised portraits of selfhood. The slum interior in all its vivid decay is no longer simply a static 'still life'

---

[97] Jonathan Rose, *The Intellectual Life of the British Working Classes*, 2nd edn. (New Haven: Yale University Press, 2010), p. 3.

[98] See, for example, John Burnett (ed.), *Useful Toil: Autobiographies of Working People from the 1820s to the 1920s* (London: Allen Lane, 1974); David Vincent, *Bread, Knowledge & Freedom: A Study of Nineteenth-Century Working Class Autobiography* (London: Methuen, 1981); Regenia Gagnier, *Subjectivities: A History of Self-Representation in Britain, 1832–1920* (New York: Oxford University Press, 1991). Helen Rogers' digital archive *Writing Lives* is an important recent addition to the field of working-class life writing and its interpretation: www.writinglives.org/.

backdrop which merges seamlessly with its occupant. These memoirists cast their own critical, disobliging eye over the domestic spaces which constituted their home. Indeed, it is crucial to note that these writers are writing retrospectively of these places from which, exerting their own agency, they have moved away to 'rooms of their own': into interiors marked by cleanliness (and whiteness), privacy and literacy. As will be seen, the autobiographical story of the writer from the slum is framed, for the most part, as a narrative of self-preservation and escape.

As Rose so effectively shows in *The Intellectual Life*, the narrative of the autodidact is usually one in which the attainment of knowledge and literacy is correlated with what are thought to be bourgeois principles of autonomy and individualism:

> Their motives were various, but their primary objective was intellectual independence. For centuries autodidacts had struggled to assume direction of their own intellectual lives, to become individual agents in framing an understanding of the world.[99]

But, Rose argues, 'there is nothing distinctively "bourgeois" in this desire for intellectual freedom'.[100] What differentiated working-class autodidacts was a matter of material reality rather than aspiration – specifically, their lack of access to the time and space that reading and writing demand. As he puts it, 'for authors who had to work in cramped tenements, Mrs. Woolf's essay was a sour middle-class joke'.[101] And although it may well have been a sour joke, many working-class memoirists demanded precisely the type of space for reading, writing and thinking that Woolf envisaged. Indeed, the desire for a room of one's own is arguably part of the very lexicon and cultural narrative of working-class writers whose self-education, as Rose and others have shown, derived from reading material which set in place powerful cultural images of privacy and self-identity.

George Acorn's *One of the Multitude* (1912) is paradigmatic in this regard. His memoir conforms to the traditional before-and-after sequence of conventional autobiography, leading from an impoverished childhood in an East London neighbourhood portrayed as antithetical to reason, civility and artistry, to an escape into the light of self-preservation and

---

[99] Rose, *Intellectual Life*, p. 12.
[100] Rose, *Intellectual Life*, p. 13. In this way, Rose departs from Gagnier's interpretation of working-class autobiographical writing that struggled to conform to a middle-class literary model and ideology, leading, she argues, to the 'disintegration' of the narrative and the 'personality' constructed within its pages (*Subjectivities*, pp. 45–46).
[101] Rose, *Intellectual Life*, p. 451.

the act of penning the memoir itself. In Acorn's account, the slums of his childhood are not only overcrowded places of impoverishment, but also of verbal deficiency. In line with a long list of social reformers who seem as scandalised with the 'filthy' language in the slum as they are with the poverty and life-threatening conditions, Acorn repeatedly characterises the environment of his childhood as comprising three linguistic factors: illiteracy, cliché and silence. He notes, for example, that his parents had never learned to read or write (although Acorn's ability to read at the age of three remains curiously unexplained), and poverty is portrayed as inhibiting communication itself: 'When I got home after school I found my father and mother sitting silently facing each other. They had nothing to talk about except trouble, so they remained silent.'[102] Acorn thus projects domestic life in the slums as one in which language is a borrowed, second-hand and worn-out affair, like a linguistic version of the shabby furnishings and objects so often described in these dwellings.[103] In one of many echoes of Matthew Arnold, Acorn deplores the 'mechanical lives' of these inhabitants that result in 'many a slum-child's scars':

> A certain conventional set of words constitutes an insult. They feel little, or no, affront, but take up and carry on a quarrel by means of a conventional harangue which increases in anger and ends with fight. The mind is not used at all; it is simply animal against animal, via conventional routes.[104]

At one point, Acorn embarks on a school trip which will constitute a transformational journey, away from Bermondsey tenement life to the rural location of Reading. On his arrival back to Morocco Street in the East End, he is struck by an acute sense of the narrowness and dirtiness of home life:

> When I returned the air of our street was choking to me – I was sorry to have returned. Instead of the neat orderliness of a farm-house, was the untidy litter of a family in one room, in a mean house, in a mean street.[105]

He soon turns on his 'illiterate' parents, and a chapter which is ostensibly about his early discovery and enjoyment of reading is underpinned by a

---

[102] Acorn, *One of the Multitude*, p. 34.
[103] George Orwell would contribute to this characterisation of the deficiency of speech in the slums. In a passage which virulently describes the apparent squalor of a family-run lodging house, Orwell notes: 'The most dreadful thing about people like the Brookers is the way they say the same things over and over again. It gives you the feeling that they are not real people at all, but a kind of ghost for ever rehearsing the same futile rigmarole'; *The Road to Wigan Pier* (Orlando: Harcourt, 1958), p. 17.
[104] Acorn, *One of the Multitude*, p. 65.   [105] Acorn, *One of the Multitude*, p. 10.

concern for sanitary domestic arrangements: 'I tried to point out to my parents the need, and the possibility, of greater cleanliness, for which I was harshly scolded and severely punished.'[106]

The movement he traces in his memoir thus originates in what is presented as the sullied shared orality of the slums and ends in the self-contained space of clean, private literacy. He thus rehearses a pattern of association between light, literacy, privacy and cleanliness that evokes nineteenth-century reform discourse, turning the sanitary idea into a metaphor and condition for learning and knowledge. The book's individualist ideology is signalled by Acorn's eventual attainment of a house of his own away from the slum and is compounded by his production of the memoir itself as a type of display of property and ownership. To this end, he announces in the memoir's dedication that 'the book is but an imperfect record, – a poor thing, maybe, but "One's" own'.[107] The production of the memoir is moreover represented by Acorn (and in the memoir's Foreword by the writer A. C. Benson) as a type of symbolic triumph against the odds over the slum that militates against art and self-expression. In this way, the home and the text are thus closely correlated as symbols of proprietorship.

In many memoirs by working-class writers, the narrative arc moves spatially from the location of the book's title, indicating a particular locality or street of origin, to a concluding endpoint consisting of the attainment of the writer's room. Willy Goldman's *East End My Cradle: Portrait of an Environment* (1940), for example, ends with two chapters bearing the title of not one, but two, of the most common domestic clichés articulated in the first half of the twentieth century: 'A Room of One's Own' and 'No Place Like Home'. Acorn's account itself is structured by his rejection of the family home and a longing for what he considers 'an ideal existence – that of a lodger in a room tastefully furnished, and all to myself'.[108] The implications of the material and symbolic importance of solitude have already been noted, but Acorn's emphasis on taste is significant here too. It crucially marks Acorn's social mobility, signified by the way in which objects and furnishings – which in the slum were commonly deemed only to be functional, 'homely', cosy or religious – are now indicators of social choice and status. This is a case of what Bourdieu defines as the disposition of taste to achieve distinction, functioning 'as a sort of social orientation, a "sense of one's place"'.[109] When Acorn finally

---

[106] Acorn, *One of the Multitude*, pp. 10–11.   [107] Acorn, *One of the Multitude*, p. vii.
[108] Acorn, *One of the Multitude*, p. 191.   [109] Bourdieu, *Distinction*, p. 466.

takes a room for himself in lodgings, he furnishes it with unsold furniture stock from his day job but also decorates the room with a selection of the 'Hundred Best Pictures' series issued in the early twentieth century by Whiteley's, the department store. Settled into his rented room of his own, the final sections of the memoir end with a proclamation of the self, underpinned by a sanitary metaphor, reminiscent of Hill's principles of domestic reform. The new room has rejuvenated him, in contrast to the ageing second-hand propensities of the slum: 'How bright and beautiful the world seemed! In the silence of my room, after retiring from such scenes, I sought to know myself; ardently I longed to purge my soul of any dross it possessed.'[110] The word 'dross' itself – so typical of slum literature – evokes once again the trope of abject, residual, impure or comingled matter that must, at all costs, be cast away from the self. Acorn's accession to a type of bourgeois domesticity is finally sealed by the description of his wife, an Agnes Wickfield to his David Copperfield, laying out the dinner at the table in the final chapter 'Home'.

But like many autobiographies based around a rigid plot of individual progress, Acorn's tale of what he suggestively labels his own 'self-culture' is riven with contradiction (a fact which ironically militates against the book's tendency towards a tone of righteousness). For if, as he argued, tenement life prevented forms of articulacy and self-expression, how did Acorn himself evade this linguistic fate? He seems unreflective of the irony that the culture of the slum armed him with the tools for bourgeois self-reliance and advancement:

> I was well aware that I had little in common with my companions and environment. . . . As I grew older and learned the great lesson of the slum – to depend entirely upon myself – I came to see that my place and position in life depended more upon myself than anybody else, that I was not like a section of a jigsaw puzzle, formed simply for the purpose of fitting into one particular corner of the social picture; but that if I kept my ideal of a steady, ordered, cultured existence constantly before me I should certainly attain it.[111]

In Acorn's account, the net effect of overcrowding and poverty results not in a sense of collectivity or solidarity but in a deep-seated desire for privacy and autonomy. For while he observes a strong working-class 'community spirit' and comments on the typical 'openness' of the slums (a clichéd observation that permeates so much of the Victorian literature of social exploration),

---

[110] Acorn, *One of the Multitude*, p. 287.   [111] Acorn, *One of the Multitude*, pp. 81–82.

he also identifies the necessary culture of secrecy among locals which carefully established discrete boundaries around households and families. He remarks that

> our neighbours were a curious lot of people, living curious lives; and though a common sympathy and help in the troubles of life was in evidence from neighbour to neighbour, the real facts as to how they got their living, or of their relation to the outer world, and the police, were guarded very closely indeed.[112]

Significantly, Acorn suggestively implies that architectural openness does not necessarily indicate that people's lives could be easily read. Thus while he notes that the door to his house remained open to the street day and night, yet 'the house we were living in was a mysterious place, being let by the landlord in separate tenements, so that nobody knew exactly who did live there'.[113] Working-class sexuality (which piqued the interest of so many social investigators) may well have been the source of neighbourhood gossip and speculation, but as Acorn seems to suggest, it was actually economic secrets to do with money, income and rent that were the real object of concealment in the community.

vi Whitewashing the future: Kathleen Woodward's *Jipping Street: Childhood in a London Slum*

The sanitary metaphor that links the interior, character and textuality also appears as a key motif in Kathleen Woodward's idiosyncratic, semi-fictional memoir *Jipping Street* (1928). In this strange form of memoir (Woodward changed many of the biographical details, including the precise geographical location of her childhood), she recollects an Edwardian childhood in a Bermondsey slum, in a text that is strikingly populated by female characters and relegates men to bit parts as invalids or shadowy tyrants.[114] In many ways, Woodward's intricate description of an inner life forged in the Jipping Street house signals a return to the more sensationalist aspects of nineteenth-century slum discourse. The house is a death trap and place of entrapment, exemplifying the debilitating effects of architecture on the bodies of the poor. Indeed, the effect of brute poverty on the body is crystallised in the bleak opening assessment of

---

[112] Acorn, *One of the Multitude*, p. 83.   [113] Acorn, *One of the Multitude*, p. 168.

[114] For a detailed discussion of the complex fictional parameters of this ostensible memoir, see Carolyn Steedman's introduction to the Virago edition; 'Introduction', Kathleen Woodward, *Jipping Street: Childhood in a London Slum* (London: Virago, 1983), pp. vi–xvi.

her mother's life: 'She knew, she said, only two certain things: death – and the landlord.'[115] The poor home's potential to damage the bodies that reside within it is summed up by what Woodward describes as one of the only pictures decorating the two-bedroom living quarters: a framed certificate recording the death of her abusive maternal grandfather, which makes note of the grim detail that his body was 'washed up at Mortlake'.[116] This representation of death as décor serves as one of many details of the brutality of the Jipping Street home, ranging from the birth of a stillborn child to scenes of graphic domestic violence.

Like earlier descriptions of slum housing, Woodward is attentive to the peculiar boundaries of the public and the private world inherent to her depiction of a childhood home. Thus in an appropriation of the familiar referencing of the tumble-down nature and openness of the slums – features which defy rigid separations of interior and exterior or public and private – the house is portrayed as shifting and permeable: 'Two- and three-roomed houses were reared unbrokenly up each side of Jipping Street; the street was long and narrow, and the substance of the houses dissolved on the slightest provocation; frequently the half or whole of some one's ceiling fell in.'[117] This intrusion of the external environment into the confines of the home is signalled by the smells of the surrounding industries – beer hops, tanyards, a pickle and jam factory and, most significantly, London Bridge Hospital – which infiltrate and pollute Woodward's childhood interior. The proximity of the hospital is itself meaningful, underscoring a sense of the vulnerability of the body and death, which characterise Woodward's own experience of home:

> There by the hospital Horror walked briskly up and down, stark, without cloth or covering, and Pain writhed and anguished past on a police ambulance, crowds swarming after – men, women, children irresistibly drawn; and Suffering, mysterious, consuming, physical suffering displayed no lineament new or strange to our eyes.[118]

The view from the back window of the canal reveals the weekly ritual of the retrieval of dead bodies which are laid out on the canal banks before being taken away to the mortuary. But it is important to note here that the slum interior, for once, is not simply observed but is a viewpoint – specifically one which renders the surrounding environment through a notably stylised, modernist idiom. The child's-eye perspective thus gives

---

[115] Woodward, *Jipping Street*, p. 1.   [116] Woodward, *Jipping Street*, p. 3.
[117] Woodward, *Jipping Street*, p. 24.   [118] Woodward, *Jipping Street*, p. 25.

these grisly scenes a poetic quality, as Woodward observes how she gazes out of the window in order to 'resolve strange, moving shapes and forms in the dissolving lines of the barges and cranes on the wharf-side'.[119]

The violence, dirt and disorder of the domestic interior are, however, contained in the text by Woodward's preoccupation with the practices of cleaning and hygiene. Her deeply ambivalent portrayal of her mother, for example, is typified in a particular image associated with the cleaning that was her livelihood:

> You must see my mother as she most familiarly comes back to me: From out of the washhouse in Jipping Street, forever full of damp, choking, soapy steam from the copper, which settles on the broken windowpanes and in a moment becomes a thousand little rivulets falling drunkenly down the surface of the windows and hangs in tiny, tremulous drops on the ledges which I can watch as I wait to turn the wringer.[120]

The passage's depiction of drops of water settling on her mother's body and the interior window panes of the washhouse gives the ritual of cleaning – as paid work and as a sanitary measure – an iconic visual significance. Symbolic of the labour that working-class women spent on cleaning, this passage suggests the extent to which the removal of dirt represented one area where with obscene amounts of effort, women could have a degree of control over their environment and how they were perceived by the local community. Indeed a recognition of working-class women's preoccupation with hygiene, the removal of dirt and the sanitary self-policing in which they engaged, needs to be seen as a counterpart to what is frequently ascribed as an exclusive or marked trait of bourgeois identity.[121]

The frontispiece to the 1928 edition of the work, by the sculptor and illustrator Leon Underwood, is itself based on this passage of the book. Underwood places the mother at the imposing centre of the scene, defined by her strong, flexed arms as she cleans the clothes using a washing dolly, with the boarded-up windows of tenements visible in the background. The steam from the washing furnace provides a frame for the positioning of the daughter who is seated apart from the mother she observes, her separation compounded by the book she is holding, signalling the divisive fact of her literacy which will guard the girl from a lifetime of working

---

[119] Woodward, *Jipping Street*, pp. 28–29.   [120] Woodward, *Jipping Street*, pp. 11–12.
[121] For an account that emphasises the importance of forms of working-class agency in the labour of cleaning, see Victoria Kelley, *Soap and Water: Cleanliness, Dirt and the Working Classes in Victorian and Edwardian Britain* (London: I.B. Tauris, 2010).

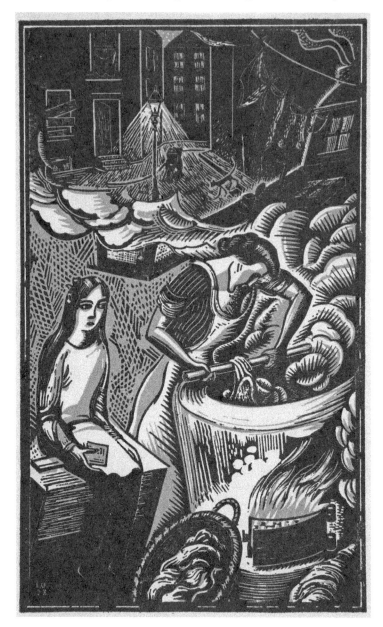

Figure 3   – Frontispiece by Leon Underwood, from Kathleen Woodward, *Jipping Street: Childhood in a London Slum* (New York: Harper & Brothers, 1928).

with her hands. The illustration conveys, however, the sheer force and energy inherent to the act of mothering that keeps the young Kathleen in clean clothes. It is a powerful image of the physicality of so much female work, as well as the strong significance of a mother-daughter bond that is marked by bodily relations. For in Woodward's account, the labour of the mother's body is her gift to the daughter and that which circumscribes the relationship. As the young girl notes of her mother: 'She sweated and laboured for her children, equally without stint or thought; but was utterly oblivious to any need we might cherish for sympathy in our little sorrows, support in our strivings. She simply was not aware of anything beyond the needs of our bodies.'[122] As in Acorn's *One of the Multitude*, Woodward's fantasy of the possibility of escape from the slum housing–scape takes the form of a wish for a separate space of her own that underpins the narrative structure of the memoir. It is presented as an iconic expression for a self-contained room – with all the resonance of that phrase:

> One day it came to me strong and clear – the end of all desires, the longing beneath all longing; and there shaped in my dreams a little room with white walls, clean, whitewashed walls, and bare floor boards, set far away on the brow of a hill I had never seen, remote, inaccessible. Swirling, fugitive, at the foot of the hill, the world pressed on – Jipping Street.
>
> In the centre of the room was a square, solid, white deal table, for scrubbing; there was a chair I could scrub and, in magnificent array about the room, the bookshelves I myself had builded [sic], supporting the books I had most strangely become possessed of; and in the room there dwelt peace and cleanness in perfect accord and sanctity.[123]

In this daydream, the coveted house is located at the top of a hill, in accordance with the principle of the social and topographical gradient in the Victorian industrial city by which wealthier residents moved steadily upwards, away from the factories, crowds and riverbanks.[124] Woodward's constructed interior reveals a specific desire to get away from the fleshy proximity of bodies in close quarters. 'How I sickened of people, loathing them!', Woodward exclaims, following her childhood room reverie. 'From morning until night, and again in the morning; people, people, in travail

---

[122] Woodward, *Jipping Street*, pp. 20–21.   [123] Woodward, *Jipping Street*, p. 53.
[124] See Mona Domosh and Joni Seager, *Putting Women in Place: Feminist Geographers Make Sense of the World* (New York: Guilford Press, 2001), p. 77. For a discussion of the spatialisation of class divisions in London by 1901, according to a scale of elevation leading from riverside areas, see Les Back, *New Ethnicities and Urban Culture: Racisms and Multiculture in Young Lives* (London: Routledge, 1996), pp. 16–17.

with their insufferable burdens. . . . I shrank from them because they scattered and refuted my dreams, with their tired eyes and indomitable endurance.'[125]

The eleven-year-old Woodward's strange domestic dream is eventually realised as she takes a job at a factory and is able to pay the rent on a back room located in the house of a 'tolerably clean' landlady.[126] In this room, she strips the 'dirty and verminous' wallpaper, applies whitewash to the walls, scrubs the floor 'white and clean' and mounts her book collection on a shelf made of Tate & Lyle sugar boxes.[127] The room is her 'citadel' and a 'world apart'; a space for private thoughts and dreaming but crucially one which is closed to the presence of other people.[128] As Sally Alexander points out, Woodward's imagining of this ideal space bears 'uncanny filiations' with Woolf's polemic *A Room of One's Own*, which was written in draft form in the year in which Woodward's memoir was published.[129] Linking the 'wish for a room' in these texts, Alexander argues, is a common longing 'for an individual Utopia, a momentary withdrawal from human relationships, an intense self-centredness rare for women. The room was a demand for a place for reverie, to study in peace, to reflect, for somewhere to discover other worlds alone.'[130] The material desire for an intense, solitary privacy based around the more metaphysical ideas of literacy and aesthetics is all the more striking, as Alexander's argument makes clear, because of the emergence of both texts at a time when political feminism had achieved crucial gains in realms of suffrage and property. For there is significantly a fervent urge to move away from everyday life and forms of collectivity, including the social presence of others.

Like Woolf's room, Woodward's interior signifies interiority – a solitary space for the cultivation of the 'inner life' – and has a practical function. But the differences in the kind of detail each writer gives to the ideal room are telling. Woolf's room, a space for writing and contemplation in the essay, remains unspecific in detail, except for the mention of book-lined shelves and the crucial need for a lock on the door. By contrast, Woodward's ideal room is positively defined by its pared-down and prescriptive form; it is almost bare of objects, scrubbed and whitewashed. This emphasis on hygiene in conjunction with textuality – in a book that is structured around images of cleanliness and bodies – is striking;

[125] Woodward, *Jipping Street*, p. 54.   [126] Woodward, *Jipping Street*, p. 93.
[127] Woodward, *Jipping Street*, p. 134.   [128] Woodward, *Jipping Street*, pp. 134–35.
[129] Sally Alexander, 'Room of One's Own: 1920s Feminist Utopias', *Women: A Cultural Review* 11:3 (2000), 273.
[130] Alexander, 'Room of One's Own', 275.

indeed, one of the few fixtures that Woodward mentions is an implement for cleaning ('a square, solid, white deal table, for scrubbing').[131] Woodward's sterile, whitewashed and bare interior thus appears to present a tabula rasa: 'Oh, the inexpressible balm of its bareness!', Woodward exclaims of a room which the landlady likens suggestively to a hospital. 'No odds and ends; no cheap china pieces with inflexible countenances; nor photographs nor stuffed chairs smelling with age and the need for fresh air – none of these things which made up the real Gethsemane of my childhood.'[132] It is possible to read the geometric shape and white colour of the room as signalling the shift from late-Victorian and Edwardian décor to a distinctly modernist aesthetic. Indeed, in one sense, as Eileen Cleere argues, the 'transition to a sleek, seamless modernism in British art and architecture looked less like an aesthetic revolution than the inevitable effect of Victorian sanitary reform'.[133] In this sense, Woodward's proto-modernist room foreshadows in microcosm the effect of governmental housing reforms and a postwar design movement which, as Richard Hornsey notes, moved towards 'designed interiors' and 'defiantly planned spaces'. These, he argues, 'introduced a layer of abstraction between the material body and the interior itself . . . through the intellectual workings of the mind, which sought to control – through prior design – the operations that the body could subsequently perform there'.[134] While postwar décor would resist the bodily trace of the bourgeois home (symbolised by Benjamin's image of the imprint left by the body on coverings made of plush), Woodward's room depicts a vision of household living which banishes the corporeal memory of her mother's labour and heralds the sterile, unfleshly interior space allocated to the postwar citizen. Whitewash – which had been associated for so long as an external marker of the homes of the poor – is redeployed here as a form of interior decoration: producing a blank slate, and apparently new start, for the slum escapee.

vii A people with history: Pat O'Mara's *The Autobiography of a Liverpool Irish Slummy*

A work that goes against the grain of these memoirs of slum life is Pat O'Mara's dynamic and engaging account of growing up in the slums of

---

[131] Woodward, *Jipping Street*, p. 53.   [132] Woodward, *Jipping Street*, p. 141.
[133] Eileen Cleere, 'Victorian Dust Traps', in Cohen and Johnson (eds.), *Filth*, p. 135.
[134] Richard Hornsey, *The Spiv and the Architect: Unruly Life in Postwar London* (Minneapolis: University of Minnesota Press, 2010), p. 220.

Liverpool around the turn of the twentieth century. *The Autobiography of a Liverpool Irish Slummy* (1934) might appear on the surface to be a continuation of the anti-domestic memoir of urban life, for O'Mara certainly depicts in stark detail the deprivation and violence that existed in some of the poorest Liverpudlian courts. As Liam Harte writes, O'Mara's 'vivid recollection of his abjectly poor childhood reads like an Edwardian version of Frank McCourt's *Angela's Ashes* (1996), complete with violent, alcoholic father, pious mother, doomed infants and serial evictions, though without McCourt's self-pitying sentimentality'.[135] The idea, proposed by decades of social explorers, that some homes may be so 'homely' as not to be homes at all is certainly borne out in O'Mara's descriptions of dilapidated living quarters, horrific domestic violence against women, the death of young children (including five of his own siblings), and the familiar mood-setting of the slums ('Huge cats continually stalked the place, their eyes an eerie phosphorescence in the darkness').[136]

Yet O'Mara's text evades the clichés of the genre in a number of distinctive ways. As noted in the previous section, a common characteristic of tenement life – at least as presented from the perspective of external onlookers – is a recurrent sense of stasis: fixed set pieces of domestic suffering and estrangement witnessed by individuals who visited before moving on swiftly to the next house in the row. By contrast, however, O'Mara's memoir presents a sense of the movement and peripatetic nature of these dockside lives in what was a major port city (known as 'the gateway to Empire'). His own domestic situation consists of a series of forcible ejections, being 'put out' or 'dispossessed' from rooms in rented courts – with the family belongings bundled into a handcart and wheeled to the next location.[137] Indeed, it is this constant locomotion, from the point of view of people on the move, which gives the narrative its form. If home is an unstable, violent and changeable place, then the memoir profits from the multifarious anecdotes and characterisations of the families and people with whom the O'Maras are repeatedly forced to share accommodation. The shadowy, degenerate figures of earlier slum narratives are replaced here with an individualised cast featuring the idiosyncratic faces and voices of a community of families living at extremely close quarters.

[135] Liam Harte, *The Literature of the Irish in Britain: Autobiography and Memoir, 1725–2001* (Basingstoke: Palgrave Macmillan, 2009), p. 153.
[136] Pat O'Mara, *The Autobiography of a Liverpool Irish Slummy* (London: Martin Hopkinson, 1934), p. 32.
[137] O'Mara, *Autobiography*, pp. 43–44.

The idea of the 'room of one's own' takes on added meaning in this environment where, quite simply, the room often is the home itself. Indeed, the issue of working-class privacy has usefully been considered by a small number of social historians, who have noted in particular the way in which households produced forms of resistance to the intrusion of external inspectors and health visitors.[138] But O'Mara's memoir makes clear that his major preoccupation was achieving a private space away from his own family members rather than representatives of the state. A lack of living space is a constant preoccupation for this author who was born into a windowless back room located on the third floor of a tenement house shared by other families. Indeed, in a bleakly ironic moment, mother and son try to get away from O'Mara's inebriated and violent father by hiding in the communal toilet of the tenement: 'It stank in this place as it always did, but the quietness and peace impressed me and I said, "Couldn't we put a few shelves in here mother and live in it? It's so quiet here."'[139] It could be argued that Woolf's paradigmatic call for a room of one's own makes its way into this text in demotic form (O'Mara uses Woolf's phrase – with a significant modification – as he expresses his ambition 'to achieve my mother's life-long dream, a room of *our* own, away from our father' [emphasis added]).[140] In fact, as in so many other working-class memoirs (including many of those examined later in Chapter 3 of this book), illness paradoxically enables the young individual to gain solitude and space. At the age of eleven, O'Mara is sent away to West Kirby sanatorium in the Cheshire countryside, where institutional life has the effect of making him feel 'fully appreciative of the loveliness of this strange, new place'.[141] As in Brendan Behan's later rather ironically bucolic vision of rural, incarcerated life in his memoir *Borstal Boy* (1958), O'Mara's health and spirit improve in the pastoral setting near the Irish sea in an atmosphere of 'unadulterated happiness', marred only by the trouble he runs into with the sanatorium nurses for the 'slummy' habit of spitting on the walls.[142] Returning to the Brick Street shack in Liverpool, the crude spatial contrast produces a pivotal moment of class self-awareness. Laughed at by the other children

---

[138] Martin Hewitt, for example, presents evidence of carefully controlled privacy and self-policed thresholds in working-class homes in 'District Visiting and the Constitution of Domestic Space in the Mid-Nineteenth Century', in Bryden and Floyd (eds.), *Domestic Space*, pp. 121–41.

[139] O'Mara, *Autobiography*, pp. 92–93. Roberts similarly notes that the water closet in the Salford backyard was 'the only place where a member of the household could be assured of a few minutes' privacy'; *The Classic Slum*, p. 164.

[140] O'Mara, *Autobiography*, p. 132.   [141] O'Mara, *Autobiography*, p. 101.

[142] O'Mara, *Autobiography*, p. 102.

for the 'clean collar' he has acquired during his sojourn at the sanatorium, he now notices with embarrassment his mother's 'discarded navvy boots'.[143] On returning to the one-bedroom abode, mother and son address each other in a moment fraught with the underlying, unspoken tensions of incipient social mobility:

> 'You don't want to come back home, do you, Timmy?'
>
> 'Yes, yes', I lied again, staring at the mattress on the floor and the spit-covered walls, only roughly cleaned, and the buckets.[144]

A form of developing class consciousness and a palpable sense of guilt are revealed in this exchange, whereby the young boy returns to see his home through the critical lens of an outsider.

Yet part of the achievement of O'Mara's autobiography is the vivid prose which brings a sense of energy and life to the depiction of the Liverpool courts. O'Mara's confidence of tone and outlook are crystallised by the surprising setting of the opening, in which the self-professed 'slummy' speaks neither from the emigrant endpoint of America (where the author wrote and published the book), nor the 'lowest depths' of the courtside slums, but from a sweeping viewpoint, gazing down at his city from the Liverpool Overhead Railway. In its presentation of a sweeping view stretching over to Birkenhead, Port Sunlight and the extensive docks, the opening recalls a famous passage from Mayhew's *Morning Chronicle* letters, in which the social explorer ascends to the Golden Gallery at St Paul's Cathedral to obtain a 'bird's-eye view of the port' and finds himself gazing on 'the giant sublimity of the city that lay stretched out beneath . . . such as one might see it in a dream'.[145] O'Mara's appropriation of this visionary stance, denoting a sense of proprietorship, says much about the relationship of the 'slummy boy' to his city of Liverpool and forces a reconsideration of familiar assumptions about panoptic viewpoints, who holds them and what they denote.[146]

---

[143] O'Mara, *Autobiography*, p. 105.   [144] O'Mara, *Autobiography*, p. 106.
[145] Mayhew, Letter XLVII, 11 April 1850, *Morning Chronicle*, vol. IV, p. 97.
[146] For Raymond Williams, the raised perspective is characteristic of the surveying poise of the landowner but is also emblematic of the viewpoint of the working-class protagonist, such as Jude the Obscure looking out over to Christminster, who possesses a 'way of looking at that life which can see other values beyond it'; *Country and the City*, p. 198. It is, moreover, one that Williams deploys to symbolic effect in his autobiographical novel *Border Country* (1960) as the protagonist, Matthew, looks out over the Welsh valley of his childhood in a stance which represents rooted belonging, as well as the power 'to abstract and to clarify'; *Border Country* (Cardigan: Parthian Press, 2006), p. 365.

This opening stance serves, in symbolic terms, to mark the way in which O'Mara has 'raised' himself out of and above tenement life, but it also points to his equally important sense of a residual attachment and belonging to his place of origin. Thus while he maps the 'sinewy arteries' of slum streets that branch off from the seven miles of docks, thereby charting and describing their existence, his cartography crucially marks him as being *of* this housing environment rather than remotely detached from it.[147] This is an important distinction because O'Mara's self-identification with the Liverpool courts, as well as the sense that these places themselves are a part of – and belong – to the city, are key motifs. Unlike other accounts of the slum that emphasise their separateness from the city (whereby abject poverty is equated with exclusion), O'Mara gives these tenement quarters a distinctive sense of history, ethnic complexity and culture. These places of residence are notably multi-ethnic, multi-lingual, often divided along sectarian lines, socially mixed and geographically distinct.[148] Sims' earlier sweeping claim that one slum is much like another is simply not borne out by these recollections of Liverpool life.

O'Mara presents his own self-formation as being deeply influenced by the culture of these neighbourhoods. But rather than the familiar model of the young child who is passively shaped by the mean streets, he exhibits a strong sense of ownership or proprietorship over this space. This is marked at the level of language, specifically in the way in which O'Mara deploys a set of verbal variations on the word 'slum' itself. O'Mara's use of the word 'slummy' in the title of the work is in fact the first recorded use of the word to denote a person from the slums (the destitute father, for example, who perpetuates a myth of a Cheshire family estate frequently chides his wife's family with his 'stock criticism': 'You're all bloody slummies and were raised in S[hit]-houses').[149] O'Mara's rehabilitation of the word 'slummy', which he often uses as an affectionate appellation, can therefore be seen to signal his wider project of rooting the past, and that of his family, in a particular historical space. In the penultimate chapter, this affectionate, almost nostalgic sense of the term is apparent. Now settled in America, O'Mara recalls a trip back to Liverpool where he

---

[147] O'Mara, *Autobiography*, p. 10.
[148] A sense of cultural and racial difference is similarly highlighted in Willy Goldman's autobiography of an East End childhood in which he states: 'Our street, like the larger world, was a "divided" community. . . . It flourished on its multitude of "differences"'; *East End My Cradle: Portrait of an Environment* (London: Faber & Faber, 2011), p. 147.
[149] O'Mara, *Autobiography*, p. 37.

hears a familiar song played at the Palais de Luxe concert hall, prompting a flood of memories:

> My eyes closed; in that darkness I was once again the little slummy in the bare feet munching his sandwiches and dreaming his dreams! ... I am thinking of Joe and Harold and Berny and the two Johnnies and Henry and Mickey; of my mates still alive; of Aeroplane Joe, the bobby; of St. Peter's School and Mr. McGinnis; of all those strange slummies ...[150]

As well as denoting an affirmative identity ('like good slummies we were all more or less sentimental'), he also consistently uses 'slummy' as a neutral term simply to denote people from particular areas.[151]

The idea that the slums are formative of identity, as implied through O'Mara's semantic deployment of the word, makes an important wider social point. Rather than serve as a metonym or byword for abjection and social disorder (as per much Victorian discourse), the slums here are an integral – albeit brutal space – for a significant section of the Liverpool population. To use the cartographic image with which the memoir begins, the slums are not off the map at all, nor do they appear, as in some forms of Victorian slum writing, 'wrested from their quotidian contexts so that they appear in darkness, contextless'.[152] Instead they are perceived to be a social space with specific formations and identities – in other words, they are places in history.[153] This sense is apparent in O'Mara's recollections of the way in which these Liverpool courts experienced and recorded historical and national events, including the outbreak of World War I; the death of Lord Kitchener in 1916; the Liverpool Police Strike of 1919; armistice and the process of interwar rebuilding. O'Mara's Liverpool 'slummies' are players in history, experiencing, for example, the exhilarating 'strange newfound happiness' of patriotism and excitement that accompanied the outbreak of war in 1914, and the tragic loss of the younger male population: '"Wiped out" could be placed against most of the raggedy young manhood that when war beckoned, had rushed eagerly from these cess-pools.'[154] And yet while the slums are part of the national story, the memoirist is also

---

[150] O'Mara, *Autobiography*, p. 304.   [151] O'Mara, *Autobiography*, p. 52.

[152] Bernstein is specifically referring here to George Gissing's treatment of the slum environment; *Celebration of Scandal*, p. 9.

[153] Jeremy Seabrook and Imran Ahmed Siddiqui's study of slum communities in Kolkata makes precisely this nineteenth-century association between the placelessness of slum areas and a commensurate lack of history (thus somewhat contradicting the book's intention to give historical and cultural specificity to precisely these communities). They write: 'Slums, trackless and impermanent, have no geography. They have no history either'; *People Without History: India's Muslim Ghettos* (London: Pluto Press, 2011), p. 9.

[154] O'Mara, *Autobiography*, p. 221.

aware of the way in which these narratives of tenement lives produce their own distinctive versions of family, home and history. Describing the impact of the end of war, he notes that 'among the bourgeoisie there had been erotic after-the-war tragedies and all that sort of "civilized" stuff. But none of this in our slums – it was simply economics, economics in everything including love'.[155]

O'Mara finally achieves a type of room of his own as he begins work on the ships departing Liverpool. Once again, in contrast to the idea of stasis or 'residuum' used to depict the lives of people in British urban slums, O'Mara maps the movement of his fellow 'slummies' who participated in the seafaring life of Liverpool, a centre for global trade networks and population movement. In fact, as he goes on to reveal, his ambition to be a writer developed during these long voyages across the Atlantic. For the uncomfortable, claustrophobic setting of the ship's hold during the cross-ings to New York has the advantage of providing him with the writer's luxuries of time, space and solitude:

> the loneliness of ship life did foster one great urge within me – the desire to write. The fact that I had no training for a literary career did not occur to me as an objection; I wanted to write and write I would.[156]

O'Mara's presentation of his development as a writer during this cross-Atlantic movement serves to reinforce the way in which his 'escape', and the eventual publication of the memoir as a New York émigré, are not based on any total rupture with his origins. The dockside tenements and its inhabitants form a powerful imaginary of home to which he returns repeatedly, like a seafarer, through intermittent visits and processes of memory.

Conclusion

If nineteenth-century slum discourse is typically viewed as ascribing passivity to the 'multitudes' living in the overcrowded tenements of the modern city, this chapter has tried to demonstrate that there are significant variants that disrupt this model, from Mayhew's enigmatic interiors, to O'Mara's memoir of flux and agency. Indeed, the examples of working-class life writing addressed in this chapter conform to a version of bourgeois subjectivity and the literary self, defined by Regenia Gagnier as 'belief in creativity, autonomy, and individual freedom; self-reflection as

---

[155] O'Mara, *Autobiography*, p. 281.   [156] O'Mara, *Autobiography*, p. 243.

problem-solving, especially in writing; and a progressive narrative of self, especially in relation to family and material well-being'.[157] Such expressions of classic individualist principles – the desire for private lives and private spaces – are hardly surprising. For studies of housing and domestic life make it abundantly clear that it has never been just the middle classes and elite who staked a claim for adequate dwelling space and forms of seclusion. In the context of eighteenth-century England, for example, Amanda Vickery examines the 'mundane tools and everyday tactics used by ordinary Londoners to draw physical and psychological boundaries within doors, and to control access to space and possessions'.[158] She attests to the fact that

> a concern with personal space can be found throughout the social pyramid, even if its enjoyment was unequally distributed. Life with no vestiges of privacy was understood to be a most sorry degradation, which stripped away the defences of the spirit.[159]

Thus while some modernist writers evoke in redolent detail the 'history of every mark and scratch' of a room, working-class writers who lived in urban dwellings were often keen to cast off the interiors of the past and embrace the whitewashed, decluttered, solitary or, in the case of O'Mara, floating rooms of their own.[160] These accounts of domestic interiors produced in the early decades of the twentieth century articulated forms of working-class subjectivity that are visionary and individualised, terms rarely ascribed to working-class subjects by the middle-class observers of slum interiors.[161] These texts also reiterate the fact that a particular ideal of domesticity was not simply the preserve of the middle-classes but formed an influential part of the working-class social lexicon and imaginary of home in the early decades of the twentieth century. As Chapter 3 will show, this conservative model – framed around precepts of domesticity and individualism – was subject to further disruption and rearrangement by later twentieth-century writers in their retrospective accounts of working-class childhoods.

---

[157] Gagnier, *Subjectivities*, p. 169.   [158] Vickery, *Behind Closed Doors*, p. 46.
[159] Vickery, *Behind Closed Doors*, p. 29.
[160] Virginia Woolf, 'Old Bloomsbury', in Jeanne Schulkind (ed.), *Moments of Being* (London: Grafton, 1978), p. 161.
[161] Troy Boone, for example, argues that Victorian and Edwardian imperialist writing presents 'a consistent representation of the middle classes in terms of visionary subjectivity and the working classes in terms of an increasingly mechanized physicality'; *Youth of Darkest England: Working-Class Children at the Heart of the Victorian Empire* (New York: Routledge, 2005), p. 1.

CHAPTER 2

Boarding and lodging houses
At home with strangers

It is not to be supposed indeed that utter strangers would go and live together without some strong inducements; and these inducements are generally money on the one side and society on the other.

–Henry Mayhew, *London Characters and the Humorous Side of London Life* (London: Stanley Rivers & Co., 1871), p. 231

Introduction: Boarding and lodging houses in history

Boarding and lodging houses in British writing are emblematic forms of the social interior and constitute a significant setting for the cohabitation of strangers. Like the slum tenements that appeared to function in material and symbolic terms as the spatial 'other' to the middle-class bourgeois home, the atypical domesticity of boarding and lodging houses has sometimes led these places to be cast as inauthentic and even potentially illicit spaces. But as places of temporary accommodation which bring together disparate individuals in often straitened circumstances, they exemplify the way in which home is often governed by contingency and the principles of getting by and getting along with the 'other'.

In the twenty-first century, the idea of the boarding house is both peculiarly evocative and anachronistic. Its former role – as the comfortable resting place for the lower middle-class travelling salesman, the home for the widowed single woman getting by on a slim annuity, or the accommodation of choice at the British working-class seaside resort – suggests that it occupies a rather marginal place in housing and cultural history. Yet in one of the relatively few academic studies of boarding and lodging houses in the nineteenth and twentieth centuries, Leonore Davidoff effectively shows how these places of accommodation, far from being culturally peripheral, in fact reveal much about the history and economics of the family, urbanisation, labour in the home and the complex imbrications of the so-called public and private spheres.[1] In fact an essential point that emerges from a closer look at the cultural history of rented rooms reminds us that the nuclear family living under one roof is a relatively recent historical construction (and assumption). For as Davidoff puts it, contrary to expectations, 'there have always been strangers or "sojourners" living with the basic nuclear family, although the definition of who belongs to this category has varied'.[2] In this regard, Amanda Vickery notes how nine out of ten homes in Georgian England were rented and that the privilege and status that came with occupying a house were not excluded from those who leased rather than owned their properties. 'The history of home', she emphasises, 'is not a saga of home ownership'.[3]

The fact that before 1914 the vast majority of people lived in Britain as renters rather than homeowners is significant for constructions and ideologies of privacy and neighbourliness. For as Vickery demonstrates, the architectural evolutions of spaces of privacy in the home were developed not because of widespread home ownership, but precisely because individual space was so hard to achieve. Thus the oft-repeated invocation of home as a place of seclusion away from prying eyes is itself a rather recent 'truism'. Vickery adds:

> The perimeter of the 'private house' represented a sacred frontier, but it was emphatically not the case that once over the domestic threshold all was secluded. Living cheek by jowl with comparative strangers robbed the London house of any automatic association with privacy as we understand it. Indeed, more solitude and anonymity was probably found outside the house than in.[4]

In the literature examined in this chapter, which features boarding houses and rented rooms as central locations, it will become clear that the spatial topography that it represents reflects this more fluid or blurred sense of the public and the private. The short stories and novels of working-class and lower-middle-class tenants feature, perhaps against expectation, a great sense of mobility and travel as the various characters find themselves on the move between their lodgings and a counter-sphere of cafés, pubs and the sitting rooms of family friends – spaces which could permit a greater sense of freedom and autonomy.

---

[1] Leonore Davidoff, 'The Separation of Home and Work? Landladies and Lodgers in Nineteenth- and Twentieth-Century England', in Sandra Burman (ed.), *Fit Work for Women* (New York: St Martin's Press, 1979), pp. 64–97.
[2] Davidoff, 'Separation', p. 68.   [3] Vickery, *Behind Closed Doors*, p. 7.
[4] Vickery, *Behind Closed Doors*, p. 33.

Boarding and lodging houses, moreover, are inextricably linked with gender and class. They often explicitly stage the marital status of their lodgers and are governed by an overt economic framework (the room you inhabit is paid for on a weekly or monthly basis). It is perhaps not surprising then that the subject of lodging has often been a charged issue in social discourse, particularly in sanitary reports and urban surveys. As Davidoff notes of nineteenth-century writing on the topic: 'The idea that lodging was an evil, although possibly a necessary one, acted as a powerful force in middle-class attitudes towards working-class housing and living arrangements.'[5] This tendency to denigrate the lodging house was perhaps due to the fact that it represented a living arrangement which departed from the normativity of the family and the idea of 'separate spheres' (as recent as those ideological formations might have been). Lodging houses also presented a challenge to the idea of home as enabling rootedness in a specific place, since they often provided shelter for people who moved about: travelling salesmen, sailors, immigrants and itinerants. As Davidoff remarks in this regard, the mobility that these places of temporary residence came to signify 'implied a casualness of relationships, the mixing of age, sex and social groups which was also viewed with revulsion by Victorian middle-class observers who were hypersensitive to social boundaries'.[6] Indeed, as Sharon Marcus argues, 'low' lodging houses in Victorian social discourse served as a metonym for much that was wrong with the urban landscape. She notes that 'almost every book about London published between the 1840s and the 1870s singled out lodging houses and lodgings as exemplars of urban dirt, disease, crowding, and promiscuity'.[7] One cause of this negative characterisation of lodging, Marcus comments, was precisely the lodging house's apparent signification of the 'antidomestic' – in part because it was associated with the city itself (and thus social intermingling) but also 'because the imagery of dirt and contagion contradicted the domestic ideal's emphasis on cleanliness and order'.[8] Like Davidoff, Marcus observes that it was the lodging house's peculiar quality of architectural impermanence, taken to indicate a type of urban decay, which seems to have provoked the wrath of many nineteenth-century commentators.[9] This idea of impermanence relates to the lodging house's improvisational character, as a site of accommodation that cropped up according

---

[5] Davidoff, 'Separation', p. 71.   [6] Davidoff, 'Separation', p. 71.
[7] Marcus, *Apartment Stories*, p. 104.   [8] Marcus, *Apartment Stories*, pp. 104–05.
[9] Marcus, *Apartment Stories*, p. 105.

to demand, but also to its properties as a place which was internally partitioned – spatially as well socially – as multiple families sheltered under a single roof (a 'calamitous medley... of divisions and subdivisions' according to one Victorian commentator).[10]

The issue of gender in the context of the lodging/boarding house formation is given particular complexity by dint of the fact that these were often female-led economic enterprises. As John K. Walton points out in his study of the Blackpool landlady as a cultural figure, boarding houses were historically a predominantly female-headed business arrangement (although, he adds, it is difficult for a variety of reasons to establish the exact number of landladies that existed at any given time).[11] Walton notes the significance of the fact that even when a married couple ran a guest-house business, it was the name of the woman that presided above the front door.[12] One reason for this is that in the nineteenth century, with growing migration to urban centres, the provision of lodging had provided single women with a key source of income, allowing them to gain financial rewards while maintaining their own households and thus a sense of propriety. This was thus a form of 'homework' for which the woman received a direct remuneration for her domestic labour. In fact, not only could the landlady transform her home into a profitable source of income, but she was also recompensed for the usually unpaid position of matriarchal arbitrator. For as Davidoff explains, part of the landlady's role was to act as peacekeeper: 'to keep the emotional atmosphere on an even keel, to apportion scarce resources of time as well as things, to sooth ruffled feelings and to arbitrate between lodgers, servants and her own family'.[13] And yet the figure of the landlady is often shrouded with suggestive ambivalence in popular culture and literature, perhaps precisely due to her economic role collecting rent for services that women were expected to provide for free within the normative family structure.[14] Such ambivalence underpins the landlady's caricature as an imposing, intrusive matriarch, whose 'fierce-ness, volubility, cunning and intimidating bulk ... often contrasted with the puny insignificance of her downtrodden spouse'.[15]

---

[10] Anonymous contributor to *The Builder*, quoted in Marcus, *Apartment Stories*, p. 105.
[11] John K. Walton, 'The Blackpool Landlady Revisited', *Manchester Region History Review* 8 (1994), 28–29. For research into this historical form of female entrepreneurship, see also John K. Walton, *The Blackpool Landlady: A Social History* (Manchester: Manchester University Press, 1978), and Alison C. Kay, 'A Little Enterprise of Her Own: Lodging-House Keeping and the Accommodation Business in Nineteenth-Century London', *London Journal* 28:2 (2003), 41–53.
[12] Walton, 'Blackpool Landlady', p. 29.   [13] Davidoff, 'Separation', p. 89.
[14] Davidoff, 'Separation', pp. 89–91.   [15] Walton, 'Blackpool Landlady', p. 24.

It is perhaps useful here to add a brief caveat about my use of the terms 'boarding house' and 'lodging house'. Traditionally, boarding houses have been defined as a residential setting in which lodgers are provided with meals – board – by (usually) the landlady who runs the establishment. But there is a distinct fluidity between the terms used to describe rented rooms – particularly between 'lodging' and 'boarding' – which means that they are often notably used interchangeably. Historically, as Davidoff notes, the slippage between a 'lodger', 'boarder' and 'visitor' was problematic for state regulatory institutions, census recorders and the police. The Registrar General in 1851, for example, reflected on the difficulty of distinguishing between these categories, but 'specifically saw the *lodging and boarding house* as "an intermediate form between the institution and the private family"'.[16] In fact, the traditional bed-and-board model of the boarding house became increasingly obsolete in the postwar period, in part because of the difficulty landladies had recruiting sufficient domestic workers in order to run the business successfully, and the practice of 'board' was replaced by a more ad hoc system of lodging (whereby the landlady might live in the house but would not necessarily provide communal meals). While this chapter looks at a variety of rented domestic spaces – the traditional room-and-board house, lodging houses, furnished rooms and bedsits – I sometimes use 'boarding house' as an umbrella term, not least because of its suggestiveness. For as Richard Brown and Gregory Castle show in their analysis of James Joyce's short story 'The Boarding House', the semantic variations inherent to this term nicely suggest 'an underlying ambiguity, contingency, and open-endedness': from *border*, *boredom* and the expression *treading the boards*, to *bawdy*, *bawdry* and *boardelhouse* (as it appears in *Finnegans Wake*).[17] Like the space of the boarding house in literature itself, an apparently bland and unassuming outward facade can mask unlikely shapes and forms.

My reading of the interior spaces of literary boarding houses, bedsits and rented rooms begins in the Victorian period, but moves on from the interwar period where Davidoff finishes her account (years in which she identifies the decline of lodging as a 'recognised social experience').[18] For while it is clear that there is a shift in the mid-twentieth century towards the valorisation of the nuclear family, accompanied by the demise of

---

[16] See Davidoff, 'Separation', pp. 74–78 (p. 78).
[17] Richard Brown and Gregory Castle, '"The Instinct of the Celibate": Boarding and Borderlines in "The Boarding House"', in Vicki Mahaffey (ed.), *Collaborative Dubliners: Joyce in Dialogue* (Syracuse: Syracuse University Press, 2012), pp. 145–48.
[18] Davidoff, 'Separation', p. 92.

domestic service, lodging arguably undergoes important transmutations in its social character and plays no less a significant role. As changing settings, both in the historical record and the social imaginary, boarding and lodging houses afford narrative possibilities that give shape to the sense of being at home – or not – with strangers.

i   The lodging plot in the boarding house stories of Charles Dickens and James Joyce

My survey of boarding-house literature begins with a consideration of two short stories by Charles Dickens and James Joyce, both structured around the familiar twin themes of marriage and money. In both cases, the boarding house serves as a type of stage set – a means of displaying the performances and behaviours of a disparate group of people within the unities of time, action and place that this distinctive dwelling place affords. Both stories ostensibly centre on a plot of romance, but this theme is undercut either comically or with dark irony by the fierce economic imperatives that are the boarding house's *raison d'être*. In these cases, the boarding-house short story does two things to the expansive marriage plot of the nineteenth-century novel: it condenses it spatially and chronologically, and it strips the idea of romantic love away in order to reveal base economic interests. As Henry Mayhew had noted in a section on lodging and boarding houses in Victorian London (in a chapter tellingly entitled 'Outsiders in Society and Their Homes in London'):

> There is always a large admixture of people who go there for the sake of society; and of this number a considerable proportion is sure to consist of widows or spinsters of extremely marriageable tendencies. The result is that, unless the residents be very numerous, individual freedom is lost, and, instead of living an independent life as at an hotel, the members of a 'circle' find themselves surrounded by such amenities as may be supposed to belong to a rather large and singularly disunited family.[19]

The social aspects of boarding-house life that Mayhew touches upon here – the potential for marriage matches, the notion of a 'disunited family' – are all present in Dickens' story 'The Boarding House', which originally appeared in *The Monthly Magazine* in 1834 and was later reprinted in *Sketches by Boz*. Dickens' landlady, Mrs Tibbs, conforms to the generic figure of the hard-nosed matriarch who brow-beats her husband while

---

[19] Henry Mayhew, *London Characters and the Humorous Side of London Life* (London: Stanley Rivers & Co., 1871), p. 233.

maintaining hold of the economic reins of the household by letting out rooms to boarders. Traditional kinship patterns are turned on their heads in this carnivalesque *mélange* of couples and residents; the landlady's husband, Mr Tibbs, for example, is relegated to cleaning 'gentlemen's boots' in the kitchen and barred from entering the parlour (except on Sundays). Payment for lodgings and matrimony are always closely associated throughout the story. When the naïve Mr Tibbs suggests that one of the recently arrived two young resident daughters might 'set her cap' at one of the existing lodgers, Mrs Tibbs expresses outrage at the prospective financial repercussions of any liaisons among her paying guests: "'I beg you won't mention such a thing," said Mrs T. "A marriage, indeed! – to rob me of my boarders – no, not for the world."'[20] She is, however, shrewd enough to know that the promise of matrimonial exchange is good for business:

> Mrs Tibbs [had] considered it an admirable little bit of management to represent to the gentlemen that she had *some* reason to believe the ladies were fortunes, and to hint to the ladies, that all the gentlemen were 'eligible'. A little flirtation, she thought, might keep her house full, without leading to any other result.[21]

The tight economy of the boarding house, in which the residents are themselves revenue, is carefully steered by Mrs Tibbs, who is the literal and figurative keeper of the keys and who thus attempts to stage-manage the household scene.

Yet throughout Dickens' comedy of errors, Mrs Tibbs' cunning designs are constantly undermined by the propensity of her boarders to cross house borders in order to form ill-fated alliances (one such *dénouement* takes place on the 'public' staircase and landing – a domestic thoroughfare which serves as a perfect location for the laying of various plots). Ultimately, the story, in which a number of marriages end badly or fail to take place, finds its comedy in the mercantile motives that underlie romantic entanglements. Thus the punchline to the story's first section offers a sidelight on the relations between the boarding house and normative domesticity: 'this complication of disorders completely deprived poor Mrs Tibbs of all her inmates, except the one whom she could have best spared – her husband'.[22] The domestic shenanigans, together with the pace

---

[20] Charles Dickens, 'The Boarding House', in Michael Slater (ed.), *Sketches by Boz and Other Early Papers, 1833–39* (Columbus: Ohio State University Press, 1994), p. 276.
[21] Dickens, 'Boarding House', p. 278.   [22] Dickens, 'Boarding House', p. 287.

of the plot, also serve to remind the reader that, as Jane Hamlett notes, 'lodgings offered the possibility of great pleasure'.[23]

James Joyce's later short story from *Dubliners*, also called simply 'The Boarding House', replaces the ribaldry of Dickens' tale with a far darker tone. Here the lodging place is no longer Dickens' shabby-genteel London, but the singular 'twilight' social zone that would characterise the image of the boarding house in the first half of the twentieth century. Joyce's boarding house is almost a microcosm in form and content of the inter-linked stories of *Dubliners* itself, all of which feature in some sense the insecure living conditions of a lower-middle class caught in the stultifying atmosphere of a colonial city. As Seamus Deane has noted of the characters in *Dubliners*: 'These people are shades who have never lived, vicarious inhabitants of a universe ruled by others. Highly individuated, they are nevertheless exemplary types of a general condition in which individuality is dissolved'.[24] In so far as Joyce's 'The Boarding House' typifies this condition, it makes the lodging house symbolically central (despite its marginal social status), rendering explicit the tenuous sense of home and family in early twentieth-century Dublin.[25] On a wider level, Julieann Veronica Ulin lays emphasis on the trope of the 'stranger in the house', as a reference to the structuring principle of the boarding house (which functions to bring unfamiliar people together in intimate proximity) as well as Britain's enduring colonial presence within Irish national space. She writes that 'the boarding house, by its very nature a space between spaces, a temporary home, offers a fitting image of the Ireland of Joyce's time, an island in-between'.[26] Thus Ulin points to images of openness in Joyce's story which highlight the fluid threshold between the not-so-private interior space of the house and the outer street and city. These range from the repetition of detail concerning various doors and windows that are left opened or forcibly entered, to the 'open-ended' narrative structure itself that leaves the reader with suggestive questions as to the literal nature of the marriage plot established between Mrs Mooney's daughter and the travelling salesman, Mr Doran.[27]

[23] Hamlett, *Material Relations*, p. 166.

[24] Seamus Deane, 'Dead Ends: Joyce's Finest Moments', in Derek Attridge and Marjorie Howes (eds.), *Semicolonial Joyce* (Cambridge: Cambridge University Press, 2000), p. 21.

[25] For a discussion of the impact of emigration and domestic service on the nature of the family household in Ireland, see Clair Wills, 'Rocking the Cradle? – Women Studies and the Family in Twentieth-Century Ireland', *Bullán* 1:2 (1994), 97–106.

[26] Julieann Veronica Ulin, 'Fluid Boarders and Naughty Girls: Music, Domesticity, and Nation in Joyce's Boarding Houses', *James Joyce Quarterly* 44:2 (2007), 282.

[27] Ulin, 'Fluid Boarders', p. 266.

Like Mrs Tibbs' establishment, the boarding house in Joyce is headed by a seemingly omnipotent matriarch who is in charge of the household economy and arbitrator of the lodgers' relations. Having disposed of her feckless, drunken husband, Mrs Mooney, the 'butcher's daughter', manages her household in a cold-blooded and efficient manner, memorably dealing with 'moral problems as a cleaver deals with meat'.[28] She reveals herself to be something of a stage manager of social and moral conventions, constantly observing people and proceedings before taking executive action. While her household may be made up of what Joyce labels a 'floating population' of tourists, artists, local clerks and travelling salesmen, she operates a tightly run system with surprisingly firm boundaries (even the sugar and butter are kept 'safe under lock and key').[29] Moreover, the commercial base of this homely establishment is always in the foreground, and pecuniary metaphors repeatedly appear in Joyce's prose. Thus Mrs Mooney 'governed her house cunningly and firmly, knew when to give credit, when to be stern and when to let things pass. All the resident young men spoke of her as *The Madam*'.[30] As the term used by the 'young men' implies, the sexual implications underlying the idea of rented rooms throws up, if only allusively, the boarding house's suggestive proximity to another often female-run enterprise which rents rooms for profit – the brothel (as featured later in Joyce's *Ulysses*).

Rather than presenting the boarding house as an anomalous perversion of an ideal home, however, Joyce's story in fact suggests that this mode of accommodation only renders explicit the transactional nature, or economic materialism, at the heart of all family affairs. Thus, like Mrs Tibbs, as she manages her household Mrs Mooney must tread a fine line between using her daughter Polly as an attractive incentive for the lodgers, giving her 'the run of the young men', and ensuring that she does not get embroiled with the less promising ones ('none of them meant business') while holding out for the maximum price (the metaphor of gambling that runs throughout the story underscores this point).[31] But whereas Dickens' Mrs Tibbs had laid an elaborate and comedic plot to catch the individual courting her maidservant, Agnes, red-handed, Mrs Mooney more cunningly allows Mr Doran, who is involved with her daughter Polly, to lay his own trap within the deceptively homely space of the boarding house. Indeed there is an apparent sense of inevitability about his dalliance with Polly (who drifts

---

[28] James Joyce, 'The Boarding House', in *Dubliners* (New York: Penguin Classics, 1993), p. 58.
[29] Joyce, 'Boarding House', pp. 56, 59.   [30] Joyce, 'Boarding House', pp. 56–57.
[31] Joyce, 'Boarding House', pp. 57–58.

through one of the oft-mentioned open doors in the seduction scene), as it becomes clear that the apparent fluidity of borders within the house are not quite as enabling for the boarders as they appear. The open thresholds and fluid space to which Ulin draws attention, for example in the sensuous detail of the boarding house's 'lace curtains [which] ballooned gently towards the street beneath raised sashes', are not indicative of homeliness and hospitality, but serve in Joyce's story as stage-managed props for the carefully planned seduction.[32] In other words, the airiness and intermingling belie to some extent the degree to which the interior space of the boarding house – in what I will show to be a characteristic of the genre – is simultaneously carefully controlled and regulated by the residents' fear of exposure, the disapprobation of the lodgers' looks exchanged over the stairwell and, in particular, the landlady's overseeing eye. Boarding houses may well have been inscribed in external social commentary as places of dangerous, fluid liaisons, but the literature itself reveals internal operations that impose strict codes and conventions on the domestic inmates.

ii   The trouble with people: Patrick Hamilton's *The Slaves of Solitude* and Brian Moore's *The Lonely Passion of Judith Hearne*

The boarding-house setting of two novels written in the postwar years, Patrick Hamilton's *The Slaves of Solitude* (1947) and Brian Moore's *The Lonely Passion of Judith Hearne* (1955), develops important motifs in relation to this location in literature. That is, the boarding house as a place of heightened class consciousness, the commercial nature of domestic life, the fraught transactional relationships between strangers (and intimates) and the idea of an internal domestic surveillance that inhibits individual privacy and meaningful social relationships. Hamilton and Moore put these elements to work in the very different and specific historical and social contexts of, respectively, a London suburb in the final years of the Second World War and postwar inner-city Belfast. Both novels are structured around the developing subjectivity of female protagonists and trace their difficult and desperate attempts to find forms of self-identity and partnership in these necessarily makeshift accommodations. In these texts, the boarding house features again as a social space of intermingling that serves to produce not greater collective bonding but a regressive sphere of petty-mindedness. The claustrophobia and tightly monitored restraints allow for social comedy, but the underlying sense, in which the collective

---

[32] Joyce, 'Boarding House', p. 58.

space of rented rooms functions only to warp individuality and genuine human connection, is as dark in tone as anything in *Dubliners*.

The setting of these novels in relation to the Second World War bears particular significance. Historians and critics have noted how the interwar and postwar period saw the proliferation of a rhetoric of home in national discourse, as the notion of a steadfast 'home front' became a rallying cry in an age of mass slaughter abroad.[33] As David Kynaston observes:

> Above all, across the country, it was on the home that most people's hopes and concerns were really focused. 'Home means a place to go to when in trouble,' a female Mass-Observation panellist declared in 1943. 'A place where bygone days were happiest. A place sadly altered by the war. A place where you can do as you like without landladies to consider. . .'[34]

As the last phrase here indicates, the boarding house sits uneasily within this national mood of domestic retreat. On the one hand, it seems almost to typify the state-driven prescription of 'homeliness' – a regimented place of enforced community; on the other hand, it is the domestic other to the heroic, nuclear family home, emblematised in the wartime film *Mrs. Miniver* (1942). But while it remains peripheral to dominant images of home, the boarding house in this period is by no means culturally irrelevant. In sociohistorical terms, for example, this location is important for the emergence of new gender roles, including working single women, and men who, for various reasons, had not been mobilised in warfare. In this latter regard particularly, the boarding houses of Hamilton and Moore's novels are places in which fierce, economically minded female proprietors nurture and supervise the non-war-faring, inactive, unmarried men.

Moore's *The Lonely Passion of Judith Hearne* was published after Hamilton's *The Slaves of Solitude* and contains many of its motifs (the boarding house setting, the inclusion of a primly named 'ageing' heroine who is solely referred to by her last name, an American love interest, and a narrative centred around pitfalls of drink and sociality). But I choose to look at Moore's novel first here, particularly as it presents a continuation of Joyce's setting and tone in *Dubliners*, not least in his characterisation of the boarding house as a conservative institution that stifles its residents in its cold-spirited economy.

---

[33] See Judy Giles, *The Parlour and the Suburb: Domestic Identities, Class, Femininity and Modernity* (New York: Berg, 2004), and Alison Light, *Forever England: Femininity, Literature, and Conservatism Between the Wars* (London: Routledge, 1991). In *The Spiv and the Architect*, Hornsey traces the growth of interior design and DIY culture from this period, emblematised by the *Britain Can Make It* and the *South Bank Exhibition* displays.

[34] David Kynaston, *Austerity Britain, 1945–51* (London: Bloomsbury, 2007), p. 50.

Moore's presentation of the boarding house as a transitory yet stagnant place for the misfits and outcasts of a firmly stratified class society is very specific to its mid-century Belfast setting. In the mid-fifties, Belfast was still struggling to re-emerge from the devastation of the bombing campaigns of the Second World War; as Gerald Dawe notes, 'if Joyce's turn of the century Dublin was a city of paralysis, post-Second World War Belfast was deadly – a cramped and dampening place'.[35] It is presented in the novel as an austere and sectarian city, dislocated from the island of Great Britain and divided internally as a consequence of the partition of Ireland in 1921. The sense of social decline is apparent in Moore's description of the street in which the boarding house is located in a 'university bywater':

> once a good residential area, which had lately been reduced to the level of taking in paying guests. Miss Hearne stared at the houses opposite and thought of her aunt's day when there were only private families in this street, at least one maid to every house, and dinner was at night, not at noon. All gone now, all those people dead and all the houses partitioned off into flats, the bedrooms cut in two, kitchenettes jammed into linen closets, linoleum on the floors and 'To Let' cards in the bay windows.[36]

In this passage, the house appears to emblematise the instability of the family in mid-twentieth-century Belfast. For as in *Dubliners*, the idea of home is degraded by its apparent commercialisation, notably in the fact that single-family homes are cleaved into sites for multiple occupancy in order to increase rental profit. The windows of what were once private houses have effectively become advertising boards for the space within, signifying a sense of real and symbolic 'vacancy'. This selling off of private space correlates with the personal circumstances of the eponymous Judith Hearne. Miss Hearne, as she is referred to throughout the novel, is a woman of middle-class origins who has been 'reared for private life', yet who has fallen foul of the marriage market in a country depleted of eligible male matches and earns insufficient private income to live independently within her own home.[37] Shackled to her past (in particular the stultifying years spent looking after her dying aunt) and to Catholic strictures, she ekes out an impoverished existence by teaching increasingly irregular piano lessons. Miss Hearne occupies an indeterminate space in Belfast society as

---

[35] Gerald Dawe, 'The Revenges of the Heart: Belfast and the Poetics of Space', in Nicholas Allen and Aaron Kelly (eds.), *The Cities of Belfast* (Dublin: Four Courts Press, 2003), p. 204.
[36] Brian Moore, *The Lonely Passion of Judith Hearne* (New York: NYRB Classics, 2010), pp. 7–8.
[37] Mary Gordon, 'Afterword', in *Lonely Passion*, p. 225.

a single woman over the age of forty, with few social attachments and very little material possibility of establishing an independent base. Her condition is typical of, but ironically exacerbated by, residency in the liminal social zone of the boarding house.

The idea of the boarding house as a liminal space that lies between the family and various forms of institution (the prospect of which haunts Miss Hearne throughout the novel) is fundamental to Moore's novel. As noted above, in the nineteenth century, boarding houses were deemed to be transitional and in-between spaces – an 'intermediate form between the institution and the private family' according to the Registrar General – at a time which saw a rise in the number of institutions designed to house those who 'did not come under the domestic rubric', such as orphanages, workhouses, hospitals and barracks.[38] Thus in Moore's novel, the house effectively serves as an interim place from which Miss Hearne shuttles dispiritedly between her occasional social visits to the gregarious middle-class home of her friends the O'Neills (in scenes reminiscent of Maria's meagre visitation rights in Joyce's story 'Clay' in *Dubliners*) and from which she eventually descends through alcoholism to the ward of the Catholic 'Earnscliffe' nursing home.

As in Joyce's short story from *Dubliners*, the liminality of the boarding house in *Lonely Passion* does not promise any radical or liberating potential for its characters. Instead, this shared home harbours a demoted fiefdom of petty rivalries and trivial affairs, made all the more acute by the claustrophobic limitations of all-too-intimate lives played out in too small a space. As is also the case in Hamilton's *Slaves of Solitude*, the lodgings are depicted as being cut off and peripheral to the urban and national metropolis, and yet a common scene in these novels takes the form of a bitter, divided 'state of the nation' argument in which narrow parochial and nationalist sentiment presides. In the case of *Lonely Passion*, religious antagonisms underpin much of the conflict; the lodgings themselves are stipulated as being a 'Catholic house', which explains its location in the cheaper real estate near the university.

In fact the unstable hierarchies of postwar Belfast, a city in which a Protestant majority had political, economic and cultural ascendency over a Catholic minority, are embodied in the intensely self-conscious interactions of the boarding-house guests. But the boarders are not simply divided by religious tensions but also by class. Economic imperatives constantly underlie the residents' interactions; thus the characters' sudden infatuations with

---

[38] *Census*, 1851, quoted in Davidoff, 'Separation', p. 78.

other lodgers (and equally rapid removal of affections) – the forces which impel the fast-moving, at times ruthless, pace of the boarding-house narrative form – are propelled by the characters' crude or misguided economic speculations and manoeuvres. Thus the potential marriage plot within the novel (centring on Miss Hearne and the unsavoury former American hotel doorman, Mr Madden) is fuelled by economic rather than romantic interest, while a series of interior monologues in chapter 6 presents each boarder pondering relentlessly over pecuniary motives: who isn't paying up, who has cash stashed away, who might come into money. Private life, or the idea of interiority (in the sense of self-reflexiveness and self-identity), are unsparingly stripped back to the more base notion of how much people are really worth.

This economic imperative inflects the relationships between women and men, but particularly those among women. This is especially noticeable in the dynamic of servility, class and economic obligation that exists between Judith Hearne and her landlady, Mrs Rice. In one instance, Mrs Rice tries to make Miss Hearne feel at home by engaging in a conversation regarding a new servant, a traditional social gambit between women of the middle classes:

> 'She's a new girl, you know,' Mrs Henry Rice said, nodding towards the door. 'I got her from the nuns at the convent. A good strong country girl. But they need a lot of breaking in, if you know what I mean.'
>
> Miss Hearne, completely at home with this particular conversation, having heard it in all its combinations from her dear aunt and from her friends, said that if you got a good one it was all right, but sometimes you had a lot of trouble with them.[39]

This exchange works simultaneously to establish Mrs Rice's confident stance as a contractor of female domestic work, and points to the landlady's assumption that Miss Hearne must be familiar with households possessing servants (the irony being underscored by the line which indicates she is 'completely at home' with this subject matter). Yet the conversation also serves to indicate that Miss Hearne is dispossessed of such a household – hence her need to rent a room. She is in the peculiar position of being able to profit from the maid's service, although she is significantly not the maid's 'mistress'. Moreover, any allusion to domestic servitude also brings to mind the fact that Miss Hearne had formerly, in some sense, performed domestic work herself as the carer for her deceased aunt.

[39] Moore, *Lonely Passion*, p. 16.

The ambiguous performance of class codes continues in the scene with the arrival of the servant herself, Mary, on whom Miss Hearne immediately reflects that 'she would do very nicely indeed. If you were civil to these girls, they often did little odd jobs that needed doing'.[40] But when she is later handed a hammer with which to hang her picture of the Sacred Heart in her private room, the intricacy of the class stratification is revealed as Miss Hearne 'fumbled with it, saying thank you, and that she would return it as soon as she had finished hanging her picture'.[41] Her uncertain positioning between paying guest and impoverished dependent is sealed when the landlady distractedly asks Miss Hearne at one point to 'just wet the tea' in the scullery.[42] When Miss Hearne later falls into drunken rages, she has only the more symbolic forms of class distinction at her disposal, dismissing Mrs Rice as a 'fat old landlady' and 'merely a common lodging-house keeper'.[43]

Mrs Rice, however, is seemingly indomitable; in control of her household and reaping its financial rewards and stability, she presents the opposite of Miss Hearne's descent into uncontrollable alcoholism and eventual institutionalisation. Thus Mrs Rice has her own sitting room, in the space of the former kitchen, demarcated by a 'curtained door' just off the communal guest dining room.[44] Although 'not in the best of taste', as Miss Hearne is quick to observe, this parlour is, all-importantly, 'cosy' and littered with doilies, lamps and ornaments – signifiers of homeliness.[45] By contrast, Miss Hearne's downfall is to be found precisely in the isolation of her private rented room, in which she is prey to her own addictions (in the form of alcoholism and food restriction). For while Miss Hearne is in the communal spaces of the boarding house, she is able to maintain an air of respectability or at least of insouciance, but in her room she seeks the solace of the bottle that, in contrast to her self-abnegating rituals of food deprivation and religious sacrifice, replenishes her quickly:

> The yellow liquid rolled slowly in the glass, opulent, oily, the key to contentment. She swallowed it, feeling it warm the pit of her stomach, slowly spreading through her body, steadying her hands, filling her with its secret power. Warmed, relaxed, her own and only mistress, she reached for and poured a tumbler full of drink.[46]

[40] Moore, *Lonely Passion*, p. 17.   [41] Moore, *Lonely Passion*, p. 17.
[42] Moore, *Lonely Passion*, p. 92.   [43] Moore, *Lonely Passion*, pp. 96, 107.
[44] Moore, *Lonely Passion*, p. 8.   [45] Moore, *Lonely Passion*, p. 9.
[46] Moore, *Lonely Passion*, p. 99.

Far from being a refuge from the mean society of the Belfast boarding house, Miss Hearne's room is a place of self-imposed surveillance – most memorably in the form of her silver-framed photo of her aunt with the 'stern and questioning' eyes that she significantly places at the 'exact centre of the mantelpiece' as well as an oleograph of the Sacred Heart ('His place was at the Head of the bed, His fingers raised in benediction, His eyes kindly yet accusing').[47] The room is full of other eyes that see her otherwise submerged shame, from the long panel mirror that runs the length of her wardrobe with its ornamental pattern of 'whorls and loops' and wood circles that 'seemed to her like eyes, mournful wooden eyes on either side of the reflecting mirror nose' to the little buttons on her shoes that she imagines 'winking up at her. Little shoe-eyes, always there'.[48] Even the 'little travelling clock' inherited from her aunt performs a similar panoptical role, taunting its occupant with the length of her activity-less days and insomniac nights, enforcing the strictures of meal times in the boarding house (reinforced by the imposing patriarchal symbol of the grandfather clock in the dining room), and eventually humiliating her with the lost time of her drinking sprees.

No less panoptic in its effects is the narrative voice and form of the novel that pursues Miss Hearne into various confining places, constantly exposing her to the reader in merciless fashion. Thus her concluding stay in an institutional nursing home is offered as a type of narrative just deserts for her fanciful (and, it is implied, rather ridiculous) dreams of romantic partnership and a 'real' home. For as Monica Cohen notes in relation to institutional 'homes': 'they are places that can only imitate home with residents who can only pretend to be a family. In other words, they are not authentic; they are not "true"'.[49] If the boarding house, as institution, strives to maintain the appearance of normalcy, albeit at the expense of a fair amount of play-acting, the grim 'Home' to which Miss Hearne is finally confined admits of no such domestic pretensions. It is her final resting place, although only after she briefly occupies a private room at an upscale Belfast hotel so the contrast may be all the more grotesque (this hotel room comes at a price, of course, and is paid for by her 'good friends', the O'Neills, who wish to remain unencumbered by this tiresome family friend). Abandoned by friends, thrown out of the boarding house, and left to live out her days in the 'white, stripped, still' single-sex dormitory of the nursing home, Miss Hearne takes solace in the two personal objects that

[47] Moore, *Lonely Passion*, p. 7.   [48] Moore, *Lonely Passion*, pp. 19, 223.
[49] Cohen, *Professional Domesticity*, p. 57.

accompany her in all her unstable residences: the photograph of the frowning aunt and the disapproving Sacred Heart.[50] 'Funny about those two. When they're with me, watching over me, a new place becomes home', she observes in a final play on the dark irony and inversion of that slippery term.[51]

Like Moore's *The Lonely Passion of Judith Hearne*, Hamilton's *The Slaves of Solitude* also deals with the ruthless class warfare underlying the apparent gentility of a boarding-house environment. The novel simultaneously uses this domestic setting to capture a particular national mood, while remaining alert to the way in which boarding-house life remains distinctly peripheral. Thus *Slaves* is summed up by one writer as 'one of the very best English novels written about [the Second World War] – yet it contains no descriptions of combat or death and destruction of warfare'.[52] In fact, the boarding house in this work engages with the more tangential domestic effects of war, with the constant implication that the real action is taking place elsewhere. Hamilton's distinctive ironic narrative voice in the novel repeatedly highlights how this particular suburban lodging house is no heroic domestic front for civilian resilience. The cast of minor residents are instead determined by their extremely unproductive activity: from the vicious, perennial small-hotel resident Mr Thwaites, to the amateur dramatist Mr Prest, an off-duty, hard-drinking American lieutenant, and the heroine of the story, Miss Roach, a copy editor who lacks work and meaningful social company.

For Hamilton, the boarding house in the fictional suburban town of Thames Lockdon (its name signifying its status as a poor relation to 'London' and hinting at the claustrophobic implications of 'lock down') is a choice venue for his favourite themes of the grand and even murderous melodrama caused by petty class and sexual jealousy. *Slaves* subsequently revels in portraying the specifically British counterpart of wartime heroism, characterised by Philip Ziegler as 'snobbishness, selfishness, the spirit of *sauve qui peut*'.[53] If the boarding house is a microcosm of the nation, Hamilton's novel seems to suggest, then Mrs Payne's boarding house, still bearing its prewar name 'The Rosamund Tea Rooms', is a knock-down version exposing an alternative national narrative of decline, isolationism and petty feuding. Indeed, the very appearance of the house itself conveys a mood of restriction and anachronism: it is a 'somewhat narrow,

[50] Moore, *Lonely Passion*, p. 222.   [51] Moore, *Lonely Passion*, p. 223.
[52] David Lodge, 'Introduction', in Hamilton, *The Slaves of Solitude* (New York: NYRB, 2007), p. x.
[53] Philip Ziegler, *London at War, 1939–45* (New York: Alfred A. Knopf), p. 1.

three-storied, red-brick house' with 'faded gilt letters' announcing its obsolete and meaningless name.[54] Inside, its communal hallway reinforces the strictures of the living space, as the landlady's reception areas, whose function is ostensibly to offer a welcome to visitors, advertise the house's punitive spirit and limited resources:

> A small, dim oil-lamp burned in the hall, just illuminating the hall table, the bright, tinny, brass Oriental gong, and the green baize letter-rack criss-crossed with black tape. Mrs. Payne had put a stop to electricity on the landings simply by taking all the bulbs out – thus succouring her hard-pressed country, the spirit of the black-out generally, and her own pecuniary resources.[55]

Everything in this transitional home is designed to militate against comfort and well-being, from the dull lighting and tinny gong to the prohibitive markers and bulb-less lights.

The novel traces the (mis)fortunes of the sympathetic protagonist, the single Miss Roach, a type of internal refugee who has been bombed out of her Kensington home, retaining only a few possessions in her current 'room of her own at the top'.[56] This room at the top, however, provides neither cosy nor bohemian seclusion. Seen from the 'feeble light' of a single bulb shaded by 'pink parchment', Miss Roach surveys the room with an outsider's critical eye:

> She saw the pink artificial-silk bedspread covering the light single bed built of stained-oak – the pink bedspread which shone and slithered and fell off, the light bedstead which slid along the wooden floor if you bumped into it. She saw the red chequered cotton curtains (this side of the black-out material) which were hung on a brass rail and never quite met in the middle, or, if forced to meet in a moment of impatience, came flying away from the sides; she saw the stained-oak chest of drawers with its mirror held precariously at a suitable angle with a squashed match-box. . . . She saw the pink wall-paper, which bore the mottled pattern of a disease of the flesh; and in one corner were piled her 'books', treasures which she had saved from the bombing in London, but for which she had not yet obtained a shelf.[57]

As a cheap pink boudoir, the room confronts Miss Roach with the fact of her lack of marital status but also, in its detail of slippery threadbare coverings, foreshadows the novel's depiction of the fickleness and deception of affairs of the heart. The black-out curtains, a recurrent detail and metaphor,

---

[54] Patrick Hamilton, *The Slaves of Solitude* (New York: NYRB Classics, 2007), p. 4.
[55] Hamilton, *Slaves*, p. 5.   [56] Hamilton, *Slaves*, p. 7.   [57] Hamilton, *Slaves*, pp. 5–6.

further signal the sharp and unforgiving delineation of the outside world and the enforced retreat to the claustrophobic interior that the war established.

As an 'ardent lover and pursuer of privacy', Miss Roach struggles with new codes of public and private living throughout the novel, a representation of the way in which the war offered women a particular brand of freedom and opportunity as well as specific constraints and limitations.[58] For the Second World War produced changing patterns of work and mobility (not least through eviction and evacuation), which resulted in new encounters and configurations for both genders in traditionally defined public and private spaces. For women in particular, the war marked a turning point in terms of spaces that were deemed permissible, including those of the factory and the public house. But *Slaves* tempers this celebratory, retrospective view of the cultural advances of the war years. For the boarding house in this novel is indeed a place for arbitrary encounters and the mingling of nationalities (the complexities of cross-cultural encounter underpin Miss Roach's relations with her ostensible love interest, the American lieutenant, and her future adversary, the German Vicki Kugelmann), but the result is less an effect of cosmopolitan encounter than of the intensification of rigid class codes and conventions. The very fact of occupying a room in a boarding house, Hamilton seems to imply, makes its residents self-conscious and defensive about their own class status: 'For nearly all who lived in the boarding-houses of Thames Lockdon were conscious of having descended in the world, of having arrived where they were by a pure freak of fate, and of courteously but condescendingly acting a part in front of their fellow-boarders'.[59] Thus the dining room in which the boarders meet at their 'system of separate tables' (a phrase that Terence Rattigan used as the title for his drama of boarding house manners) is described as being 'peculiarly and gratuitously hellish', a place in which the gloomy silence and social awkwardness are forever on display.[60] Indeed, it is the very enforced proximity of the breakfasting guests that seems to lend itself to the utter self-estrangement of this provisional community:

> For, in the small space of the room, a word could not be uttered, a little cough could not be made, a hairpin could not be dropped at one table without being heard at all the others; and the general self-consciousness

---

[58] Hamilton, *Slaves*, p. 91.   [59] Hamilton, *Slaves*, pp. 73–74.
[60] Terence Rattigan, *Separate Tables* (1955) (London: Nick Hern, 2010); Hamilton, *Slaves*, pp. 8–9.

which this caused smote the room with a silence, a conversational torpor, and finally a complete apathy from which it could not stir itself.[61]

Because the residents of the boarding house are not 'at home' in the conventional sense and therefore cannot display or project themselves through their surroundings (as per conventional domestic ideology), social distinction has to be enacted through the performative display of dress and speech. Thus while Mr Prest may be the Tea Rooms' resident small-time actor, all the characters are engaged in amateur dramatics of some kind. It is representative of what Alison Light sees as the stagey quality of inter-war life, captured by 'middlebrow' writers such as Ivy Compton-Burnett and Agatha Christie, who show a 'society of strangers whose social exchanges have become theatrical and dissevered from a sense of place'.[62] Again, the fact that the boarding house brings together disparate people, whose origins are often obscure and whose backstories remain concealed, reinforces the sense in which only the performative survive. Everyone has to play a role, or become a caricature in some sense, in order to get by or to preserve their own fragile sense of self. 'Private life' is ruthlessly reduced to the baser notion of who has the money to escape from this place where hell truly seems to be other people.

The interior space of Hamilton's boarding house effectively conveys a form of community in its most rudimentary and unidealised form. This sense is encapsulated in a description of the aural soundscape of guests waking up in their separate rented rooms:

> This perception, on the part of the guest, of his animal self, was made even more dreary by certain impressions which were now wafted towards him of the coarser bedroom selves of his fellow-guests. These impressions were conveyed to him in partially ghostly and mysterious ways – in the uncanny gurgling and throbbing of unlocated water-pipes, which seemed softly and eerily to answer each other all over the house: in the sound of unidentified windows shrieking open or being slammed shut: in sudden furious rushes of water from taps into basins: in the sound of bumps, and of thuds: of tooth-glasses being rattled with tooth-brushes, and of expectorations: of coughs, and stupendous throat-clearings: of noses being blown: even of actual groans. . . . Mrs Payne, pettishly hitting at her gong below, announced the proper commencement of day, and the end of privacy.[63]

As the passage shows, the boarding house permits its inhabitants little opportunity for social veneer or facade; privacy is brief and insufficient, and the architecture of the house militates against seclusion.

---

[61] Hamilton, *Slaves*, p. 9.   [62] Light, *Forever England*, pp. 61–62.   [63] Hamilton, *Slaves*, p. 63.

Like Moore's *The Lonely Passion of Judith Hearne*, Hamilton's novel is finely tuned to the way in which the structural arrangement of the boarding house enables particular narrative trajectories and set pieces. Indeed, there is a clear sense that he considers the boarding house itself to be a characteristic space of its own, an impression confirmed by his frequent adjectival use of the word ('pretty ordinary boarding-house specimens', 'in boarding-house and landlady psychology', 'the boarding-house tempest', 'petty boarding-house lassitude', 'boarding-house life').[64] The novel's structure thus reflects and heightens the atmosphere of crowding and claustrophobia which defines the interior spaces of the Rosamund Tea Rooms. Hamilton's characteristic relentless attention to trivialities of speech and behaviour, along with his overanalysis of the minor, the implied and the unsaid, can be seen to be indicative of the tendencies of the idle, overcurious boarders themselves. Thus in typical manner, Hamilton might start a new chapter which, far from offering the sense of a new setting or at least some respite from the wrangling of the previous chapter, will in fact turn out to be a direct continuation of the previous scene or dialogic exchange. It is a narrative device that enacts the boarding-house ethos of refusing to offer any diversion or reprieve to its residents – simply a momentary pause before the next onslaught of obsessive detail or rumour-mongering. In this, the text mimics formally the interiority of the boarding house: the architecture of thin walls, easily breached boundaries and encroaching overintimacy.

Yet like the role of the boarding house itself, the narrative plot of *The Slaves of Solitude* provides a precarious mixture of conventionality and an undercurrent of something more transgressive. On the surface, the house is characterised in conservative ways as a stereotypically 'feminine' space: apolitical, trivial and concerned with petty romance. Thus Hamilton frequently uses a mock-heroic tone to lampoon the passions and cruelties of the effeminate 'Tea Rooms':

> It was not for the piano-tuner to know that in this still, grey, winter-gripped dining-room, this apparent mortuary of desire and passion (in which the lift rumbled and knives and forks scraped upon plates), waves were flowing forward and backward, and through and through, of hellish revulsion and unquenchable hatred!
>
> It was not for him to know that between these two women there existed a feud almost unparalleled in boarding-house, or indeed feminine, history...[65]

---

[64] Hamilton, *Slaves*, pp. 158, 208, 216, 237, 240. In fact, Hamilton's family lived for extended periods in English boarding houses which might explain this anthropological sensibility.
[65] Hamilton, *Slaves*, p. 158.

But while the boarding house and femininity are bywords for triviality in passages such as these, it is possible to argue that *The Slaves of Solitude* bears elements that disrupt stereotypical plots of gender and sexuality. To begin with, Hamilton places an unusual focus on his female characters and ascribes to them alone the three-dimensionality of complexity, depth and interiority. This is true even for the enigmatic Vicki Kugelmann, whom the story keeps necessarily at a certain distance but portrays in subtle and nuanced hues, at least in comparison to the rather insipid and overrated American lieutenant. Indeed, the deliberate blandness of this ex-'Laundry king' from Detroit, whom both women view as a potential husband, is crucial to the plot's pivot: the relationship between the wary Miss Roach and her intrusive next-door neighbour Vicki, the disruptive late arrival to the boarding-house community. Like Dickens and Joyce before him, Hamilton takes pleasure in skewing the traditional novelistic marriage plot – in his case, through a parodic and carnivalesque *menage-à-trois* under the auspices of the (three-storey) boarding house. Indeed, as in his other novels, in particular the *Twenty Thousand Streets Under the Sky* trilogy (1935) and *Hangover Square: A Story of Darkest Earl's Court* (1941), Hamilton's plots are driven by the thrills and despair engendered by the 'three-cornered meeting', a dynamic often fuelled by copious alcohol consumption.[66] As the narrative of *Slaves* progresses, the heteronormative duality of the traditional romantic and sexual encounter is constantly punctured by this structuring role of the threesome – Miss Roach, the American lieutenant and the German (and possibly Jewish) Vicki.[67]

According to René Girard's delineation of 'triangular desire', romantic plots often present a situation in which the depth of feeling between the male rivals in love at times exceeds the relation between the admirer and the female object of desire.[68] The result, Girard contends, is that the dominant relationship of rivalry is in fact centred upon the two male figures who compete over the same woman, thus revealing the disguised homosocial (and potentially homosexual) relation at the core of the narrative. Extending this analysis to *Slaves*, the closeness between the two women who start out as firm friends before they find themselves simultaneously divided and drawn together over their rivalry for the

[66] Hamilton, *Slaves*, p. 89.
[67] While Vicki is identified as German throughout the novel, the significance of her last name ('Kugel' is the name of a traditional Jewish pudding) and the landlady's eventual abrupt ejection of her from the house hint that she might be a Jewish refugee.
[68] See René Girard, '"Triangular" Desire' in *Deceit, Desire, and the Novel: Self and Other in Literary Structure*, Yvonne Freccero (trans.), (Baltimore: Johns Hopkins Press, 1965), especially 40–49.

attention of the American guest, is also a product of the boarding-house space itself, in which Vicki is roomed next door to Miss Roach.[69] Thus superficially at least, Miss Roach appears to become increasingly irate at Vicki's casual manner of entering her room in order to engage in the intimate actions of gazing at herself in Miss Roach's mirror and using her hairbrush. But in doing so, Vicki posits herself simultaneously as the object of Miss Roach's gaze while interpolating herself within Miss Roach's private space. This blurring of subject and object, particularly in the context of sexual desire, is an underlying motif in the novel and the narrative frequently plays on the lack of specificity as to the identity of the object of desire. Paralleling Eve Kosofsky Sedgwick's delineation of the male homosexual bonds that are forged in the guise of a heterosexual plot, Hamilton's erotic triangle articulates latent sexual desire between the two women.[70]

This aspect is once more generated by the spatial confines of the boarding-house interior which keeps the characters – in a blur of love objects, enemies, allies and snoops – in frustrating proximity to one another. The eroticism of private rooms, too easily encroached upon, is signalled as Miss Roach lies awake in her bed and vividly imagines Vicki undressing in the room next to her, fuelled by her hypersensitivity to the suggestive sound of keys in locks. For while at a surface level the narrative indicates only that Miss Roach's obsessive alertness to the sounds of her neighbours is related to her jealousy vis-à-vis the lieutenant, it also implies that Vicki herself is the coveted object of desire.

The boarding house in Hamilton's novel can thus be seen to operate not simply as a suburban backwater to national life but as a potential 'third space' for nonheteronormative romantic alliances. 'It was all rather queer', the narrative proposes suggestively: 'Nothing definite, but rather queer'.[71] The term 'queer' itself derives from *across*, serving, as Sedgwick notes, to capture 'a continuing moment, movement, motive' – a sense that suits the layout of the boarding house with its interior space constituted by connective landings, thoroughfares and hallways.[72] And as Sarah Waters reveals in her wartime novel, addressed later in this chapter, the abnormalities of

---

[69] In this way, the novel reconfigures the heterosexual unrequited-love-through-thin-walls relations between Bob and Ella, a barman and barmaid who live above The Midnight Bell pub, in Hamilton's trilogy, *Twenty Thousand Streets Under the Sky* (London: Vintage, 2004).

[70] Eve Kosofsky Sedgwick, *Between Men: English Literature and Male Homosocial Desire* (New York: Columbia University Press, 1985).

[71] Hamilton, *Slaves*, p. 160.

[72] Eve Kosofsky Sedgwick, *Tendencies* (London: Routledge, 1994), p. xii.

blacked-out wartime life could produce a queering of all levels of the physical and social landscape.[73] "'Love", like drink', Hamilton's narrative rather cryptically asserts, 'under the influence of the war, was exerting a new sort of pressure everywhere, affecting people it would not have affected before, and in an entirely fresh way'.[74]

iii   Refuge: The rented room in a time of war

In the novels of Hamilton and Moore, the interior space of the boarding house functions in part as a peripheral setting for individuals who are apparently excluded from a masculinist, 'heroic' national narrative. This sense of marginality produces heightened dramas of class and unbelonging, where the fragile social bonds of disparate individuals united by straitened circumstances prove to be brittle. Boarding houses in these texts, I have argued, serve to atomise individuals living cheek by jowl in an 'inauthentic' home. They can function as a setting for pettiness and mean-mindedness, in which social appearances are mercilessly stripped away to expose damaged and vulnerable souls. Hamilton's *Slaves*, however, suggests that there is a transgressive potential in the space of the boarding house which, by its nature, queers the heteronormative structure of the traditional family home. In this next section, I turn to literary representations of lodgings as types of emergency accommodation and a complex form of refuge – an important trope at a time when the physical and social landscape of Britain was undergoing radical change.

The rented rooms in Rose Macaulay's short story 'Miss Anstruther's Letters' (1942), and Sarah Waters' historical novel, *The Night Watch* (2006), serve as a temporary shelter for two female characters who – like Miss Roach – have been bombed or displaced from their 'original' homes. Again, then, the lodging house is by definition a secondary site of inauthenticity: a transient and insufficient bad copy of 'home'. But while they are a poor compensation for the individuals who are forced to take refuge in them, the temporary lodging spaces in these texts serve as a fitting projection of the women's sense of themselves as ghostly doubles, inhabiting a world that appears as a pale imitation of what went before.

In these texts, the loss of the female characters' prewar home is shown to be commensurate with a sense of personal and national uprooting.

---

[73] Indeed, Sarah Waters' most recent publication, *The Paying Guests* (London: Virago, 2014), plays precisely on the queer erotics of the postwar lodging house.
[74] Hamilton, *Slaves*, p. 238.

This is pertinent in a historical context in which bodies and architecture had become distinctively linked: literally, in the context of a war in which civilians were bombed in their own houses, and metaphorically, since bombed houses were often likened to, or stood in for, the large-scale devastation of lives. Thus contemporary depictions of neighbourhoods ravaged after bombing raids constantly invoked a surreal landscape of craters and ghostly absences where houses once stood. As Rod Mengham argues, 'the bombed houses of the Second World War provided British culture with some of its most disturbing images of the domestic interior', resulting in the exposure of what he calls (in a suggestively gendered term) the 'denuded interior' that exposes what should be a citadel of privacy to a public gaze.[75]

The exposure of private life – and, indeed, closely held secrets – is at the root of 'Miss Anstruther's Letters', in which the eponymous female character finds that her London home and all her possessions have been obliterated in an air attack. In a quietly devastating opening sentence, Macaulay lays out the brute effects of the bomb:

> Miss Anstruther, whose life had been cut in two on the night of 10 May 1941, so that she now felt herself a ghost, without attachments or habitation, neither of which she any longer desired, sat alone in the bed-sitting-room she had taken, a small room, littered with the grimy, broken and useless objects which she had salvaged from the burnt-out ruin around the corner.[76]

There appear to be no ambiguities in the aftermath of the devastation. 'Everything was doomed', the narrative voice observes, taking in the smouldering remains of the collapsed Edwardian house: 'furniture, books, pictures, china, clothes, manuscripts, silver, everything'.[77] Miss Anstruther's crucial letters, mementoes penned by her dead lover and carefully conserved, have been cruelly burned by the fire that has consumed the emblematic, Victorian-style locked rosewood desk.

Macaulay's short story presents a symbolic demolition of the cherished Victorian bourgeois interior and its associated values of security, sanctuary and protection from the exterior world. The idea of a room and its objects exhibiting secure individualism has, in this short story, been apocalyptically

---

[75] Rod Mengham, '"Anthropology at Home": Domestic Interiors in British Film and Fiction of the 1930s and 1940s', in Aynsley and Grant (eds.), *Imagined Interiors*, p. 251.
[76] Rose Macaulay, 'Miss Anstruther's Letters', in Anne Boston (ed.), *Wave Me Goodbye: Stories of the Second World War* (London: Penguin, 1989), p. 65.
[77] Macaulay, 'Letters', p. 70.

blown to dust; the fire has reduced personal objects and familiar furnishings to 'blackened fragments [lying] in indistinguishable anonymity together' and a 'chaotic mass'.[78] Likewise, the subdivided, multi-storeyed Edwardian house, within which Miss Anstruther privately occupied a floor, has been savagely merged with the hall and outside street: 'scrambled and beaten into a common devastation of smashed masonry and dust'.[79] The temporary bedsit in which Miss Anstruther now resides, a 'strange, littered, unhomely room', is the very opposite of what a home should be – and yet paradoxically turns out to be exactly expressive of her current condition of shell-shocked blankness.[80] This is encapsulated in the use of that uncanny word again, 'unhomely', which emphasises the bedsit's role as the negated version of a real home and Miss Anstruther's sense of leading a form of life-in-death. For Miss Anstruther has survived the bomb only to now exist as a 'drifting ghost' who is impelled to haunt the site of her trauma – rummaging through the ruins of her house and former life like a 'revenant'.[81]

While Macaulay's story partly invokes a nostalgic longing for this ruthlessly burnt-out world, it also invites a possible critique of the fetishisation or overvaluation of the clutter and trinkets of the prewar interior. Miss Anstruther, for example, castigates herself for not retrieving her precious letters, having salvaged instead an array of useless ornaments: 'a china cow, a tiny walnut shell with tiny Mexicans behind glass, a box with a mechanical bird that jumped out and sang, and a fountain pen'.[82] In the end, it is the more intangible aspects of memory and language that offer her some kind of salve. Thus towards the story's conclusion, Miss Anstruther's despairing reflection on her ruined home, epitomised by the illegible remaining scraps of love-letters, sparks an epiphany of heightened consciousness and revelation (much like Gabriel Conroy's epiphany concerning his marriage in 'The Dead', in which 'moments of their secret life together burst like stars upon his memory').[83] For while the narrative deals with a life reduced to fragments, the modernist ending, in which flashes of memory recall the past and its lost objects, offers some kind of redemption and mitigation against material desecration, recalling T. S. Eliot's lines: 'These fragments I have shored against my ruins'.[84] Set in Miss Anstruther's desultory bedsit, filled with the charred, ruined fragments of a former world, the narrative conveys the idea that the relations of the past may only persist in disrupted and intangible forms.

---

[78] Macaulay, 'Letters', p. 66.   [79] Macaulay, 'Letters', p. 68.   [80] Macaulay, 'Letters', p. 67.
[81] Macaulay, 'Letters', pp. 67, 73.   [82] Macaulay, 'Letters', p. 69.   [83] Joyce, *Dubliners*, p. 214.
[84] T. S. Eliot, 'The Waste Land', in *Collected Poems, 1909-1962* (London: Faber and Faber, 1974), p. 79.

The rented room as a space of physical and psychic recovery in face of the actual destruction of a physical home is also present in Waters' novel of domestic 'refugees'. Waters' reverse narrative charts the interrelated stories of four central characters who alternately love, betray, rescue and abandon one another. It is effective precisely for the way in which Waters characteristically creates a deep interiority for each character, binding the cast together in a social web which encompasses not only love affairs between women, but also the complex relations of friendship and guardianship. It is a social narrative framework, one which is adept at revealing the strength and yet ultimate fragility of fleeting and finite correspondences.

Reminiscent of 'Letters', *The Night Watch* begins from the vantage point of the shell-shocked heroine, Kay, who has retreated into a rented room in a dilapidated 'crooked house', full of the dusty paraphernalia of the Victorian home and with 'lurid Edwardian angels' on its threshold.[85] Again, life inside the bedsit is used to evoke a type of historical hiatus and stagnation, a post-traumatic state of recovery (in Kay's case, a place to recuperate from her stint as an emergency response ambulance worker and abandonment by her lover Helen). Kay, like Miss Hearne in *Lonely Passion*, has become 'a person whose clocks and wrist-watches have stopped'. And like Miss Anstruther, it seemed to her that 'she really might be a ghost ... that she might be becoming part of the faded fabric of the house, dissolving into the gloom that gathered, like dust, in its crazy angles'.[86] For Kay's room is once again physically and figuratively indicative of substitute and makeshift accommodation, having been converted from its original use: 'The walls were empty, featureless, just as they had been when she'd moved in. She'd never hung up a picture or put out books; she had no pictures or books; she didn't have much of anything'.[87] In one sense, of course, the room 'reflects' precisely Kay's sense of loss and ghost-like uprooted existence; but in another echo of Miss Anstruther, the narrative serves to reveal precisely the way in which subjectivity is incommensurate with the material nature of the interior.

The opening description of the lodgings from which Kay looks out, two years after the war had ended, encapsulates Waters' dominant motif in the novel of the house as body. Despite its outdated appearance, this crooked house in which she has taken refuge is a site of exposed vulnerability and

---

[85] Sarah Waters, *The Night Watch* (London: Virago, 2006), pp. 7, 4.
[86] Waters, *Night Watch*, pp. 2–3.   [87] Waters, *Night Watch*, p. 5.

endurance: 'For it was the last surviving building in what had once, before the war, been a long terrace; it still had the scars, on either side, where it had been attached to its neighbours, the zig-zag of phantom staircases and the dints of absent hearths'.[88] Throughout *The Night Watch*, the house exteriors, like the outward appearance and gait of the novel's characters, are shown to be misleading 'fronts' (in both senses of the term):

> It looked forbidding in the darkness, the flat Georgian houses seeming smooth as well-bred bored blank faces – until [Helen] moved, and saw the sky behind the windows, and realized that many of them had been gutted by blast and by fire.[89]

But while the houses are humanised, the victims of war are reduced to material parts, dislocated and scattered (a woman whom Kay rescues tells her, 'I feel like tinder. . . . Just like tinder').[90] Yet the fates of houses and people are not always so neatly correspondent; as an emergency response ambulance worker, Kay comes across intact houses in which the occupants have perished, while at other times, she bears witness to collapsed buildings in which unscathed families have miraculously and surreally survived. In other cases, the collapse of interiors and exteriors creates a dreadful intermingling of bodies and architecture and gives the anthropomorphic trope a vivid distressing materiality. As Kay and others enter the rubble of bombed buildings, they are sometimes confronted with shards of the building, household objects, and the fractured body as a type of scattered object, in a grotesque domestic ensemble.

In one house, the effect of the bombing has turned a home into historical ruins:

> The chaos was extraordinary. Every time Kay put down her feet, things cracked beneath them, or wrapped themselves around her ankles: broken window-glass mixed up with broken mirrors, crockery, chairs and tables, curtains, carpets, feathers from a cushion or a bed, great splinters of wood. . . . What amazed her, too, was the smallness of the piles of dirt and rubble to which even large buildings could be reduced. . . . She supposed that houses, after all – like the lives that were lived in them – were mostly made of space. It was the spaces, in fact, that counted, rather than the bricks.[91]

---

[88] Waters, *Night Watch*, p. 8. This description interestingly evokes Rachel Whiteread's ghostly white plaster sculpture of the 'absent space' of a demolished Victorian terraced house on Grove Road, East London; 'House' (1993–94), www.artangel.org.uk/projects/1993/house.

[89] Waters, *Night Watch*, pp. 358–59.   [90] Waters, *Night Watch*, p. 292.

[91] Waters, *Night Watch*, p. 201.

Waters' shattered houses cleverly play on the tension between what is simultaneously an act of exposure and burial; the uncovered domestic interior is in fact a form of internment. For as in Miss Anstruther's tale of self-revelation, the mangled mess exposed by the bomb is finally shown to be meaningless, while more significance is given to the immaterial possessions of memory and shared experiences in a common space. The character Viv subsequently reflects: 'She'd never thought of that before, about all the secrets that the war must have swallowed up, left buried in dust and darkness and silence. She had only ever thought of the raids as tearing things open, making things hard'.[92]

As in Macaulay's story, it is narrative itself that offers the possibility of some kind of reparation. *The Night Watch* uses an effective form of reverse chronology, beginning in the immediate postwar years of 1947 and advancing – or perhaps retreating – back to 1940–41, during the Blitz, thus engaging at a structural level with motifs of loss, haunting and healing. Because of the reverse narrative structure, Waters' novel begins with the broken and scarred postwar London terrain and concludes with the adrenaline-fuelled optimism that characterised the emergency period of a few years earlier. Like a miraculous act of reconstruction (or rehabilitation), the shift back in time serves textually to repair the shattered interiors with which the novel opens. It is a technique that promotes an unnerving sense of nostalgia that aptly captures a particular strand of longing in the years of British austerity for the relations, and perhaps imaginary 'wholeness', of a former way of life. Yet the reversal of sequential narrative form also produces a sense of ambivalence: the past can be regained, but it is always foreshadowed by loss.

The book's final section is thus also a return to a historical moment in which women in particular found themselves unanchored from traditional spaces and roles. It is a change in the structure of feeling that Waters addresses in a commentary on her novel:

> This literal opening-up of London had its corollary, of course, in people's emotional lives. Everyone felt the impact of the temporary, anonymous intimacies that sprang up in shelters, in queues, in trains – in any of the places where people were newly obliged to be cooped up together for many dull or frightening hours. Elizabeth Bowen, one of the war's most eloquent chroniclers, describes living through the bombings 'with every pore open'. 'Sometimes I hardly knew where I stopped', she writes in her postscript to the wartime stories *The Demon Lover*, 'and somebody else began. The

---

[92] Waters, *Night Watch*, p. 309.

violent destruction of solid things, the explosion of the illusion that prestige, power and permanence attach to bulk and weight, left all of us,
equally, heady and disembodied.'[93]

In a wartime world which was rationing even private space, the characters
in *The Night Watch* are impelled by circumstance to forge new makeshift
domesticities in varying types of accommodation and household settings:
rented rooms, fire escapes, a boathouse on the Thames. Waters conveys
the delicacy and impracticality of sociality in these transient interiors,
the hastily constructed codes between lovers and neighbours as well as
the way in which intimacy, strangeness and estrangement are perhaps less
surprising bedfellows than are often imagined. In that sense the novel
reflects the shift, marked by cultural historians, in the levelling of domestic arrangements, the reordering of family structures, and the creation of
new, emergency spaces where strangers might take refuge in the dark.

iv   Windrush: Cultures of lodging in black British writing

This man, this room, this city; this story, this language, this form.
—V.S. Naipaul, *The Mimic Men*
(New York: Vintage International, 2001), p. 97

The notion of boarding houses and rented rooms as practical shelters, as
well as symbolic places of refuge from hostile social conditions, becomes
increasingly significant in the postwar period, particularly in the context
of increased immigration from Commonwealth countries. The 493 West
Indian passengers on the *Empire Windrush* who docked at Tilbury in
June 1948, for example, found themselves temporarily housed by the
Ministry of Labour in the rehabilitated space of Clapham South Under-
ground Station, which had been used as an air shelter during the war.
Having spent weeks in ship dormitories, the newly arrived citizens were
to spend their first night in fitted bunks literally under the ground of the
'Mother Country'. Their sojourn in the 'clearing house' or 'transit camp'
of the Deep Shelter, captured in evocative photographs, highlights the
way in which immigrants found themselves directly caught up in Britain's postwar housing crisis, a result of the wartime bombing of British
cities (which destroyed two million homes), the rapid pace of the Labour
government's slum clearance schemes, and the war's interruption of plans

---

[93] Sarah Waters, 'Romance Among the Ruins', *Guardian*, 28 January 2006, www.theguardian.com/
books/2006/jan/28/fiction.sarahwaters.

to build new homes.[94] The fact that this was captured in photojournalism is itself telling of the way in which public and private boundaries were experienced differently for migrant people. As Wendy Webster has commented: 'It was on arrival, often within hours, that they discovered that although their labour was required in Britain and gave them access to places defined as public, there were no places for them to live'.[95] The housing issue was particularly acute for migrants who did not have the economic resources to enter the home ownership market and who were ineligible for the type of council housing that typically accommodated working-class and displaced residents (waiting lists were long and, in any case, required a three-year minimum residency). Moreover, excluded for the most part from the council sector, immigrants also faced overt racism in the private housing sector.[96] Representations of this discrimination form well-known images and anecdotes from the period, from the infamous signs which explicitly prohibited them from renting rooms ('Europeans only', 'White people only') to the less overt, but no less pernicious, apology ('We personally don't mind, but the other people in the house do').[97]

The figure of the black person as a renter of rooms in this period is thus historically and culturally significant. Indeed, the familiarity of what Stuart Hall labels the 'now overtypical and over typified so-called "documentary" shot of the man looking at the sign which reads "Rooms to Let. No Coloured Men"' suggests the way in which housing and the question of migrancy were frequently correlated.[98] As always, one group's exclusion from the council sector and mainstream rental market presented a financial opportunity for others, and private estate agents and landlords found they could rent rooms of poorer quality to West Indian

---

[94] 'Clearing house' and 'transit camp' are the terms used in the document 'SS *Empire Windrush* – Jamaican Unemployed: Memorandum by the Secretary of State for the Colonies, Arthur Creech Jones, 15 June 1948', in Panikos Panayi (ed.), *The Impact of Immigration: A Documentary History of the Effects and Experiences of Immigrants in Britain Since 1945* (Manchester: Manchester University Press, 1999), p. 39.

[95] Wendy Webster, *Imagining Home: Gender, 'Race', and National Identity* (London: Routledge, 1998), p. 151.

[96] See Chris Hamnett, *Unequal City: London in the Global Arena* (London: Routledge, 2003), pp. 121–23. Mohan Luthra describes this as the 'laissez-faire' period of immigrant housing history in *Britain's Black Population: Social Change, Public Policy and Agenda*, 3rd edn. (Aldershot: Arena, 1997), p. 305.

[97] See Ruth Glass, *Newcomers: The West Indians in London* (London: Centre for Urban Studies, 1960), pp. 58–62.

[98] See Stuart Hall, 'Reconstruction Work: Images of Post-War Black Settlement', in Ben Highmore (ed.), *The Everyday Life Reader* (London: Routledge, 2002), p. 260.

immigrants at a much higher premium. Confirming the key importance of questions of housing to the lives of immigrants and to the way in which they were perceived in the culture at large, James Procter points out in his important study of depictions of living space in black British literature that

> the dwelling place was, perhaps more than the official point of entry, the site at which the regulation, policing and deferral of black settlement were most effectively played out. It was around housing that the national panic surrounding black immigration tended to accumulate and stage itself in this period.[99]

Much contemporary British literature of the period – including Harold Pinter's *The Room* (1957), Shelagh Delaney's *A Taste of Honey* (1958) and Lynne Reid Banks' *The L-Shaped Room* (1960) (as well as the 1962 film adaptation of this novel directed by Brian Forbes) – uses the bedsit/rooming house as a setting for explorations of (often female) alienation, where the black lodger features in racist portrayals as an inscrutable or threatening presence. In these texts, the visibility of a black man in close living quarters with the white characters is frequently intended to produce a shock effect, one which depends precisely upon the sexualisation of black men in cultural portrayals.[100] It also projects the sense, articulated by contemporary sociologists such as Sheila Patterson, that housing was the contact zone between black migrants and the white working class: 'the chief source of competition and potential conflict with the local population'.[101] Indeed, the tensions surrounding housing are all too evident in the historical and sociological writing of the period, often expressed in an idiom that betrays a fear of the impact of economic depreciation in areas populated by migrants, sometimes framed as a euphemistic anxiety about a 'lowering of tone'. Thus the demonisation of the lodging house, familiar from Victorian commentary, seeps back into mid-century popular and media discourse, producing a discursive anxiety relating to urbanisation, the breakdown of the nuclear family and the presence of so-called strangers in the national landscape. As Frank Mort shows in his study of the Rillington Place murders in the 1950s, words like 'unsettled' or 'disturbed', in the context of descriptions of particular urban environments, were often

---

[99] James Procter, *Dwelling Places: Postwar Black British Writing* (Manchester: Manchester University Press, 2003), p. 22.

[100] For the way in which fears of 'black sexuality' permeate descriptions of housing and places of accommodation in the 1950s and 1960s, see Procter, *Dwelling Places*, pp. 24–26.

[101] Sheila Patterson, *Dark Strangers: A Sociological Study of the Absorption of a Recent West Indian Migrant Group in Brixton, South London* (London: Tavistock, 1963), p. 173.

used obliquely in this period to imply racial otherness.[102] The Rillington Place case in question concerned John Christie, a tenant of a sublet flat in a run-down, three-storey lodging house in the poor and racially mixed area of North Kensington, who murdered and encased his female victims within the walls of the home. Mort argues throughout that the gruesome rooming house murders drew together many of the prevailing social anxieties of the time concerning urban change, sexuality and 'an accelerating debate about the cultural impact of Caribbean migration on the indigenous character of one problem zone in the inner city'.[103]

Emblematised by the Clapham air shelter with which this section began, there was something particularly makeshift and improvisational about the housing conditions that faced postwar black communities. As Ruth Glass noted in *Newcomers* (1960), the traditional areas associated with an influx of migrant groups, such as London's East End or its areas south of the river, which had historically provided the first port of call for French Huguenots, Irish immigrants and Jewish populations, were not amenable to Caribbean immigrants (largely due to slum clearance schemes as well as the particular housing type and tenureship in those areas).[104] West Indians thus found themselves occupying what amounted to de facto segregated zones of the most dilapidated housing on the rental market in parts of West London (Paddington, North Kensington and Notting Hill) and South West London (Brixton), areas where large and inexpensive houses could easily be subdivided and let out to multiple renters and households. But the fact that transitory housing spaces were key locations for immigrants led to common expressions of concern; Patterson, for example, quotes one interviewee who complained that 'Now Brixton and Kennington are one vast lodging-house'.[105] Evidently the lodging house had become a metonym for social decline, one that bore strong racial and racist implications.

In fact, many immigrants were settling in the crumbling remains of a decaying British infrastructure, literally taking up residence in the holes and debris left by the war (many rooming houses were located in terraces with gaps in the middle where houses had fallen down). As the historian

---

[102] Frank Mort, 'Scandalous Events: Metropolitan Culture and Moral Change in Post-Second World War London', *Representations* 93:1 (2006), 109. Webster also notes the characteristic depiction of black males in this period as 'rootless and adrift'; *Imagining Home*, p. 49.

[103] Mort, 'Scandalous Events', p. 108. It is striking that in a case which is presented as being about racial anxiety, the murderer and his victims were white Londoners. The sense that a migrant community could provide a 'backdrop' (and implicitly a type of motive) for what was effectively a 'white-on-white' crime is itself a crucial part of the racial discourse that Mort seeks to critique.

[104] Glass, *Newcomers*, p. 47.   [105] Patterson, *Dark Strangers*, p. 50.

Ron Ramdin notes, these were the 'so-called "streets of transition" where a large number of West Indians found rooms. Not surprisingly bombed out sites formed part of the surroundings'.[106] The fact that these groups inherited this urban dilapidation is important, particularly in view of an emergent social discourse that equated urban degradation and poor standards of living with the arrivals of the immigrants themselves. Demonstrating that housing space in the postwar period was a highly politicised and charged issue, Procter and Mort allude to the way in which already rundown housing and newly arrived immigrants became conflated in this period. Indeed, repeating tropes of the discourse concerning impoverished people and poor housing that I analysed in Chapter 1, the anthropomorphic language of housing, so prevalent in Victorian observation of slums, was put to work again. Glass, for example, noted that 'West Indians find rooms in streets where the tall houses, covered with grime and peeling plaster, display their decay. . . . The faces of the buildings tell whether they are the ones in which the migrants are concentrated'.[107] This figuration of 'faces' (a term used for buildings since the sixteenth century) as an architectural signifier for the new arrivals is noted by Procter: 'Privileging the domestic façade as the site at which to diagnose and make sense of the new immigrant communities, Glass' account is indicative of a much larger body of writing to appear in the 1950s and early 1960s to evoke a black presence *through* the dwelling place'.[108] But the condition of the house interior could be used to counteract this narrative of 'reading' lives from the exteriors of houses. One report into the housing conditions of immigrant families living in Slough in 1964 unequivocally stated:

> The interiors of virtually all the many dwellings visited during the study were visibly clean and neat. . . . Our observations disclosed that it is quite possible for a building exterior to be drab and untidy, for entrance halls to be dingy, but for the individual living rooms to be acceptably clean throughout. The cleanliness of actual living space was, in fact, the rule rather than the norm.[109]

The report went on to commend this population for their domestic resourcefulness and 'considerable ingenuity' in dealing with a very British housing problem.[110]

[106] Ron Ramdin, *The Making of the Black Working Class in Britain* (Aldershot: Gower, 1987), p. 193.
[107] Glass, *Newcomers*, pp. 48, 50.   [108] Procter, *Dwelling Places*, pp. 21–22.
[109] Slough Council for Social Services, *Colour and Community* (1964), in Panayi, *The Impact of Immigration*, p. 71.
[110] Slough Council, *Colour and Community*, p. 71.

Georgian and Victorian 'tall houses', rented out by the room (of which 10 Rillington Place was an example), afforded an economically viable means of cramming multiple people and families under one roof. But this change of use added to the general perception of a social downturn (Glass notes how 'each of the rooms, once scrubbed by servants, is now often occupied by a separate group of people – by a family; the remnants of a family; by one lodger, or by several who pay their rent jointly').[111] Thus as in Moore's Belfast-based *The Lonely Passion of Judith Hearne*, the subdivision and reinvention of space for commercial purposes signalled to some observers the demise of the middle-class family serviced by domestic help and the rise of a more transient population (specifically the unattached single lodger). It was not only the houses but also the rooms themselves that could be subject to multiple occupancy, as represented in Sam Selvon's *The Lonely Londoners* (1956) in descriptions of the multifunctional single room 'where you have to do everything – sleep, eat, dress, wash, cook, live'.[112]

The subdivided lodging house arrangement often worked against forms of community and well-being, a point repeatedly made in writing of the period. Thus Patterson articulates a sense of atomisation and transience in her description of the worst parts of the London 'ghettos':

> Certain streets become the dormitories of the restless, the unsuccessful, the unattached, the antisocial, and the newcomers who have nowhere better to go, together with the white misfits who have drifted into the coloured orbit. These are the streets of the nameless, of the undelivered letters, of the lodgers who do not know the names of those on the floor below, of the migrants who change their rooms as they change their jobs, for the difference of half-a-crown a week, for a brusque word, or because of some inner restlessness.[113]

Here the disconnection of the rooming house is presented as the logical outcome of the economy and society in which immigrant groups operated. This sentiment is captured in Selvon's text in which a group of West Indian men struggle to forge forms of self-identity and solidarity with others in an environment which fosters isolation, self-dependency and the need to 'hustle' to get by. Thus the central character, the Trinidadian Moses Aloetta, observes the way in which the migrants live peripatetically, staying in rooming houses at the volatile whim and discretion of the

---

[111] Glass, *Newcomers*, p. 49.
[112] Sam Selvon, *The Lonely Londoners* (Harlow: Longman, 1985), p. 137.
[113] Patterson, *Dark Strangers*, p. 214.

landlady or landlord and are forced to keep moving in order to live close to the place of work. Selvon's Moses sums up this paradoxical condition of mobile stagnation (as opposed to social mobility) by remarking 'how after all these years I ain't get no place at all, I still the same way, neither forward nor backward'.[114] In this sense, the subdivision of the rooming houses represents a far wider process of atomisation and retreat. Commenting on the working-class area on the Harrow Road, its houses 'old and grey and weatherbeaten, the walls cracking like the last day of Pompeii', Moses comments:

> It have people living in London who don't know what happening in the room next to them, far more the street, or how other people living. London is a place like that. It divide up in little worlds, and you stay in the world you belong to and you don't know anything about what happening in the other ones except what you read in the papers.[115]

Throughout the novel, Selvon's characters are mostly depicted away from the cheap lodging houses they have to call home, walking around the London streets and sights, gaining at least a geographical sense of being 'central' as they stake a claim on tourist hotspots like Piccadilly Circus.

A sense of deracination and a lack of fixed boundaries between public and private space are borne out by the literature depicting men and women feeling 'home-sick' in their own rooms.[116] George Lamming's novel *The Emigrants* (1954), for example, reverses Selvon's outdoor focus and features few descriptions of urban London despite its 'inner city' setting. As one critic comments, 'with no outdoor scenes and few place names – indeed, with every scene in its 150 pages of London narrative taking place in a room (typically a basement one) – the effect of its rather ponderous, fragmentary, and disorienting narrative is of people barred entry to the very city they have crossed the Atlantic to inhabit'.[117] The novel's London section, 'Rooms and Residents', thus begins with the men's descent into the dark, bare basement barbershop that will become a regular meeting place for the West Indian (and African) men: 'it was dingy and damp, a hole which had lost its way in the earth; and they put their hands out along the wall and over the floor like crabs clawing for security'.[118] Surveying the interior of the basement, the Trinidadian ex-RAF pilot Tornado is struck

---

[114] Selvon, *Lonely Londoners*, p. 129.   [115] Selvon, *Lonely Londoners*, p. 74.
[116] Ramdin, *Black Working Class*, p. 193.
[117] John Clement Ball, 'Immigration and Postwar London Literature', in Lawrence Manley (ed.), *The Cambridge Companion to the Literature of London* (Cambridge: Cambridge University Press, 2011), p. 226.
[118] George Lamming, *The Emigrants* (University of Michigan Press, 1994), p. 129.

by the room's only small window: 'a long narrow window, railed perpen-
dicularly with bars of iron which made somber shadows against the thick
green glass'.[119] The window offers no view onto the outside city; providing
not perspective but enclosure, its bars and sea-green glass evoke the ship on
which the men and women arrived. In another basement dwelling, a lower
floor space shared among different groups, including in one room a
Jamaican man and his girlfriend, and in another three men who work
together at the same factory, brings people together in a paradoxical form
of atomised self-consciousness:

> They had worked, returned home, and now in the early night which had
> suddenly grown thick outside they were together in a small room which
> offered no protection from the threat of boredom. . . . In another climate, at
> another time, they would ramble the streets yarning and singing, or sit at
> the street corners throwing dice as they talked aimlessly about everything
> and nothing. Life was leisurely. But this room was different. Its immediacy
> forced them to see that each was caught in it. There was no escape from it
> until the morning came with its uncertain offer of another day's work.
> Alone, circumscribed by the night and the neutral staring walls, each felt
> himself pushed to the limits of his thinking. All life became an immediate
> situation from which action was the only escape. And their action was
> limited to the labour of a casual hand in a London factory. It was here in the
> room of garlic, onions and mist that each became aware, gradually, anx-
> iously, of the level and scope of his private existence. Each tried to think, for
> that too was a kind of action.[120]

This representation of male characters oppressively confined within rooms
also serves as a reminder that the traditional image of the interior as a
feminine space of entrapment is racially contingent. Here, it is the men,
identified by their blackness as 'strangers', who do not feel they have access
to the public space of the city in their paradoxical status as the racial
'other' – at once invisible and overvisible. Black feminist thought notably
argues precisely that the conflation of privacy and family, as well as the
setting apart of a public sphere of work against a 'private' sphere of
domesticity, is radically disrupted in the context of historical communities
of colour for whom privacy may well mean a space free from racist
oppression.[121] As Tornado, who lived in England previously, forewarns
his fellow passengers on board the ship heading to England, no matter

---

[119] Lamming, *Emigrants*, p. 136.   [120] Lamming, *Emigrants*, p. 192.
[121] See, for example, Patricia Hill Collins, 'The Sexual Politics of Black Womanhood', in *Black
Feminist Thought: Knowledge, Consciousness, and the Politics of Empowerment*, 2nd edn. (New
York: Routledge, 2000), pp. 123–48.

what ideas and dreams they may hold about the Mother Country: 'You ain't home, chum'.[122]

Nevertheless, within the literature under consideration, there is also a sense that the interior spaces of the rooming house – as basic as they were – present an important site in which individuals might exert a degree of control and a freedom from the antagonism and racism of the city. For, as Procter crucially notes, dwelling space in the literature is often depicted as a medium in which characters demonstrate the 'ability to manipulate and manage spatial environs to their advantage'.[123] Indeed, partly because housing was the primary source of exclusion and discomfort in Britain, it could also be, as Michael McMillan argues, the site of forged solidarity among immigrants.[124] Thus, in the novels, the rudimentary interiors can appear as unexpected sites of community. In *The Lonely Londoners*, for example, Moses' room becomes a meeting place for the migrants who gather for regular 'get-togethers'. A sense of space, belonging and solidarity among the men is created not through objects or display – the traditional markers of the 'homely' domestic interior – but through conversation and sociability: 'liming in Moses room, coming together for a oldtalk, to find out the latest gen, what happening, when is the next fete'.[125] Likewise, in Lamming's *The Emigrants*, the makeshift women's hairdressing salon in the rented basement room of a house offers little domestic comfort: it is 'low and narrow, with its faded rugs carefully placed over the floor. . . . the view was abruptly blocked by houses which came up like a wall between two foreign territories'.[126] But it is again also a sociable place where the women can sit and talk together: 'The world passed by on the outside, intent or callous, but ignorant of the intimacy and the warmth of this house, in this corner, where those women were seated around a table'.[127] Like Selvon, Lamming stresses how a sense of collectivity is established primarily through language, where the phatic and social elements of talk provide individuals with defence and succour against the isolating effects of poverty and racism.

While such depictions of rooming houses present the possibility of sociality and community, other novels, such as Andrew Salkey's *Escape to an Autumn Pavement* (1960) and V. S. Naipaul's *The Mimic Men* (1967), show them to be bases for the exploration of self-identity. Both novels

---

[122] Lamming, *Emigrants*, p. 67.   [123] Procter, *Dwelling Places*, p. 39.
[124] Michael McMillan, 'The "West Indian" Front Room: Reflections on a Diasporic Phenomenon', *Small Axe* 28 (2009), 140.
[125] Selvon, *Lonely Londoners*, p. 138.   [126] Lamming, *Emigrants*, p. 155.
[127] Lamming, *Emigrants*, p. 148.

diverge from the works of Selvon and Lamming by focusing not on a group of West Indian immigrants but on the figure of a male individual: Salkey's Johnnie Sobert, a Jamaican, and Naipaul's Ranjit Kripalsingh (also known as Ralph Singh), a Caribbean 'colonial' exiled in London. In Salkey's novel, the boarding house is, in a now familiar scenario, teeming with sexual opportunity and tinged with danger, as Sobert has to choose between his attraction towards a white female lodger (and rent collector for the house) and his below-stairs neighbour, a white man. Significantly, the rooming house in this novel is explicitly the site for the exploration of the social taboos of interracial relationships and homosexuality. Likewise, self-contemplation and sexual opportunity feature in Naipaul's novel, in which a Kensington boarding house provides the material and symbolic basis for an exiled colonial's exploration of the difficulty of establishing his own sense of a place in the world. Interestingly, in this case, it is precisely the sense of inauthenticity and lack of apparent rootedness engendered by the boarding house that allows Ralph Singh to find some sort of solace. His 'tall, multi-mirrored, book-shaped room', and the motley assembly of fellow lodgers who view him somewhat vaguely as being of a higher class, provide an ideal base for this writer who reviles the 'suburban semi-detached house' favoured by those other middle-class colonial subjects who have tried to make a life for themselves in England.[128] Paradoxically perhaps, he seems to find kinship in the limited performativity of his fellow boarders, as they appear 'two-dimensional, offering simple versions of themselves'.[129] For Singh, who self-professedly finds it easier to act out parts allotted to him by other people and who struggles to reach any sense of his own 'originality', the role of drifter and outcast, and what he labels the 'boarding-house character', is a part he can play with ease.[130] As Naipaul self-reflexively suggests in the epigraph at the start of this section, the relations between the male protagonist, the interior and its place in the wider urban environment ('this man, this room, this city') lend themselves to the production of story, language and form.

What is thus striking about these examples of early black British writing is the presentation of a cohesive aesthetic sensibility set in the boarding houses and bedsits of a drab postwar London that bore the visible scars of war. The stylisation of the prose in these works conveys the sense of personal identity and creativity being forged among the residents of these lodgings, for whom improvisation and new occupancy are a necessary way of life.

---

[128] V.S. Naipaul, *The Mimic Men* (New York: Vintage International, 2001), pp. 7, 13.
[129] Naipaul, *Mimic Men*, pp. 17–18.   [130] Naipaul, *Mimic Men*, p. 31.

A distinct homosocial world of immigrant fraternity emerges, forged in melancholy and straitened circumstances, and yet of vital importance to male characters who are alienated from their new home city and cast as embodiments of the national 'stranger'. Thus while it is true that self-fulfilment is shown to be difficult, uncomfortable and fraught for the central characters, it is nonetheless the presiding theme of these highly self-reflexive and often experimental works. In this sense, these novels present the development of what Mark Stein terms the voicing of an identity; 'the black British novel of transformation does not predomin-antly feature the privatist *formation* of an individual: instead, the text constitutes a symbolic act of carving out space, of creating a public sphere'.[131] From this perspective, the indeterminate endings of the novels are indicative, for the future seems to be open and choice is a daunting but valid option. And yet the deeply gendered nature of this narrative form of self-possession is also significant. In these makeshift, temporary homes – set apart from traditional forms of family and kinship – the focus is on male bonds and male speech; female characters are for the most part relegated to the background, or serve as the object – desired or derogated – of masculine 'talk'.

v   'The whole Empire in little'?: Forms of accommodation in Andrea Levy's *Small Island*

Revealingly, one of the most dominant female presences in these early works by West Indian authors, as well as in the sociological surveys by Patterson and Glass, is that of the white landlady: the keeper of various houses who can give or deny shelter to newly arrived men and women. As in Wole Soyinka's poem 'Telephone Conversation' (1960), she is the fearsome adjudicator, quick to exercise power when it becomes apparent that her potential lodger is black ('Considerate she was, varying the emphasis–/ "ARE YOU DARK? OR VERY LIGHT?"').[132] Interestingly, the landlady figures as the central and defining character in Andrea Levy's contemporary novel *Small Island* (2005), which reimagines postwar London life. Arguing that 'isolation is the hallmark of male migrant narratives of 1950s London', Sarah Brophy contends that in *Small Island*,

---

[131] Mark Stein, *Black British Literature: Novels of Transformation* (Columbus: Ohio University Press, 2004), p. 30.
[132] Wole Soyinka, 'Telephone Conversation', in Gerald Moore and Ulli Beier (eds.), *The Penguin Book of Modern African Poetry*, 3rd edn. (Harmondsworth: Penguin, 1984), p. 187.

by contrast, Levy 'brings into view what her predecessors saw in rare glimpses, but ultimately judged next to impossible in postwar Britain: possibilities for intimacy, community, and a multiracial future'.[133] Written more than fifty years after the Selvon generation, Levy's historical novel opportunely returns to the arrival of the *Windrush*; the lodging house of a white landlady in Earls Court becomes the thematic and structural setting for a story which is more deeply concerned with the wider cultural implications of sharing space, accommodation and hospitality.

Queenie Bligh's lodging house is the new face of her marital home which she has converted in the absence of her husband Bernard, missing in action in the Second World War. Against the wishes of her neighbours, she rents out rooms to West Indian men and women, including a Jamaican lodger, Gilbert Joseph, who has recently returned from service in the British Royal Air Force. He is soon joined by his prim schoolteacher wife from Jamaica, Hortense, who has been looking forward to living the life of a respectable lady in the long-dreamed-of mother country. The boarding and lodging house, as this chapter shows, has often tended to be presented as a rather base, spatial 'other' to dominant national or metropolitan narratives of home; a place containing unruly, multiple households; or a rather sad assortment of singletons. In *Small Island*, however, Levy engages precisely with the representation of the maligned rooming house in British culture by questioning the very ideology underpinning domestic display as a form of national narrative.

This is manifest from the novel's effective opening prologue in which Queenie reminiscences about a childhood daytrip to the British Empire Exhibition at Wembley. This event, which opened on 23 April 1924 and ran for two summer seasons, promoted trade throughout the British Empire by 'displaying' the fifty-eight countries of the Commonwealth. 'I thought I'd been to Africa. Told all my class I had', Queenie states, in lines which initiate the motif of the national 'imagined community' as well as invoking implicitly the disappointment that attends this ideal.[134] The British Empire Exhibition, like countless other international exhibitions before it – most notably the 1851 Great Exhibition – aimed to render abstract ideas about Empire into tangible and visible forms of display. The exhibitions thus enacted and depended upon the scopic regime of Western imperialism, with its anthropological assumption that 'seeing things' and

---

[133] Sarah Brophy, 'Entangled Genealogies: White Femininity on the Threshold of Change in Andrea Levy's *Small Island*', *Contemporary Women's Writing* 4:2 (2010), 100.
[134] Andrea Levy, *Small Island* (London: Review, 2004), p. 1.

knowledge are coterminous. Housed under the three roofs of the Palaces of Industry, Engineering and Arts, the 1924 exhibition rendered the British Empire by way of an interiorised form: a type of national parlour staging a specific version of the past, which, like the most effective of those bourgeois interiors, was designed to tell a public story about its 'owner-occupiers'. Remembering the visit, Queenie comments:

> The King had described it as 'the whole Empire in little'. Mother thought that meant it was a miniature, like a toy railway or model village. Until someone told her that they'd seen the real lifesize Stephenson's Rocket on display. 'It must be as big as the whole world,' I said, which made everybody laugh.[135]

From the monarchical claim to objectify Empire, to the mother's incisive understanding that to miniaturise something is to change its nature into a 'play' version, to the young Queenie's hesitating grasp of the relations between symbols and wider realities, the novel sets up from the start a concern with ideologies of models and public display.

For Didier Maleuvre, museums and the concept of the bourgeois domestic interior share a common ideological function; both serve to express a sense of belonging and ownership through a visual semiotics of display, particularly through the idea of the spectacle of a collection of objects. He notes:

> Collecting is a way of taking possession of the world, a way of domesticating the exotic by keeping a tribal mask on the mantelpiece, of securing the distant past through an antique statue, and of enshrining personal memory by means of a souvenir. All this has the effect of making the home the center of a wide temporal and geographic circle at the core of which the world is encapsulated in miniature form. The home thus becomes the domestic keeper of all things far and near, the center of gravity of ownership at the basis of the bourgeois world.[136]

But no such domestic interior exists in the lodging house in *Small Island*. Levy moves swiftly in the novel from the inaugural and emblematic British Empire Exhibition to the run-down, converted lodging house which is evidently not intended for public show (indeed, Queenie takes great efforts to hide her domestic enterprise from disapproving neighbours). The lodging house's distinct aberrance is all the more significant in the context of an increasing drive towards the postwar planned and designed 'model home' for family living. Queenie's hastily converted or rehabilitated

[135] Levy, *Small Island*, p. 2.   [136] Maleuvre, *Museum Memories*, p. 115.

lodging house, which is open for business, is therefore very much at odds with a national narrative about the ideal home (itself the subject of an exhibition since 1908).

The Earls Court lodging house is even a disappointment to its Jamaican tenants who are deeply familiar, through the processes of colonial education, with cultural images of the British homestead. On her arrival from the ship, for example, Hortense observes the shabby, but grand, London house and assumes it is the sole residence of her husband Gilbert. The deceptive semiotics of architectural form are once again manifest as she reassures herself that 'this house could once have been home to a doctor or a lawyer or perhaps a friend of a friend of the King. Only the house of someone high-class would have pillars at the doorway'.[137] Her subsequent realisation that Gilbert only rents one of a number of multipurpose rooms is a disenchantment on many levels, exacerbated by her illusions about standards of living in the 'mother country'. In a line which neatly undercuts contemporary media perceptions of West Indian domestic habits and expectations, she goes on to exclaim of the dark and dingy room: 'Is this the way the English live?'[138] Yet Gilbert jumps to the defence of the postwar British lodging house, its windows pathetically patched up with cardboard and tape, by telling her: 'There been a war here. Everyone live like this'.[139] In this context, run-down housing is posited as a great social leveller.

Small Island also implicitly questions the relations between knowledge (in the form of display) and national identity that the prologue introduces. Like Waters, Levy turns her eye to the scarred, bombed-out setting of war-torn Britain that serves as the landscape of home for its 'natives' and 'newcomers'. And as in *The Night Watch*, Levy portrays the brutal, graphic reality of the exposure of home interiors that the war brought about, an effect which presented a very different kind of domestic truth to the smoothly executed artifice of the exhibition spectacle:

> A house had had its front sliced off as sure as if it had been opened on a hinge. A doll's house with all the rooms on show. The little staircase zigzagging in the cramped hall. The bedroom with a bed sliding, the sheet dangling, flapping a white flag. A wardrobe open with the clothes tripping out from the inside to flutter away. Empty armchairs sitting cosy by the fire. The kettle on in the kitchen with two wellington boots by the stove.[140]

---

[137] Levy, *Small Island*, p. 12.   [138] Levy, *Small Island*, p. 22.   [139] Levy, *Small Island*, p. 21.
[140] Levy, *Small Island*, p. 304.

The likening of a bombed residence to a doll's house is striking, once again disrupting conventional ideas about domestic interiors as ordered displays for public view. The metaphor bears particular significance in view of the fact that the Queen Mary's doll's house (built for Queen Mary in recognition of her role in World War I by the British architect Sir Edwin Lutyens) had been one of the centrepieces of the 1924 Wembley exhibition.

While Levy's presentation of the lodging house serves in part to parody and demystify a particular version of the house as an exemplary display, or microcosm of the nation, as the novel progresses it increasingly comes to embody a more progressive version of home. But the wider symbolic significance of Queenie's entrepreneurial home is not necessarily immediately obvious. Levy never sentimentalises the lodging house in the novel; it is not an obvious symbol for anything. For like other such rooming houses surveyed throughout this chapter, the Earls Court house is distinctly run-down and unaesthetic. Its very *raison d'être* is not altruistic but commercial. And Queenie herself evades some of the clichés of landlady; she is neither the nurturing mother nor the ruthless entrepreneur, although in a nice intertextual nod back to Joyce's calculating landlady, Mrs Mooney, she is also a 'butcher's daughter'. Yet Levy's choice of the words 'paying guests' to describe the house's inhabitants is particularly telling in its displacement of the ubiquitous, and implicitly racist, reference to the 'stranger' that dominates the writing and visual depictions of immigrants to Britain in the 1950s and 1960s. 'Guest' implies that these individuals deserve hospitality from the host nation, but significant emphasis rests on the word 'paying', since this serves as a reminder of the economic reasons for mass immigration to Britain, engendered by a shortage of labour in Britain and widespread unemployment in the Caribbean.[141] At a more general level, the idea of the 'paying guest' raises the issue of a British national debt owed to colonial subjects – such as *Small Island*'s Gilbert Joseph – who performed active duties in the war (many of whom 'paid' with no less than their lives).

The idea of renting, or 'paying', for dwelling space takes on an egalitarian and dignified significance when contrasted with the novel's depiction of complacent notions surrounding property and historical entitlement. This is represented by Queenie's husband Bernard, who, when he eventually re-emerges from the war, clings to an older sense of property and ownership. In one scene, Bernard surreptitiously enters the rented room of

141   The words 'host', 'guest', 'stranger', 'foreigner' – and, indeed, 'hostility' – are, in fact, nicely linked etymologically (from the Latin *hospit-em* (*hospes*)).

Gilbert, the lodger: 'Felt like a thief. Silly, I know. A man can't burgle his own home. But the turn of the key in the lock. Unfamiliar objects in the room. Odd smell. Somehow made it all feel clandestine'.[142] His path is blocked by Gilbert's large trunk (a visual metonym of migrancy) as he tries to navigate what used to be his mother's room and, before that, the room in which his father was born.[143] When Gilbert returns, the two men come to blows about who has right of passage to this room at the top. In their physical and discursive struggle, Bernard asserts himself as not only the rightful owner of the house but also proclaims he had 'fought a war to protect home and hearth. Not about to be invaded by stealth'.[144] Gilbert replies by insisting on his tenancy rights: 'Said he paid rent therefore he deserved – yes, deserved – privacy'.[145] According to tenancy laws, of course, the landlord might own the property, but it did not grant him free access into a lodger's rented room.

Throughout the novel, it is Levy's emphasis on the social relations of individuals in the boarding house interior space, rather than the objects or things on display, which mark it as a site of global and historical networks. The house is made up of complex simultaneous flows (a rendition of British history as global history over and against the 'small islander' version): the relocated remnants of a former world, the entrance of new populations and, in a decidedly unsentimental vein, the ejection of those who refuse to be accommodated to the new domestic arrangement.

Moreover, Levy's lodging house can no longer be seen as the unstable and transitory 'other' to some solid domestic ideal, since the novel – like 'Miss Anstruther's Letters' and *The Night Watch* – effectively exposes the myth of the solidity and endurance of houses. After all, Queenie had been urged to marry the dour Bernard by an aunt who had assured her: 'You're lucky there, Queenie. That man is a brick – you'll be safe as houses with him'.[146] The popular notion of things being 'safe as houses' is, in this line as elsewhere, shown to be fundamentally flawed. Drawing attention to the fragility of solid structures, Levy's novel puts faith in the political virtues of change, rehabilitation and flexibility. But unlike the problematic openness associated with Joyce's boarding house, with its suggestion of licentiousness and promiscuity, the more accommodating house of *Small Island*

---

[142] Levy, *Small Island*, p. 467.
[143] See Procter's discussion of the visual significance of 'travel bags' in photography from this period in *Dwelling Places*, pp. 202–09.
[144] Levy, *Small Island*, p. 470.   [145] Levy, *Small Island*, p. 470.   [146] Levy, *Small Island*, p. 255.

offers the possibility of surrogate and makeshift forms of domesticity that can be changed and modified over time.

In her tale of shared lodgings, Levy constantly allows a subtle and complex version of class and national belonging to emerge. For although the novel creates the expectation that this is to be a story in which an East End landlady achieves a form of social mobility through her entrepreneurial efforts, the lodging house in this text is always the site of wider, intersecting social shifts. Indeed, at least from one perspective, the novel crucially promotes the idea that the emancipation of one individual (such as Queenie Bligh) engenders the possibility of common gain for others. This motif is articulated through the central trope of maternity in the novel and the associated ideas of hospitality, guardianship and belonging. Like Hortense, Gilbert had also been rebutted on arrival by the Mother Country, the 'beloved relation whom you have never met':

> The filthy tramp that eventually greets you is she. Ragged, old and dusty as the long dead. Mother has a blackened eye, bad breath and one lone tooth that waves in her head when she speaks. Can this be that fabled relation you heard so much of? This twisted-crooked weary woman. This stinking cantankerous hag. She offers you no comfort after your journey. No smile. No welcome. Yet she looks down at you through lordly eyes and says, 'Who the bloody hell are you?'[147]

In her surrogate role, it is Queenie who steps in to offer Gilbert accommodation under her roof. This is not, however, a sentimental relationship; it is borne of practicality and financial necessity. Headed by Queenie, the house nevertheless serves as a pragmatic receiving place that at a wider level regathers survivors which the war, as Queenie puts it, had 'scattered like dandelion seeds'.[148] Indeed, the idea of the lodging house as a more equitable form of hospitality has wider implications for the novel's engagement with postcolonial tropes of the 'host' (nation) and 'guest' (immigrant).[149]

In fact, Queenie's role as an atypical matriarch had been foreseen by her father in the novel's prologue, in a scene in which he takes her to the top of the Exhibition's scenic railway to gaze down at the people below and tells her: 'See here, Queenie. Look around. You've got the whole world at

---

[147] Levy, *Small Island*, p. 139.   [148] Levy, *Small Island*, p. 113.

[149] Addressing the metaphor of the nation as a 'house', deployed for various purposes within immigration discourse, Mireille Rosello suggests that it may be more accurate 'to imagine the state as a hotel, rather than a private house'; *Postcolonial Hospitality: The Immigrant as Guest* (Stanford: Stanford University Press, 2001), p. 34. In this context, see also Sarah Gibson, 'Accommodating Strangers: British Hospitality and the Asylum Hotel Debate', *Journal for Cultural Research* 7:4 (2003), 367–86.

your feet, lass'.[150] While the episode sweetly parodies the textual cliché of (usually male) articulations of ambition from on high, more importantly perhaps, it also inaugurates the motif of the Queen-as-landlady. So while her lodgers will certainly never be 'at her feet', Queenie's self-enterprising lodging house enables her to be at the head of a very different-looking British home.

Identified as an unsentimentally maternal space, the lodging house finally oversees the birth of a child, the result of a fleeting love affair between Queenie and one of her passing lodgers, a black airman. The baby is born with 'golden skin' and eventually given up by Queenie to Hortense and Gilbert; they in turn plan to leave Queenie's house with their adopted child to become the proprietors of their own fixed-up lodging house in Finsbury Park. But their lodging house will be a determined improvement on Queenie's enterprise: 'Other room we board to people from home. Not Englishwoman rent. Honest rent you can collect up'.[151] The transience of the halfway lodging house thus becomes an optimistic space; Gilbert Joseph and his wife will operate their own lodging business according to the West Indian 'pardner' system while themselves raising their former landlady's child. The novel thus ends with an iteration of the principle of surrogacy (from the Latin *surrogātus*, meaning 'assimilated'), seeing optimism and integrity in this substitute form which displaces the authority of fixed origins. The pitfalls or dangers of home in *Small Island* are seen to occur when home is assumed to be inherited from the past as a solid structure available for owner-occupation under lock and key; the traditions that endure, by contrast, are shown to be those that adapt through change to accommodate new social formations.

The shift in tone from the anxious, restless and experimental style of the Selvon generation which often focussed on single male protagonists to Levy's more expansive narrative approach is noticeable, and the novel in some ways returns to the lightness and comedy that we see in Dickens' drama of rented rooms. In *Small Island*, then, the lodging house again serves as a setting for carnivalesque plots involving romance, coincidence and social *faux pas*. But the characters here are never mere one-note boarding-house caricatures, evolving instead in nuanced and delicate ways as their lives and histories enmesh with each other. There is no wry, distanced authorial stance which laughs at and condemns the residents to a communal hell, as found in Moore and Hamilton's novels. Instead, Levy's presentation of her protagonists' development and change results not simply in their own greater self-understanding, but in the reconfiguration of social bonds between individuals through forms of hospitality as well as an emerging sense of the global

---

[150] Levy, *Small Island*, p. 7.   [151] Levy, *Small Island*, p. 499.

and historical networks that bind the disparate lodgers. The fate of strangers thrown together in particular historical circumstances – the novel here as a type of lodging house – serves to reiterate the notion that these people are connected through a common history.

Conclusion

In 1930, the artists Eric Ravilious and Edward Bawden completed a series of murals in the refectory of Morley College for Working Men and Women, an adult education centre in Lambeth, South London. One of these images included the depiction of a Kensington boarding house presented, as one newspaper noted, as 'a modernist view of a Kensington mansion – seen like a doll's house'.[152] Indeed, lodging, as depicted in this institutional fresco, summons a simultaneously banal and fanciful scene, seamlessly merging realism and the imagination in its depiction of acquaintances from Ravilious' life alongside mythical figures; on the ground floor kitchen a landlady tends to her aspidistra, while at the very top of the house a writer is visited by a flying muse.

There exist very few utopian imaginings of boarding houses, and this one did not last very long; the college was bombed by the Luftwaffe in 1940 and the refectory murals were destroyed. But while the texts I have surveyed in this chapter present a less bucolic picture of boarding-house life, like 'Ravilious and Bawden's interior mural', they offer a sense of the narrative and spatial possibilities of rented rooms and lodging which plot social stories of class, gender and sexuality in a changing cultural landscape. For as I have shown, these places of residence serve as a setting which is governed, complicated, bounded and, at times, enhanced by the effects of communal living and shared domestic space. In these locations, there is a type of realignment of the spatial hierarchy of the parlour, bedroom and kitchen of the normative family household. For what are often deemed merely functional and peripheral domestic spaces, such as corridors, staircases and landings, here form crucial nodes of social interaction and narrative climax, acting as a connective system in which the residents meet, greet, scheme and come into conflict.

An analysis of the narrative space of lodging housing and its meanings forces a closer consideration of the significance and value (in the monetary and symbolic senses) of shared and private life. For in social commentary

---

[152] 'The "Modern Art" Boarding House: Kensington "Frescoed"', *The Sketch*, 12 February 1930, p. 280. Thanks to Elaine Andrews, Learning Resources Centre Manager at Morley College, for providing this source.

THE GRAPHIC, March 15, 1930

"LIFE IN A BOARDING HOUSE"

A Detail of the Remarkable New Frescoes by Young Modernist Artists at Morley College

Figure 4 — 'Life in a Boarding House', *The Graphic*, 15 March 1930.
Photo courtesy of Morley College Gallery.

as well as in fiction, the boarding house presents a domestic interior which is marked by sociality, but that is clearly not necessarily one of idyllic cohabitation. Interior space, the boarding house reminds us, is a crude material asset to be purchased and conserved in whatever way possible. While traditional conceptions of personhood have tended to fetishise private space and seclusion, the private rented bedroom in lodging literature is often depicted as a space not of autonomy and self-knowledge but of loneliness and estrangement. These boarding-house bedroom interiors (frequently in a down-at-heel form) can be hopelessly unreflective of the individuals they temporarily harbour, revealing the pathos of people 'cherishing very large hopes in very small lodgings'.[153] Indeed, as the Camden Town Group's early twentieth-century sequence of interiors encapsulates visually, solitary rooms in lodging houses are often incongruous settings for the glimpsed private lives of their occupants.[154]

Far from being a curiously outmoded form of accommodation on the social and historical margins, the readings in this chapter show that in material and symbolic terms, the inner worlds of lodging houses of all kinds reveal a great deal about the changing identity of self, family and nation in modern British culture. Indeed, the contemporary form of the lodging house has transmogrified once again into a place that epitomises the idea of lives in flux: specifically, the type of bed-and-breakfast emergency accommodation that is sometimes used to house refugees and asylum seekers in Britain. The tragi-comedy of boarding-house life that is represented in the literature of the twentieth- and twenty-first century therefore tells multiple and competing stories about cultural encounters and social mingling, always serving as a reminder of the way that notions of collectivity and privacy in housing forms are subjective and historically contingent. In this housing setting, home may have very little to do with roots and a sense of belonging, revealing instead the precariousness of emergency accommodation or the thrill of the hallway encounter sustained all too briefly by a dim light set on a timer. For some, the transience of the home setting is a matter of grievous regret; for others, this form of 'inauthentic' domesticity offers all kinds of possibilities. We tend to look for history, particularly domestic histories, in permanent structures, but the boarding house and rented room, and their attendant narratives and plots, reclaim the temporary and fleeting space of accommodation as culturally significant and resonant.

---

[153] George Eliot, *The Mill on the Floss* (London: Penguin, 1985), p. 506.
[154] This group of neorealist painters attempted to convey the modern sensibility of working-class and lower-middle-class urban spaces, with the lodging house interior as a recurring location; see, for example, Harold Gilman's *Tea in the Bedsitter* (1916) and *Mrs Mounter at the Breakfast Table* (1917).

CHAPTER 3

Unhomely homes
Life writing of the postwar 'scholarship' generation

Accounts of working-class life are told by tension and ambiguity, out
on the borderlands. . . . this is a drama of *class*.
                            –Carolyn Steedman, *Landscape for a Good Woman*
                                   (London: Virago, 1986), p. 22

Introduction: The Butler Act and its uncanny legacies

Turning from the world of boarding houses, rented rooms and bedsits that
offer sites of improvised or surrogate kinship networks, this chapter now
addresses representations of what might appear to be the more traditional
domestic setting of the family and childhood home. Focusing on postwar
autobiographical accounts of working-class childhood, however, this chapter engages with evocations of domestic interiors and representations of self
which are distinctly unsettled; these are works which eschew autobiographical realism for something altogether more strange. It addresses writing by
authors who formed part of the Robbins or 'scholarship' generation and
who consciously reflect upon the expansion of access to education
following the 1944 Butler Education Act. This act, which overhauled the
restricted provision of education in Britain by the introduction of universal
secondary schooling, produced radical changes in the social landscape of
the mid-twentieth century, enabling children from working-class homes to
enter the grammar school system and propelling some of them into higher
education. Among other factors, it had a marked impact on gender and the
family; girls who passed the Eleven Plus exam had the option of entering
academic schools rather than being pushed towards more vocational
options (or leaving school altogether), thereby presenting them with
opportunities that were inconceivable for their mothers. It is unsurprising,
therefore, that the narrative of the scholarship story is often framed as a
form of home leaving – a move away from a particular environment
and the entrance to a new realm of opportunity. Although this is the

accepted version, my rereading will frame it instead as a domestic narrative, albeit one of a very specific kind.

The figure of the 'scholarship' boy/girl is, as one author points out, 'that most archetypal of post-war characters'.[1] As a cultural 'type', it is found in forms of social realism and the 'kitchen sink' aesthetic – often more lyrical and experimental than its name suggests – which have constituted the dominant mode for the iconic angry young people of this era.[2] My reinterpretation of this body of life writing points to a common tendency among the writers to eschew gritty realism in favour of distinctly unrealist modes which invoke the literary apparatus of the uncanny, particularly the modern Gothic and fairy tale.[3] My account therefore seeks to redress the tendency in criticism to view mid-century working-class experience within the aesthetic parameters of social realism (a representational form whose implicit ideology serves to 'reflect' life 'as it is'). Indeed, this body of life writing could be said to display what is a conspicuous absence of reference to materialist detail or consumer and popular culture in the decades of the 1950s and 1960s. Instead, the texts steer away from realist devices, centring instead on the dynamics of class and the enduringly influential idea of the uncanny, epitomised in ideas of the strangely familiar and the unhomely home.

By focusing on representations of the recalled or reimagined homestead in the memoirs of writers from Richard Hoggart to Hilary Mantel, I show how an anti-realist aesthetic transforms working-class domestic spaces, such as the urban terraced house, into mysterious sites of unexplained phenomena, presenting scenes (real or imagined) of conflict, secrecy and even violence. The parallels and echoes among the memoirs under consideration are uncanny in and of themselves: echoes of the Victorian *Bildungsroman* and its stock narrative devices, family secrets, a history of 'bad blood', childhood sickness, the writer's self-seclusion into the world of books, doubtful parentage, questions of illegitimacy and a first-person voice which speaks uneasily of the relations between ambition, guilt and betrayal. In some of the works I address – Seamus Deane's

---

[1] Terry Eagleton, *The Gatekeeper: A Memoir* (Allen Lane: 2002), p. 52.

[2] Well-known examples of this 'archetype' feature in John Osborne's *Look Back in Anger* (1959) as well as the films of the British New Wave, such as *Saturday Night and Sunday Morning* (1960), *A Taste of Honey* (1961) and *This Sporting Life* (1965).

[3] The idea of working-class literary British Gothic remains relatively unexplored; see, however, Sarah Gamble, 'North-East Gothic: Surveying Gender in Pat Barker's Fiction', *Gothic Studies* 9:2 (2007), 71–82; Brian McCuskey, 'Not at Home: Servants, Scholars, and the Uncanny', *PMLA* 121:2 (2006), 421–36.

Reading in the Dark and Mantel's *Giving Up the Ghost* for example – domestic interiors seem to be haunted by 'real' ghosts.[4] In others, the idea of a haunting takes a more figurative dimension and serves to articulate a sense of profound division and doubleness which disrupts the individualist narrative of self-progress. As the epigraph to this chapter from Steedman suggests, the 'drama of *class*', as a story 'told by tension and ambiguity, out on the borderlands' is one that lends itself to the tropes, settings and figures that populate the realm of the uncanny.

Hauntings and ghosts imply the idea of 'seeing things' – an ambiguous phrase which implies close examination or interpretation and extrasensory perception. I explore this double meaning to address the idea of the scholarship child's sense of separation from the family and their awareness of a critical faculty, or interpretative stance, that at least in part creates this divide. To the readerly child of these memoirs, everyday landscapes may be translated into something portentous, symbolic and fused with subjectivity.

A sense of doubling and doubleness – a defining characteristic of the uncanny – recurs throughout the texts, as the writers attempt to represent their family and class origins by means of a narrative that pulls in the opposite direction towards the plot of individuation. Often self-reflexively casting themselves as the young protagonist of the nineteenth-century *Bildungsroman*, or as the orphaned figures of the classic fairy tale, the writers portray the domestic interior as a doubled space, one that is central to identity formation as well as being the site from which they must escape.[5] Of course, the rendering of a chiaroscuro escape from 'dark' poverty to educational 'enlightenment' is itself a well-established motif in nineteenth-century working-class autobiography (and endures in the type of autobiographical model used by George Acorn and Kathleen Woodward, as shown in Chapter 1 of this book). Ronald Goldman, reflecting on his experience of what Rose terms 'the climb up the scholarship ladder', uses precisely this trope: 'Being at home was like a slow death to me and leaving home felt like moving into a free world of light

---

[4] Seamus Deane's *Reading in the Dark* (London: Vintage, 1997), it should be noted at this point, is not a memoir per se (although, as I argue later, at a meta-textual level the work significantly engages with the politics of the autobiographical form in ways which make it an important addition to this chapter).

[5] For the influence of fairy tale and romance in the nineteenth-century *Bildungsroman*, see Fredric Jameson, *The Political Unconscious: Narrative as a Socially Symbolic Act* (London: Routledge, 1996), pp. 89–136, and Franco Moretti, *The Way of the World: The Bildungsroman in European Culture*, new ed. (London: Verso, 2000).

and rationality'.[6] In contrast to this ideological framework of enlightenment, however, I stress how these recent autobiographical explorations of working-class childhoods shift significantly away from a model that entails movement from darkness to light. For while the family home – and all that it represents – is at turns resisted or rejected, it continues to 'haunt' these ambivalent autobiographical narrators in significant ways.

Despite appearances to the contrary, the uncanny modes of Gothic and fairy tale are deeply engaged with material matters as well as issues of social class and its boundaries. Yet haunting, doubles, divisions, blood, bodies and border crossings are elements generally aligned with the architectural spaces of the 'big house' and landed gentry in British (and Irish) literature. Indeed, there is a type of currency or cultural capital to the Gothic, from the ghost story to the horror film, based on the assumption that it is usually the mansions of the rich and the townhouses of the middle class which are sites of intriguing disturbances involving hidden sources of wealth, long-standing family feuds and the threat to established order and respectability. Haunted houses, then, are frequently characterised by an architectural semiotics whose familiarity belies its bourgeois roots; in literature and film, hauntings tend to occur in detached, multi-storied homes, with plenty of rooms and recesses – attics and cellars, stairwells and inner chambers – in which malevolent spirits may lurk.

But the idea of the Gothic and the uncanny as a narrowly bourgeois preserve is an assumption that ignores the extent to which these literary forms themselves draw upon a rich legacy of oral culture and folktale. And this is particularly salient in the context of the Irish cultural underpinnings in the texts of three of the authors – Deane, Terry Eagleton and Mantel – that further dismantle the pedigree of the middle-class British Gothic.[7] My analysis therefore engages with the way in which the texts under consideration self-reflexively reclaim the uncanny as part of a working-class landscape. In this respect, I borrow and adapt from Anthony Vidler's influential study of the idea and aesthetic of the uncanny in forms of architecture in which he describes this modern malediction as 'the quintessential bourgeois kind of fear', an articulation of a 'fundamental insecurity: that of a newly established class, not quite at

---

[6] See Rose, *Intellectual Life*, p. 145.

[7] Deane and Eagleton engage with the topic of Irish Gothic in their academic writing: see Deane, *Strange Country: Modernity and Nationhood, Irish Writing Since 1790* (Oxford: Clarendon Press, 1997), and Eagleton, *Heathcliff and the Great Hunger: Studies in Irish Culture* (London: Verso, 1995).

home in its own home'.[8] When applied to the landscape of postwar British working-class narratives, Vidler's theorisation of the uncanny as symptomatic of profound changes in class structure is revealing. Indeed it will be central to my analysis of stories of ghosts, family secrets and transgressive acts set within an architectural landscape of terraced back-to-backs and postwar council houses, locations in which the textual figure of the scholarship child is indeed never quite 'at home in its own home'.

i   The scholarship boy: Doublings in Richard Hoggart's *The Uses of Literacy*

Beginning with Richard Hoggart's *The Uses of Literacy* is, perhaps, surprising since Hoggart's pioneering analysis of changes in working-class and popular culture in the first half of the twentieth century typifies aspects of the social realist tradition of mid-twentieth-century writing. Hoggart's pioneering ethnography – intermeshed with autobiographical recollection – looked back to the culture of working-class life in the rented back-to-back terraces and 'tunnel-backs' in Hunslet, Leeds, in the 1920s and 1930s (before the postwar slum clearances and consequent population shift to the new estates). Viewed historically, *The Uses of Literacy* is often taken as a key text in cultural studies, not least on the basis of its form and methodology, which put into practice the idea that personal experience could illuminate and transform sociological enquiry. But this methodology has also invited criticism, specifically in relation to earlier sections of the work which have been read as skewed by the author's sentimental and nostalgic view of a working-class urban culture on the wane. But the expectation that he should have been more objective or scientific in his study ignores Hoggart's own concern with the issue of subjectivity and cultural analysis within the pages of this preternaturally self-reflexive book. Thus in a retrospective comment, Hoggart declared in a significant phrase that one of his intentions was to 'lay one's ghosts', and he was explicit about the book's tendentious aim of telling the middle-class reader: 'see, in spite of all, such a childhood is richer than yours'.[9] Indeed, far from defending himself against accusations that he was overinvested in the text, Hoggart would retrospectively place a perhaps surprising emphasis on the book's autobiographical and literary qualities. He agreed with one

---

[8] Vidler, *Architectural Uncanny*, pp. 3–4.
[9] Richard Hoggart, *The Uses of Literacy: Aspects of Working-Class Life with Special Reference to Publications and Entertainments* (London: Penguin, 1991), p. 18.

commentator who described it as not a conventional academic study but instead a 'rather lyrical re-creation ... the kind of book you can only write at a certain point in your life, given the level of personal involvement'.[10]

This 'personal involvement' is manifest at the level of form, specifically in what Hoggart himself refers to as the book's 'broken-backed' structure: one that presents a type of before-and-after vision of a working-class community undergoing radical change, together with an account of the irrevocable 'progression' of the author himself.[11] It is a structure that articulates what Hoggart identifies as his own 'double relationship' of class belonging and the deep separation and loss that marks the working-class scholarship child's trajectory.[12] Two voices thus resonate throughout the pages of *The Uses of Literacy*: that of the young watchful boy of the early sections, and that of the retrospective and melancholy adult scholar. It is a form of duality, as Hoggart noted himself, which is intrinsic to the portrayal of working-class culture, language and people by someone who is 'both close to them and apart from them'.[13]

The trope of doubleness – and its implication of self-division – extends to Hoggart's recurrent emphasis on images and codes of home life in this domestic-centred text. His picture of the working-class domestic interior conforms superficially to images of the respectable Edwardian working-class home. Indeed, Hoggart aligns the dominant aesthetic of the working-class home with 'prosperous nineteenth-century middle-class style; the richness showing well and undisguisedly in an abundance of odds-and-ends, in squiggles and carvings, in gold patterns'.[14] Such homes, Hoggart acknowledges, were places that had apparently changed very little since Edwardian times; their abiding function being to present the cherished domestic virtue of 'homeliness'. Thus he presents the working-class home of Hunslet in the earlier part of the century as an intensely private world, rigorously defined by its gendered separation of spheres in which the father is master of the house and an agent in the public world of work, while the mother functions as 'the pivot of the home'.[15] Indeed, the home is defined as lying at the centre of each individual's place in the community, marked by a 'peculiarly gripping wholeness' ('wholeness' and 'centre' are terms which recur symptomatically throughout those earlier sections of the text that centre on an older working-class community).[16] In this account,

[10] See John Corner, 'An Interview with Richard Hoggart: Studying Culture: Reflections and Assessments', in Hoggart, *Literacy*, p. 387.
[11] Hoggart, quoted in Corner, *Literacy*, p. 383.   [12] Hoggart, *Literacy*, p. 17.
[13] Hoggart, *Literacy*, p. 17.   [14] Hoggart, *Literacy*, p. 149.   [15] Hoggart, *Literacy*, p. 41.
[16] Hoggart, *Literacy*, p. 68.

then, the home is a private, tangible and safe place, 'a cluttered and congested setting, a burrow deeply away from the outside world'.[17] The home furthermore exists in a neighbourhood characterised by closeness and proximity (a 'knowable community' to use Raymond Williams' term).[18] 'This is an extremely local life, in which everything is remarkably near', Hoggart notes, and people go about their daily lives 'with sights fixed at short distance'.[19] Hoggart thus presents the imagined interior of the working-class home as, above all, authentic. It operates in stark contrast to the cheap and soulless modern interior that he deems to epitomise mid-century consumer capitalism and mass media:

> Compare it with the kind of public room which may be found in many a café or small hotel today – the walls in several hostile shades of distemper, clashing strips of colour along their centres; cold and ugly plastic door-handles; fussy and meaningless wall lamp-holders; metal tables which invite no one and have their over-vivid colours kicked and scratched away: all tawdry and gimcrack. The materials need not produce this effect; but when they are used by people who have rejected what sense of a whole they had and have no feeling for the new materials, the collapse is evident.[20]

Hoggart's apparent sentimentality and nostalgia for the stability of an integral and knowable home has been the subject of some critique. Doreen Massey, for example, has questioned what she interprets as a heavily gendered depiction of home in the work of 'the Angry Young Men' in which the mother is 'not as herself a living person engaged in the toils and troubles and pleasures of life, not actively engaged in her own and others' history, but a stable symbolic centre – functioning as an anchor for others'.[21] In addition, Carolyn's Steedman's *Landscape for a Good Woman* (1986), which I address in detail below, professes to be nothing less than a response to Hoggart's depictions of working-class community, specifically the portrayal within this tradition of cultural criticism of 'a kind of psychological simplicity in the lives lived out in Hoggart's endless streets of little houses'.[22] Indeed, Steedman's device in her own autobiographical work is to present her mother as an example of a desiring, angry woman, one 'who finds no place in the iconography of working-class motherhood that Jeremy Seabrook presents in *Working Class Childhood*, and who is not to be found in Richard Hoggart's landscape'.[23]

---

[17] Hoggart, *Literacy*, p. 36.
[18] Williams defines the 'knowable community' as a 'selected society in a selected point of view' which is usually identified retrospectively as existing in the past; *Country and the City*, p. 179.
[19] Hoggart, *Literacy*, pp. 60, 92.   [20] Hoggart, *Literacy*, p. 40.   [21] Massey, *Space*, p. 180.
[22] Steedman, *Landscape*, p. 7.   [23] Steedman, *Landscape*, p. 6.

But several recent collections have sought to redress the charge of nostalgia levelled so frequently at Hoggart, and a close reading of *The Uses of Literacy*, one which takes into account its aesthetic and literary features, reveals a far more ambivalent picture.[24] What is striking is precisely the way in which Hoggart's apparently idealised portrayal of a particular kind of working-class domestic life lies cheek by jowl with the unsettling and incongruous fragments of a more submerged autobiographical account of childhood loss and poverty. This strange doubleness disrupts the text's chronological account of cultural change and presents the 'scholarship boy' story as ambivalent and discordant. Thus while Hoggart praises the pleasures of working-class domesticity, he simultaneously notes 'the prevalent grime, the closeness and the difficulties of home life'.[25] Juxta- posed with portrayals of the generalised respectable terraced house cleaned by 'Mother' are Hoggart's memories of his early childhood home, situated in a court in the Chapeltown area of Leeds, in which 'the tiny house was damp and swarming with cockroaches; the earth-closet was a stinking mire in bad weather'.[26] Moreover, a closer analysis of the text reveals the figure of the mother, 'the pivot of the home', to be a type of cultural myth drawn from the author's very loosely defined experience and his characteristic collection of cultural aphorisms and sayings. In fact, by way of the autobiographical, embedded voice, it is revealed that Hoggart's mother was widowed when her three children were still under the age of six; that she struggled to work because of ill health and that the family got by on charitable donations (although she 'thanked no one for their pity or their admiration'); and that she died five years later, leaving the orphaned children to be cared for among the extended family.[27]

Surprisingly, then, at least in light of the criticism of his supposedly hagiographic presentation of the working-class mother, Hoggart noted that his mother's own experience of life 'was too much an unrelieved struggle to be at all enjoyable'.[28] Indeed, Hoggart's brief and terse representations of his own mother in the text, to whom raising three hungry, demanding children afforded little pleasure, prefigure precisely the angry maternal

---

[24] See Sue Owen (ed.), *Richard Hoggart and Cultural Studies* (Basingstoke: Palgrave Macmillan, 2008) and Michael Bailey, Ben Clarke and John K. Walton, *Understanding Richard Hoggart: A Pedagogy of Hope* (New Jersey: Wiley-Blackwell, 2011).

[25] Hoggart, *Literacy*, p. 88.   [26] Hoggart, *Literacy*, p. 48.   [27] Hoggart, *Literacy*, pp. 47–48.

[28] Hoggart, *Literacy*, p. 48. In conversation with Ronald Goldman, Hoggart recalls his mother in the briefest of terms: 'But my mother I remember fairly well. Most of the time she was tired and ill'; Ronald Goldman (ed.), *Breakthrough: Autobiographical Accounts of the Education of Some Socially Disadvantaged Children* (Oxon: Routledge, 2012), p. 91.

figure who haunts Steedman's sociological memoir. Thus Hoggart recalls a scene from childhood which at once captures the taboo of maternal ambivalence and anticipates what he calls the 'real rage' of the working-class mother that can be found in a number of autobiographical texts throughout the twentieth century:

> On one occasion my mother, fresh from drawing her money, bought herself a small treat, something which must have been a reminder of earlier pleasures – a slice or two of boiled ham or a few shrimps. We watched her like sparrows and besieged her all through tea-time until she shocked us by bursting out in real rage. There was no compensation; she did not want to give us this, and there could be no easy generosity in the giving. We got some, though we sensed that we had stumbled into something bigger than we understood.[29]

This disturbing disruption of expectation is further mirrored by the disjuncture between Hoggart's proclamations of the centrality of the working-class father, and his text's defining silence and absence in relation to his own.

A tone of unease thus pervades Hoggart's portraits of generic and specific mothers and fathers, revealing itself in the peculiarly stilted syntax and formal diction. Likewise, Hoggart's characteristic use of quotation marks in *The Uses of Literacy* purports to represent his evidence of a distinctly oral and anecdotal working-class culture, but it also appears as a distancing technique that signals the writer's estrangement from these cultural types and experiences. Such features convey a sense of discomfort with the dual factors of debt and betrayal that weave throughout Hoggart's strange sociology. For example, in passages which detail the scholarship boy's sense of un/belonging within the domestic sphere, Hoggart notes how he is 'marked out early', quickly finding that the privacy and solitude needed for his studies require him 'to be more and more alone, if he is going to "get on"'.[30] Using the distancing third-person voice, Hoggart writes of this 'type':

> He will have, probably unconsciously, to oppose the ethos of the hearth, the intense gregariousness of the working-class family group. Since everything centres upon the living-room, there is unlikely to be a room of his own; the bedrooms are cold and inhospitable, and to warm them or the front room, if there is one, would not only be expensive, but would require an imaginative leap – out of the tradition – which most families are not capable of making.[31]

---

[29] Hoggart, *Literacy*, p. 48.   [30] Hoggart, *Literacy*, p. 294.   [31] Hoggart, *Literacy*, p. 294.

The need for private and quiet space was one of the principal problems experienced by the memoirists whose writings feature in David Vincent's study of nineteenth-century working men's autobiography. One such autobiographer, John Harris, whose memoir was published in 1882, expressed a longing for 'some obscure corner' of his own in which to write verses: 'But this was denied me, and I often sat in my bed-room, with my feet wrapped in my mother's cloak, with a pair of small bellows for my writing desk.'[32] The desire for privacy is thus portrayed as a pragmatic requirement, but one which also entails wider, more symbolic, implications.

In contrast to earlier autobiographical accounts in which literacy leads to enlightenment, intellectual freedom and autonomy (as articulated, for example, in the writing of George Acorn and Kathleen Woodward), Hoggart's narrative is marked by a crucial ambivalence. Significantly, then, his own 'imaginative leap' into a world of higher education is portrayed as a narrative of gain – he is 'very much of *both* the worlds of home and school' – as well as loss.[33] In the crucial chapter 'Unbent Springs: A Note on the Uprooted and the Anxious', Hoggart uses a defining image of division to encapsulate the predicament of the scholarship boy, separated from his class by an apparently 'stronger critical intelligence or imagination', and his educational conversion to full literacy and higher education.[34] Such dislocation is experienced as not only a psychological change but as a visceral experience: 'a physical uprooting from their class through the medium of the scholarship system'.[35] The price to pay for the scholarship boy's entry into this other world, he writes, is an 'unusual self-consciousness before [his] own situation' and a lack of physical self-ease in space, finding himself 'chafing against his environment'.[36] Thus the scholarship boy's sought-for solitude comes at a symbolic cost; the room of one's own results in a form of inhibiting interiority – 'the pressure of all this living inside oneself'.[37] Self-conscious and self-doubting, the scholarship boy in Hoggart's text is likened to 'a version of the dissident Byronic hero', one who has 'lost the hold on one kind of life, and failed to reach the one to which they aspire'.[38] Using that strangely impersonal third-person voice, set off by those formal yet anonymous quotation marks, a stylistic mode Hoggart employs for the most 'autobiographical' of his chapters, he describes the

---

[32] Vincent, *Bread, Knowledge*, p. 121.   [33] Hoggart, *Literacy*, p. 294.
[34] Hoggart, *Literacy*, p. 292.   [35] Hoggart, *Literacy*, p. 292.   [36] Hoggart, *Literacy*, p. 292.
[37] Hoggart, *Literacy*, p. 315.   [38] Hoggart, *Literacy*, pp. 315, 310.

condition of the scholarship boy as almost phantasmal. He is caught, in a phrase taken from Matthew Arnold, 'between two worlds, one dead, the other powerless to be born':[39]

> He cannot go back; with one part of himself he does not want to go back to a homeliness which was often narrow: with another part he longs for the membership he has lost, 'he pines for some Nameless Eden where he never was'. The nostalgia is the stronger and the more ambiguous because he is really 'in quest of his absconded self yet scared to find it'. He both wants to go back and yet thinks he has gone beyond his class, feels himself weighted with knowledge of his own and their situation, which hereafter forbids him the simpler pleasures of his father and mother.[40]

Importantly, the type of semi-hypothetical, semi-autobiographical, melancholy scholar who is surveyed in this section of *The Uses of Literacy* inhabits rooms that match their sense of unease, marking in their décor 'a division of experience'.[41] Such rooms

> have usually lost the cluttered homeliness of their origins; they are not going to be chintzy. The result is often an eye-on-the-teacher style of furnishing, like their favourite styles in literature; rooms whose pattern is decided by the needs of the tenants to be culturally *persona grata*, not to fall into any working-class 'stuffiness' or middle-class 'cosiness'; intensely self-conscious rooms whose outward effects are more important than their liveableness.[42]

Hoggart deems these places to be 'intensely self-conscious' – an aesthetic of the interior that is apparently hampered by its preoccupation with 'outward effects'.[43] It is a style that structures the form of *The Uses of Literacy* itself; this is a text in which the subject, with his ambivalent status as insider and outsider, is located in an uncanny threshold position which makes past and present unhomely.

ii Against revelation: Seamus Deane's *Reading in the Dark* and Terry Eagleton's *The Gatekeeper*

The Uses of Literacy can be read as a drama of conversion – or to use a telling spatial and linguistic metaphor – of translation and a 'carrying across'. It presents a parallel between the shift from working-class oral

---

[39] Hoggart, *Literacy*, p. 300. The fragment of the quotation is from Matthew Arnold's poem 'Stanzas from the Grande Chartreuse' (1850).
[40] Hoggart, *Literacy*, p. 301. [41] Hoggart, *Literacy*, p. 311. [42] Hoggart, *Literacy*, p. 311.
[43] Hoggart, *Literacy*, p. 311.

culture to populist print forms and the biographical narrative of the
scholarship boy's movement from a close-knit 'known community' into
higher education. In this regard, the use of literacy embodies a form of
loyalty (in its capacity to represent working-class culture) and betrayal (in
its placing of the narrator as an 'outside' ethnographer of his environment).
This conception of literacy as the medium of loyalty and betrayal takes on
Gothic undertones in Deane's enigmatic and unsolvable *Reading in the
Dark* – a hybrid autobiographical novel rather than an orthodox memoir
per se which combines features of the domestic ghost story, the
Bildungsroman and the Northern Irish Troubles thriller.

If the idea of the border is a recurrent and significant metaphor in the
narrative of the scholarship boy, it significantly takes on a physical and
political aspect in Deane's Derry-based work in the form of the political
sectarianism that divides the space of the city.[44] Unlike Hoggart's presentation of Hunslet, the working-class community in this text is defined
from the start not by wholeness but by borders. Accordingly, there is
nothing hermetic or safe about the home in *Reading in the Dark*, a point
which reflects the fact that in twentieth-century Northern Irish history,
home and domestic space are irrevocably steeped in history, politics and
violence. Indeed, housing has been a fraught site of political antagonism
throughout Derry's fractious twentieth-century history, particularly during
the onset of the Troubles in the late 1960s. The enduring political murals
on the sides of terraces and council houses in various parts of the city give
stark visual form to the very political nature of private life in what was, at
least from an Irish Republican perspective, an occupied territory. Indeed, it
was the issue of housing that became the catalyst for the onset of the Civil
Rights Movement in the 'Squatting at Caledon' protest in 1968.[45] Thus as
Deane demonstrates in *Reading in the Dark*, home can offer no sanctuary
in a militarised state which works precisely to infiltrate the boundaries of
the private.[46] The text presents several instances of the politicisation of the

---

[44] After the partition of Ireland in 1921, Northern Ireland formed part of the United Kingdom; it
comprised a Catholic minority population governed by a Protestant Unionist government.

[45] Dungannon Rural District Council had allocated all but one of the houses on a new-build estate,
Kinnard Park, in Caledon, County Tyrone, to Protestants. Two Catholic families had occupied
houses on the estate, and after a short period, the Catholic family that had squatted at a three-
bedroomed house at 11 Kinnard Park was evicted in favour of a single Protestant woman who was
employed by a local Unionist politician. The Northern Ireland Civil Rights Association was involved
in the case, and two weeks after the eviction, the decision was taken to hold a civil rights march from
Coalisland to Dungannon; this march – and the sectarian violence that surrounded it – is taken by
many commentators to mark the start of the Northern Irish Troubles.

[46] As Scott Brewster notes, 'the house is both an overdetermined site, and a curiously overlooked
space, in Irish culture', with writers aware of the way in which 'the topophilia of home can easily

space of the home, not least in a series of brutal invasions by the police acting on supposed tip offs. The failure of the domestic interior as a safe location is particularly acute for the book's young nameless narrator, whose family is doubly marked: they are Catholics with family links to the IRA, but they are also tainted within their own community by rumours that a family member had colluded with the British Army in the past.

While *Reading in the Dark* has more often been interpreted within the specific context of the Northern Irish conflict, I address it here in relation to the nineteenth-century novel of education and the 'scholarship boy' narrative, with their presiding motifs of literacy, social mobility and the consequent anxiety of identity. For it is arguable that the overt political story of this text occludes what I take to be an equally significant social and historical narrative: the depiction of the scholarship boy's education and his subsequent 'betrayal' of the family. As my reading will demonstrate, the boy in this tale develops into a type of domestic spy (and later an 'informer' in a precise sense of the term) – as he becomes aware of, and able to read, the complex hidden signs he glimpses on his journey away from a working-class community into that of higher education and (disappointing) enlightenment.

Set within the housing landscape of the Derry Bogside, consisting of rows of close-standing, sloping terraced streets, the family home in Deane's work is a site of secrecy, conflict and incipient meaning – one in which the repressed and unspoken tensions of the past seem to make themselves manifest through the signs of a domestic haunting. The book's opening immediately signals the haunted house genre with the announcement of a ghost and its simultaneous presence-in-absence: 'On the stairs, there was a clear, plain silence.'[47] The narrative thus commences with a moment of suspension and like the ghost on the liminal space of the landing – suspended between the living and the dead – the protagonist is midway up the stairs, about to cross to the window looking out to the Gothic St Eugene's cathedral, when he is halted by his mother's portentous warning to *stay in place*: 'Don't move. . . . Don't cross that window.'[48]

---

become territorialisation, a matter of exclusion, silence and vulnerability'; 'Building, Dwelling, Moving: Seamus Heaney, Tom Paulin and the Reverse Aesthetic', in Smyth and Croft (eds.), *Our House*, p. 143. Moreover, as Clair Wills acknowledges, dominant conceptions of 'public' and 'private' spheres are uneasily mapped onto Irish society and its specific colonial history; *Improprieties: Politics and Sexuality in Northern Irish Poetry* (Oxford: Clarendon Press, 1993), pp. 65–66.

[47] Deane, *Reading*, p. 5.   [48] Deane, *Reading*, p. 5.

The notion of haunting as symptomatic of some kind of unfinished historical business is a staple of the Gothic genre, as is the convention that the return of repressed history is often actively sought out by the protagonist of the novel. But focalised through the scrutinising eyes of the first-person diarist, in *Reading in the Dark* it is arguably the boy's subjective point of view which transforms quotidian life inside the Derry terrace into a signifying Gothic terrain. Scenes of domestic life and poverty are constantly translated by the first-person version of events, and the familiar visual idiom of the working-class home becomes a space of Gothic excess which is seemingly charged with incipient meaning.[49] Thus the young protagonist enjoys the idea of a ghost-in-residence and its transformative potential; seen through his eyes, the prosaic kitchen range has a 'red heart fire', a broken boiler 'expired in a plume of smoke and angry hissings', and 'lids of the saucepans trembled on the range and the bubbling water gargled'.[50] The overall effect is that the dreary domestic poverty faced by the family is rendered not through realist detail but through a signifying web of symbolic and dramatic significance: 'We were haunted! We had a ghost, even in the middle of the afternoon. . . . The house was all cobweb tremors.'[51]

The tension between realist principles and Gothic writing, which underpins the plot and narrative telling of the work, is best illustrated in the title chapter 'Reading in the Dark'. Like the typical protagonist of the *Bildungsroman* – from Jane Eyre to Maggie Tulliver and indeed the autodidacts of working-class autobiography – this section features the young boy engaged in a pivotal act: reading privately to himself (albeit, due to lack of space, with his bedfellow brother's knees pressed into his body). In an earlier urban Gothic novel, *Oliver Twist*, Oliver peruses *The Newgate Calendar* late at night in Fagin's den; in *Reading in the Dark,* the young boy is engrossed in *The Shan Van Vocht* ('The Poor Old Woman'), a dramatic telling of the 1798 nationalist rebellion: 'In the opening pages, people were talking in whispers about the dangers of the rebellion as they sat around a great open-hearth fire on a wild night of winter rain and squall'.[52] The book offers all the elements that fascinate and thrill the child and that he constantly seeks to find in his own family history: intrigue, danger, rebellion and conspiracy.

The boy's dramatic imaginings in this chapter are, however, abruptly interrupted by his recollection of a recent lesson learned at school:

[49] On the Gothic as a 'writing of excess', see Fred Botting, *Gothic* (London: Routledge, 1996), pp. 1–6. [50] Deane, *Reading*, pp. 6, 9, 128.   [51] Deane, *Reading*, p. 6.   [52] Deane, *Reading*, p. 19.

The English teacher read out a model essay which had been, to our surprise, written by a country boy. It was an account of his mother setting the table for the evening meal and then waiting with him until his father came in from the fields. She put out a blue-and-white jug full of milk and a covered dish of potatoes in their jackets and a red-rimmed butter dish with a slab of butter, the shape of a swan dipping its head imprinted on its surface. That was the meal. Everything was so simple, especially the way they waited. She sat with her hands in her lap and talked to him about someone up the road who had had an airmail letter from America. She told him that his father would be tired, but, tired as he was, he wouldn't be without a smile before he washed himself and he wouldn't be so without his manners to forget to say grace before they ate and that he, the boy, should watch the way the father would smile when the books were produced for homework, for learning was a wonder to him, especially the Latin. Then there would be no talking, just the ticking of the clock and the kettle humming and the china dogs on the mantelpiece looking, as ever, across at one another.

'Now that,' said the master, 'that's writing. That's just telling the truth.'[53]

The boy's own submitted account, in contrast to this essay, caused him to feel embarrassed

because my own essay had been full of long or strange words I had found in the dictionary – 'cerulean', 'azure', 'phantasm' and 'implacable' – all of them describing skies and seas I had seen only with the Ann of the novel. I'd never thought such stuff was worth writing about. It was ordinary life – no rebellions or love affairs or dangerous flights across the hills at night. And yet I kept remembering that mother and son waiting in the Dutch interior of that essay, with the jug of milk and the butter on the table, while behind and above them were those wispy, shawly figures from the rebellion, sibilant above the great fire and below the aching, high wind.[54]

Reversing the common literary and filmic convention whereby reality gives way to fantasy and imagination, the child protagonist's imagining of dramatic plots, as he reads in the dark of the bedroom, is abruptly brought down to earth by realist representational modes. The reference to the Dutch interior style is telling, for these seventeenth-century representations of intimate domesticity often capture a sensibility of stillness, order and privacy. In fact, the genre famously inaugurated the visual representation of private life situated in domestic space that was flooded by what appeared to be forms of natural light, and in which the openness and

[53] Deane, *Reading*, pp. 20–21. The 'country boy' in question, who dwells on the minutiae of the homestead, is thought to be based on Seamus Heaney, a classmate at St Columb's College grammar school in Derry.
[54] Deane, *Reading*, p. 21.

transparency figured by windows and doors were counterpoised with allusions to the individual's possession of secrecy and private property (in the form of a letter, a glance, a key in the door). The 'Dutch interior' of the 'model essay' represents a scene that appears to be inimical to Deane's young narrator, who seems excluded and baffled by its simple, passive details: the mother and son who are content to wait, a father for whom learning is 'a wonder', domestic space that is filled with the meaningless sounds of the kettle and clock. The rebel spirit of the Gothic, which is finally conjoined to the Dutch interior in the final lines of the passage quoted above, can be read as the scholarship boy's yearning for a disruptive and ambitious plot that will propel him forwards and upwards. Yet this image of a fusion between Gothic and domestic realism ultimately encapsulates what ends up being *Reading in the Dark*'s principal aesthetic achievement. For what seem to the child incompatible modes – domestic realism and melodrama – are significantly brought together through the plot and form of this urban haunted house tale.

Ironically, perhaps, it is through this self-reflexive attention to the politics of literary form, rather than any autobiographical disclosure, that Deane reveals himself most clearly. For throughout his critical writing, Deane has demonstrated a preoccupation with the way in which social conflict and the possibility of transformation are transacted precisely by way of aesthetic and literary form. Thus, as noted earlier, the narrator recollects that when discussing the other boy's essay, the teacher had instructed the class that its form of realism is 'real' writing – a way of 'just telling the truth'. But the text seems to suggest that the realism of the Dutch interior cannot represent the reality of domestic space in his 'strange country': a sectarian, surveyed community in which politics can scarcely be kept at the door (the police barracks lie a mere 300 yards from the family home). Using the metaphor of the uncanny itself, Deane wrote in an early essay that 'to live in a ghetto, is to live in a *strange homely and lethal climate*' (emphasis added).[55] In such a state, the homestead offers little sanctuary and is subject to the repeated intrusive violence of the police, as in the raid in the opening sections of *Reading in the Dark*, in which the house is described as being 'splintered open': 'The linoleum was being ripped off, the floorboards crowbarred up, the wardrobe was lying face down in the middle of the floor and the slashed wallpaper was hanging down in ribbons.'[56] This demolition of domestic space produces an almost phantasmal impression: 'Objects seemed to be floating, free of gravity,

---

[55] Seamus Deane, 'Why Bogside?', *The Honest Ulsterman* 27 (1971), 8.   [56] Deane, *Reading*, p. 28.

all over the room.'[57] The effect of this violation of the private realm is to make the aesthetic of domestic realism impossible as well as to complicate the means by which truth might be told.

Of course, 'telling the truth' is a difficult concept in this monitored community in which social intercourse is often strategically coded, and where history is subject to, or represented as, a series of misrepresentations, including gossip, rumour, secrets and lies. Indeed, throughout the work, the young boy constantly encounters the limits of dominant enlightenment modes structured by the principle of realism: history-telling, chronology, diaries, translation, interrogation and autobiography. This is not surprising, for as Deane has argued in *Strange Country*, which is concerned with Irish manifestations of Gothic (including forms of Irish Catholic Gothic as a lesser-known counterpart to the Anglo-Irish genre), a colonial legacy leaves behind a terrain in which literary realism, with its complacent discourse of veracity, cannot easily take root.[58] This is nowhere more strikingly expressed than in the fact that despite its apparent status as a detective story, Deane's text reaches no conclusions, to say nothing of convictions, a point that has frustrated some readers.[59]

Deane's Gothic scholarship boy tale is crucially about 'informers' who betray not simply a political project but perhaps also their own class or family. For one of the effects of the partitioning of Ireland was the extension of the Butler Education Act to Northern Irish citizens, including, of course, its dissident Catholic population. Thus as Liam Harte has argued, Deane's young protagonist is 'situated at a crucial conjunction of social and historical change, as the oral folk culture of his native community is about to be finally and irrevocably overlaid by the dominant state-sponsored culture of literacy'.[60] Indeed, for Harte, the young boy functions as an embodiment of the generation which would profit from the 1944 Butler Education Act; his 'educational progress is itself emblematic of the Catholic minority's rise to political articulacy'.[61]

---

[57] Deane, *Reading*, p. 28.
[58] In his discussion of a genre he labels 'Catholic or Catholic-nationalist Gothic' (which anticipates, of course, his own choice of form in *Reading in the Dark*), Deane points to the influence of James Clarence Mangan's unreliable and fantastical memoir 'Fragment of an Unfinished Autobiography' (1882); *Strange Country*, p. 126.
[59] See, for example, Gerry Smyth, *Space and the Irish Cultural Imagination* (Basingstoke: Palgrave Macmillan, 2001), p. 134; Terry Eagleton, 'The Bogside Bard', *New Statesman*, 30 August 1996, p. 46.
[60] Liam Harte, 'History Lessons: Postcolonialism and Seamus Deane's *Reading in the Dark*', *Irish University Review* 30:1 (2000), 159.
[61] Harte, 'History Lessons', 158.

Significantly and paradoxically, perhaps, the alumni of the grammar school system included Eamonn McCann and Bernadette Devlin, both of whom would become powerful figures of counterinsurrection against the British state itself.[62]

The specific interest of Deane's autobiographical novel, however, lies in its tracing of the more personal ramifications of the child's education. For the young boy's self-assigned role of amateur detective – whose job is to analyse the skein of family secrets, pull it all together and return the 'true' narrative to its central players – places him necessarily in the role of interpreter, but also results in his ultimate sense of separation from the family. As a 'scholarship' tale, *Reading in the Dark* thus presents the young protagonist's movement from oral to literate codes, from the homestead to an educational setting which will force him to pass particular kinds of interpretative judgment on the household (including the laying bare of its secrets). It is telling, therefore, that the narrator's progressive discovery of the details surrounding the execution of the informer in the family leads to his confessing that 'I could never talk to my father or my mother properly again', a division that centres on language, interpretation and knowledge.[63] And fittingly, perhaps, the means by which the father rejects the boy's repeated inquisitions about the family secrets is expressed as a prohibition on communication: 'You ask me no more questions. Talk to me no more'.[64]

The fact, then, that Deane has resisted rather predictable attempts either to confirm or deny the book's status as a truthful 'memoir' of his life is central to the text's literary politics. For autobiographical modes here are fundamentally and significantly skewed: the very notion of the revelation of self, or transparent subjectivity, is meaningfully placed in question. In a brilliant interplay of form and content, a narrative relating a mystery story involving hidden identities operates as a riddle at the level of genre and intention.[65] In this way, the book itself serves as a type of Gothic

[62] Deane's fellow alumni at St Columb's College included Seamus Heaney, John Hume, Eamonn McCann and Brian Friel; for an account which frames this generation specifically within the context of the Education Act, see Maurice Fitzpatrick's *The Boys of St Columb's* (Dublin: Liffey Press, 2010).

[63] Deane, *Reading*, p. 126.   [64] Deane, *Reading*, p. 108.

[65] The UK and US editions of the Vintage paperback used the generic visual hallmark of memoir – a black-and-white photograph of the author and his brother as children on its cover – although the book is classified as 'fiction'. While Deane has distanced himself from the autobiographical angle, partly for literary-critical reasons, his commentary on the text has also served to add to the book's generic ambiguity and opacity. On several occasions he has rebutted the suggestion that the book was a memoir, only to affirm its autobiographical truth: 'I have been insistent in saying that it's fiction,

autobiography, undoing its formal precepts at every turn. Again, this achievement rests on the use of the uncanny. As Nicholas Royle argues:

> The uncanny is a crisis of the proper: it entails a critical disturbance of what is proper (from the Latin *proprius*, 'own'), a disturbance of the very idea of personal or private property including the properness of proper names, one's so-called 'own' name, but also the proper names of others, of places, institutions and events.[66]

In *Reading*, the very protagonist is denied a 'proper name' – that stamp of value intrinsic to the novel and the autobiography.[67] But other challenges to the senses of the term 'proper' ramify throughout Deane's text in an quasi-structural way: material possession ('that which is one's own; a personal possession; private property'); attributive ownership ('belonging or relating to a specified person or thing distinctively or exclusively; intrinsic, inherent'); authenticity and truthfulness ('strictly applicable; accurate, correct; literal, not metaphorical'); and conformity ('behaving according to social norms') (*OED*).

Read in this way, the stylistic ambivalence of *Reading*, including its liminality in bordering the genres of the autobiography and the novel, has social and political resonance. For in many ways the novel constitutes its own model of critical interpretation, one in which the 'lessons' learned by the boy are key to a reading of the text. As Deane himself has remarked about the work: 'The only way out is by keeping a secret, keeping things secret. It's very un-American in that sense. There's no talking-cure, no implication that by revealing everything you will

---

it's not a memoir, but there is a good deal of autobiographical material in it' (Andrew Ross, 'Irish Secrets and Lies', *Salon*, 11 April 1997, www.unz.org/Pub/Salon-1997apr-00017); 'A lot of it [is autobiographical]. I wouldn't want to give a percentage, but in effect it's an interpretation of my own family's history' (Nicholas Patterson, 'An Interview with Seamus Deane', *The Boston Phoenix*, 8 June 1998, http://weeklywire.com/ww/06-08-98/boston_books_1.html). Furthermore, the protagonist of the work remains nameless throughout (and is significantly not given a fictional pseudonym), yet Deane does not extend this 'anonymity' to the protagonist's family members. In this regard, Deane has commented suggestively: 'I could only write when I used the real names of my sisters – if I gave them different names the narrative ceased to be true' (Nick Fraser, 'A Kind of Life Sentence', *Guardian*, 28 October 1996, p. 9). This precise inability to 'economise' with the truth on the crucial matter of the 'proper names' of his family (in a book which is preoccupied with concealment and revelation of identity) reinforces the sense that Deane is using, and challenging, the conventions and cultural expectations of autobiography and memoir.

[66] Nicholas Royle, *The Uncanny: An Introduction* (Manchester: Manchester University Press, 2002), p. 1.

[67] See, for example, the discussion of the function of 'proper names' in Philippe Lejeune, 'The Autobiographical Contract', in Tzvetan Todorov (ed.), *French Literary Theory Today*, R. Carter (trans.), (Cambridge: Cambridge University Press, 1982), pp. 192–222, and Ian Watt, *The Rise of the Novel: Studies in Defoe, Richardson and Fielding* (London: Pimlico, 2000), pp. 18–21.

somehow overcome it!'[68] Resisting narrative transparency and resolution, *Reading* provides a complex way of representing subjectivity
that is not premised on the disclosure of self. Deane's rejection of the
modes of closure and resolution offered by realism, and his refusal to
place a transparent autobiographical stamp on the work, thus takes on
political significance rather than being simply a dispute over names
and categories. At the heart of the text is a steadfast antagonism
towards the individualist precepts of the memoir form in its conventional treatment of one individual or a specific family. Indeed, as in
Toni Morrison's historical ghost story *Beloved* (1987), the haunting
of one particular house in *Reading in the Dark* serves as a canvas for
the exploration of a collective and social history of conflict and
communal memory.

Eagleton has likewise engaged with the tensions of literary realism
and Gothic in his critical writing and in his memoir *The Gatekeeper*,
which self-reflexively and knowingly engages with the grammar school
narrative and plot. In his critical work, Eagleton has identified the way
in which Gothic modes operate as a type of political unconscious that
ruptures the Enlightenment project of literary realism with its failure to
articulate the 'disrupted course of Irish history and the nonrealist
quality of its fictions'.[69] The idea of the Gothic as a countercultural,
disruptive genre is thus key to any reading of Eagleton's memoir. For as
with Deane's text, Eagleton's representation of a working-class childhood in industrial 1950s Salford is governed not by gritty social realism
but by modes of hyperbole, theatricality and excess. There is, in fact, an
irony in this (as Eagleton indicates himself in the memoir) because
Salford is the place of origin of many famous proponents of mid-
century social realism in a variety of modes, including L.S. Lowry,
Albert Finney, Shelagh Delaney and Mike Leigh. But in *The Gatekeeper*'s
rendering, the uncanny sensibility of a Salford childhood is self-reflexively
produced through an identification with the family's Irish roots and
Catholicism, 'a deeply un-English culture'.[70] A Catholic upbringing, in
this memoir, exposes the protagonist to nothing less than 'secrecy and

---

[68] Carol Rumens, 'Reading Deane', *Fortnight*, July/August 1997, p. 30
[69] Eagleton, *Heathcliff*, p. 182.
[70] Eagleton, *Gatekeeper*, p. 33. Like *Reading in the Dark*, Eagleton's text can also be seen as an example
   of the type of 'Catholic Gothic' invoked by Deane in *Strange Country*. See also Richard Haslam's
   analysis of this 'subcategory of Irish Gothic' in 'Gothic: A Rhetorical Hermeneutics Approach', *Irish
   Journal of Gothic and Horror Studies* 2 (2007), http://irishgothichorrorjournal.homestead.com/
   IrishGothicHaslam.html.

doubleness, absolute refusal, Gothic grotesquerie, gestures of extremity . . . self-immolation, death-in-life'.[71]

The identification with Catholicism and, later, the collective belonging of socialism deliberately eclipses the traditional emphasis on the self and the family household which is generic to the traditional memoir form. Indeed, the defining interior in *The Gatekeeper*, with which the text begins, is not the family home but that of the 'holy family' – the Carmelite convent in which Eagleton serves, in a defining symbolic role, as the gatekeeper to the nuns who have chosen a life of self-abnegation. Despite its unprepossessing appearance (a 'squat, ramshackle building, its roof more corrugated iron than Gothic pinnacle'), the convent's inner secret space, to which the gatekeeper has special access, is depicted as an interior that defies expectation, perspective and reason.

> For all its drab outer appearance, the convent was Gothic enough in its own way. It was really two separate spaces hinged cunningly together: the sealed interior of the nuns' quarters, and then, outside the enclosure, a few public rooms, a small chapel open to local people, and the lay sisters' dingy apartments. These two spaces met in a kind of faultline of turntables, concealed doors, secret compartments, small cupboards accessible from both sides, so that the whole building was a sort of *trompe l'oeil*, like a crazy house at a fairground or an Escher drawing. It was as though the familiar world could open at any moment on to an alternative universe, only inches away from it yet incomparably remote.[72]

The convent parlour itself is laden with spatial symbolism, serving as a 'kind of no man's land or air-lock between the nuns' enclosure and the outside world': a locale that is bare but divided by a black iron grille from which 'symbolic spikes jutted ominously'.[73]

As in *Reading in the Dark*, the settings and scenes from childhood in *The Gatekeeper* do not function to reveal the autobiographical protagonist, but form a structural tableaux: a composition of the social and aesthetic formations that frame the writer's modes of analysis and ways of seeing. For Eagleton, the socialist Catholic literary critic and intellectual, 'Catholicism was a world which combined rigorous thought with sensuous symbolism, the analytic with the aesthetic, so it was probably no accident that I was later to become a literary theorist. You did not see reason and mystery as incompatible'.[74] In a characteristic move of self-reflexivity,

---

[71] Eagleton, *Gatekeeper*, p. 40.   [72] Eagleton, *Gatekeeper*, p. 4.   [73] Eagleton, *Gatekeeper*, p. 3.
[74] Eagleton, *Gatekeeper*, p. 33.

conjoining the apparently impersonal collective space of the convent with the form of the personal life, Eagleton notes:

> It was also an image of my fissured life as a child. One moment I would be playing tag outside the corner shop, and the next moment I would slip through a black hole into a realm unimaginably remote, where my Protestant friends could not follow and where secular reason slithered to an abrupt halt.[75]

As the allusion to Lewis Carroll's *Alice in Wonderland* suggests, elements of fairy tale in the broadest sense, including grotesque shape-shifting, are used to convey the book's predominant motif: the sense of being located between two worlds. This occupation of liminal space – the border within which Deane's scholarship-boy narrator also develops – is again shown to be unsettling and enabling. And as with Deane's text, this representation is politically significant. Thus whereas Lowry's paintings depicted Northern working-class life as a study in rootedness and industrial routine, Eagleton's Salford convent suggests that things are potentially in flux. In that sense, the work presents the convent as an aesthetic space of possibility and transformation.

If the convent is thus the memoir's ironically definitive location, a place where the inhabitants 'ritually avoided the first-person pronoun' for the collective 'our', the opposite of the symbolically charged convent is none other than the family home itself, at which the autobiographer almost reluctantly arrives.[76] While the convent, grammar school and, later, Cambridge University are sites of overdetermination and larger-than-life characters, the description of the family home and its occupants is significantly pared down to a bleak minimum. Eagleton describes a childhood of poverty governed by a spirit of 'grim utility which being poor tends to foster', a way of living that is depicted as 'anti-aesthetic'.[77] Against the literary cliché of the warm, affectionate working-class hearth, Eagleton evokes a home that is singularly bare – marked by an absence of homeliness and explicit affection. In fact, invoking a theatrical comparison, he writes that the 'sparsely furnished house was like a Beckettian stage-set in which nothing ever happened, since we lacked the resources for eventfulness to occur'.[78] That mainstay of the 'respectable' working-class home, the parlour, is presented in this text as a redundant space. Indeed, Eagleton recalls how in his father's childhood home, a small terraced house

---

[75] Eagleton, *Gatekeeper*, p. 4. [76] Eagleton, *Gatekeeper*, p. 13.
[77] Eagleton, *Gatekeeper*, pp. 104, 103. [78] Eagleton, *Gatekeeper*, p. 104.

in a 'Salford slum', the family of fourteen had slept upstairs on principle so the parlour could be kept 'sacrosanct'.[79] The parlour, in this representation of working-class home life at least, 'is kept empty, as a kind of witness to the fact that you have neither time, training nor inclination for such pursuits. ... It is "kept for best", but since the best never happens it remains a shell'.[80]

Consequently the family home in *The Gatekeeper* is a rather under-determined space, from which the autobiographical protagonist departs in order to encounter a panoply of Oxbridge dons, bullying landlords and hypocritical aristocratic types. This is important because it reinforces the sense that the self in Eagleton's world is presented as being formed not by the private, familial spaces of the domestic but through the public influences of institutions, mentors, antagonists and ideologies: 'A Catholic aversion to subjectivism went along with a working-class allergy to emotional ostentation, and both were underpinned by an Irish devotion to the tribe rather than the individual'.[81] The family is thus at once an intimate part of this world – the first mention of Eagleton's mother and father is in relation to the Carmelite convent – and set apart in what becomes an almost self-orphaning text.

This symbolic hollowing-out of the domestic interior, the traditional site for the assertion of personal origins, has implications for the book's literary politics. The memoir itself subscribes to the type of 'anti-autobiography' Eagleton describes in sidelong fashion, whose aim is to supplant the 'prurience and immodesty' of the autobiography and its promise of access to the writer's 'inner life', with a stress instead on a portrait of the self through the collective institutions that lend it shape (the church, school, political party and higher education).[82] The emphasis is thus on forms of practice: 'a world of compulsive rituals, not of agonized inwardness'.[83] In this regard, Eagleton notes the impact of Catholic doctrine in and on his young childhood:

> As with the acting technique of Laurence Olivier, you built from the outside inwards, and so were at odds with a social order which made a fetish of interiority. ... You were raised, then, to be suspicious of the warm glow, the intuitive certainty, the ineffable private experience. Truth had to be publicly argued for, reasoning was to be expected, and the criteria for inner states lay in what you did.[84]

---

[79] Eagleton, *Gatekeeper*, p. 116. [80] Eagleton, *Gatekeeper*, p. 116.
[81] Eagleton, *Gatekeeper*, p. 32. [82] Eagleton, *Gatekeeper*, p. 57. [83] Eagleton, *Gatekeeper*, p. 31.
[84] Eagleton, *Gatekeeper*, pp. 31–32.

Eagleton's memoir then presents an implicit critique of the bourgeois ideology of the interior as revelatory of the self and replaces it with a narrative in which the scholarship boy gains access into the heart of institutional spaces, exemplified by his movement towards the cloistered centre of the Cambridge college.

But entry into the cultural spaces of institutional knowledge is, in this text, as in *The Uses of Literacy* and *Reading in the Dark*, also experienced as a type of family betrayal (Eagleton notably recalls how news reaches him of his father's death as he sits waiting for his entrance interview at Cambridge). As with the autobiographical works of Hoggart and Deane, *The Gatekeeper* presents an account of a life which is centrally concerned with the ambivalent relations of language and power. The story in all three of these texts is put into words by the articulate, educated son who is painfully aware of the shadow of a father who is distinguished by a type of silence. This problematic is expressed, aptly enough, in *The Gatekeeper* by a rhetorical question that alludes to Catholic theology: 'What if others win for you by their sacrifice the very largeness of mind which might tempt you to betray them?'[85] In this respect, the protagonist of Eagleton's work, like those of Hoggart and Deane, assumes the role of the insider who is also outsider. The difference is that he inherits less of the agonised doubt concerning this position, instead viewing his 'inauthenticity' as a powerful and strategic political and rhetorical weapon. Being on the inside, as it were, does not require complicity, and it is significant that Eagleton cites Oscar Wilde's role as 'a kind of fifth columnist in the enemy camp, unmasking their own complacent imperial selfhood for the fiction that it was, mocking as well as flattering their social and artistic forms by deploying them even more dexterously than they did themselves'.[86] Ultimately, what distinguishes the narrative of *The Gatekeeper* is its presentation of an autobiographical trajectory that leads towards a political version of the interior, in which access to the 'inner sanctum' of hegemonic institutions provides a means of mimicry, subversion and critique.

iii   Scholarship women and Carolyn Steedman's *Landscape for a Good Woman*

The narrative of the 'scholarship boy' or 'scholarship girl', as these enduring epithets indicate, is a highly gendered form. In popular culture, in fact, postwar social mobility has generally been emblematised by the figure of

---

[85] Eagleton, *Gatekeeper*, p. 58.   [86] Eagleton, *Gatekeeper*, p. 161.

the 'angry young man', although feminist scholarship has demanded and given greater attention to the specificity of gendered experience.[87] The second half of this chapter thus turns towards depictions of childhood interiors and domestic space in the works of female writers who also reflect, through the prism of autobiography, on the border crossing of social mobility or displacement brought about by the grammar school process.

In her introduction to an important collection of autobiographical writings by women which centre on the postwar period, Liz Heron identifies a common thread among the contributions, one determined by

> a sense of not belonging, of feeling like outsiders, either in relation to others beyond our immediate family or community, or in a more singular sense of exclusion. This very common feature of childhood and adolescence was inevitably sharpened in a period when industrial expansion and technological development led to a substantial degree of geographical and social mobility, so that the bonds of community were loosening. Housing developments and slum clearance contributed to this process, and it must also have been heightened by the forms of education which, for some of us, demanded that we separate ourselves from our class or cultural identity.[88]

Depictions of space and place are of course always crucial to narratives of class mobility, but here I will explore how female authors display an acute self-reflexivity towards the positions they occupy as writing subjects. Significantly, the reminder that interiority concerns the body, as well as subjectivity and the imagination, is brought to the fore in memoirs in which 'escapees' and 'refugees' from a particular social environment portray their passage of development as an acutely embodied experience.[89]

Ideas of space and the body are complicated by the female memoirist's identification with the body of another person – namely, that of the mother, who is often conspicuously identified with the place of home. While fathers are silent but symbolically central in the literature by male writers addressed in the previous two sections, in the works of the scholarship women, it is the mother who 'haunts' the daughter's text. The psychodynamics of mother–daughter relations have, needless to say, a prominent and complex place in feminist criticism, not least in the work

---

[87] For example, see Liz Heron (ed.), *Truth, Dare or Promise: Girls Growing Up in the 50s* (London: Virago, 1985), and Gillian Whitlock, 'Disciplining the Child: Recent British Academic Memoir', *a/b: Auto/Biography Studies* 19 (2004), 46–58.

[88] Liz Heron, 'Introduction', in Heron (ed.), *Truth*, p. 3.

[89] These are the suggestive terms used by Steedman and Kuhn, respectively, as noted by Whitlock in 'Disciplining the Child', pp. 51–52.

of Simone de Beauvoir, Luce Irigaray and Julia Kristeva. However, I intend
to focus specifically on the way in which the portrayal of mother–daughter
ambivalence in memoirs can be read in relation to postwar shifts in gender
and social mobility. For the 'angry woman' in these texts is often not the
autobiographical protagonist herself but the doubled figure of the mother.

As Gillian Whitlock points out, accounts by women of the so-called
Robbins generation frequently recall 'childhoods where the maternal role
was performed grudgingly' and include 'the embedded biography of a
mother who deeply resented domesticity and the sexual politics of married
life in postwar Britain'.[90] These were mothers, she adds, who showed their
resentment in a display of an insurrectionist 'acquired domestic incompe-
tence'.[91] The resentful mother is thus significantly aligned to the domestic
interior, with the result that the childhood home in the memoirs is a
disturbing space of seething conflict, division and a constant sense of
things only half explained. Again, then, I read the striking presence of
the uncanny in such texts – including the portrayal of various haunted
houses, ghostly apparitions, grotesque bodily transformations and maternal
figures likened alternatively to 'Cinderella' or the 'witch' – as articulations
of a conflict that can be interpreted in the context of material changes
relating to literacy, education and class mobility.

In an autobiographical account of her childhood, Valerie Walkerdine
suggestively describes her mother as 'the woman who gave her children
everything, hoping to find there some fragment of herself. My mother in
this history has no history. She lurks silently in the kitchen. She is safety.
She is danger'.[92] Walkerdine's description encapsulates many of the recurring difficulties found in these memoirs: the bitterness of maternal self-
sacrifice; the paradox of the daughter writing her own account in view of
the mother who lacks a textual history; and the edge of danger ascribed to
the maternal figure who is rooted to the home. Annette Kuhn expresses it
thus in her own memoir *Family Secrets* (1995):

> My father, sick and marginalised, was little more than a spectral physical
> presence in the house: I knew quite well where the real power lay, and
> behaved accordingly. My mother, now in her fifties and working long hours
> in the workmen's cafe she owned, was touchy, ill-tempered, and resentful of
> her daughter. The closeness between us was still there; but it had assumed a
> stifling, conflicted, unpredictable – *unsafe* – quality whose feeling-tone
> I still shudder to recall. School became the focus for everything that was

90 Whitlock, 'Disciplining the Child', p. 56.   91 Whitlock, 'Disciplining the Child', p. 56.
92 Valerie Walkerdine, 'Dreams from an Ordinary Childhood', in Heron (ed.), *Truth*, p. 75.

amiss between us. She would denounce my newly-acquired 'book learning' as useless for survival in the real world.[93]

This figure of the mother and housewife seething within domestic confines is given another notable depiction in Jeanette Winterson's recent memoir *Why Be Happy When You Could Be Normal?* (2012). Here, Winterson's adoptive mother's fearsome and extravagant proportions allow her to function as the meek 1950s housewife's veritable *doppelgänger*: 'She was a big woman, tallish and weighing around twenty stone. Surgical stockings, flat sandals, a Crimplene dress and a nylon headscarf. . . . She was out of scale, larger than life. She was like a fairy story where size is approximate and unstable. She loomed up. She expanded'.[94] 'Mrs Winterson', as the author labels her in a rather Gothic appellation, is both menacing and pitiful – a woman whom custom and economic circumstances have confined to the house. It is a situation that she retaliates against by making ammunition of her domestic utensils: 'She was a flamboyant depressive; a woman who kept a revolver in the duster drawer, and the bullets in a tin of Pledge. A woman who stayed up all night baking cakes to avoid sleeping in the same bed as my father'.[95] In the manner of fairy tale acts of metamorphosis, which are themselves so often triggered by fits of rage, Mrs Winterson is literally and figuratively unstable; she grows to extreme proportions, her body pressing against the confining walls of the small two-up, two-down Accrington terraced house. Like Kuhn's perception of her mother's power *within* the interior (in contrast to her shortage of social capital outside the house), Winterson portrays her mother as greedily taking up space for herself in the small terrace. Thus the 'larger than life' Mrs Winterson pushes out husband and daughter by growing to an excessive size in a manner which is inversely proportionate to her lack of 'economic clout'.[96]

Yet while Winterson is drawn towards fairy-tale transformations, here, as elsewhere in her writing, she also alludes to the specific tensions related to class, shame and poverty that underlie this shape-shifting creature she calls mother. For in fact Mrs Winterson, it emerges, is wracked by the sense of having 'married down' (a strikingly recurring motif among the mothers of the scholarship women), and a combination of acute class-consciousness and disappointment are said to impel many of her tirades. The mother's unappealing habit of greeting a visitor with a poker

---

[93] Kuhn, *Family Secrets*, p. 106.
[94] Jeanette Winterson, *Why Be Happy When You Could Be Normal?* (London: Vintage, 2012), p. 3.
[95] Winterson, *Why Be Happy*, p. 1.   [96] Winterson, *Why Be Happy*, p. 132.

through the letter box, for example, is revealed to be more of a defensive rather than purely aggressive gesture: an attempt to prevent outsiders from entering the house and discovering that there was no bathroom or inside toilet.[97]

The expression of the daughter's ambivalent sense of loyalty towards, and rejection of, the mother – whose story she articulates even as she simultaneously maligns her – has been accorded classic status in Steedman's key memoir *Landscape for a Good Woman*. The trope of illegitimacy – of things that are literally outside of the law or that lie at the margins of propriety – is the foundation of *Landscape*'s aesthetic as well as its politics. Again, as with *Reading in the Dark* and *The Gatekeeper*, both of which are also preoccupied with challenging the 'legitimacy' of various political and cultural forms, Steedman's text is a work that manifests deep ambivalence towards the autobiographical genre to which it uneasily belongs. For this is a work that stubbornly refuses to conform to the expectations of the genre, not least in the uncanny doubling effect created by the subtitle to the American edition of the book, 'A Story of Two Lives'.

But Steedman's story aims to be unsettling in other ways, since her stated purpose is to seek out the fissures in those 'central interpretative devices of the culture' which she deems incapable of transmitting her own family history.[98] Significantly, these interpretative devices or explanatory narratives have a distinctive spatial shape, as signalled in the under-explored idea of landscape in the title of the work itself. *Landscape* thus presents an interrogation of two types of cultural interiors. The first is what Steedman posits as the idealisation of domestic life in male working-class autobiography, together with its presentation of the romanticised mother figure.[99] Against this typology, *Landscape* renders an account of the subjectivity and psychodrama of the lives of working-class women – specifically, the desire, envy and rage she believes constitute her mother's life story. Thus using an apt architectural metaphor, Steedman describes her methodology as one that 'widens the fissure between the terraced

[97] Winterson, *Why Be Happy*, p. 100. Like 'Mrs Winterson', Steedman's mother also bans visitors from the house – a fact that is also attributed in the text to her sense of shame at the family's poverty.

[98] Steedman, *Landscape*, p. 5. Although a striking feature of the work is *Landscape*'s deep affinity with precisely some of the texts and paradigms it seeks to reject, ranging from Mayhew's oral histories of the working poor to Freud's case study form.

[99] Nicola Wilson explores the way in which the figure of the mother serves as the focus of particular accounts of working-class domesticity in 'Reproducing the Home in Robert Tressell's *The Ragged Trousered Philanthropists* and D. H. Lawrence's *Sons and Lovers*', *Home Cultures* 2:3 (2005), 299–314.

houses that Hoggart and Seabrook have so lovingly described' in order to 'open the door of one of the terraced houses, in a mill town in the 1920s, show Seabrook my mother and her longing'.[100] The second interior which Steedman aims to refurbish through her account is that of the psycho-architecture of the bourgeois household (as located in the fairy tale and psychoanalysis), with its familiar symbolic objects and narrative apparatus. Thus referring to the Freudian case study form, with a particular emphasis on the famous case of 'Dora', she notes:

> The corpus draws its images from the social world (it could scarcely do otherwise); it is made out of metaphors that look as if they describe nothing at all, but rather simply *are* the way the world is: a jewel-case, a pair of pearl ear-rings, a nursemaid, a household ordered this way, now that, a tree outside the nursery window. ... This story, the psychoanalytic story, could not use the stuff of the world outside the gate in this way: streets, food, work, dirt, can only be used to dispel the complacency of the imagery. The narrative holds within itself sets of images that represent the social divisions of a culture, and only with extreme difficulty can it be used to present images of a world that lies outside the framework of its evidential base.[101]

To be middle class, Steedman argues in effect, is to inherit a thesaurus of signifying objects that serve as convenient props or symbolic ciphers in the articulation of a life: 'The myths tell their story, the fairy-tales show the topography of the houses they once inhabited.'[102] But as a challenge to this paradigm, Steedman uses her own childhood and household to furnish an alternative account that details the specific materials which measure the grammar school girl's move up the social ladder (from the prosaic significance of acquiring a desk in her bedroom to consumer items that facilitate transformation: fashion, shoes, makeup). Alongside this, she creates her own Freudian psychodrama using the visual idiom of her childhood rented house in Streatham Hill, in which a New Look coat, magazines and a bluebell forest form an intricate network of symbolic connections. So while Steedman at times can express rigidity in her view of the way particular genres or narrative structures are aligned to class experiences, her own text in fact shows how the interior landscape can be furnished through a hybrid network of historical and cultural forms.

As a historian of reports by nineteenth-century reformers on working-class households, Steedman has effectively critiqued the politics of the representation of the working-class interior, specifically the question of

---

[100] Steedman, *Landscape*, pp. 121, 11.   [101] Steedman, *Landscape*, pp. 76–77.
[102] Steedman, *Landscape*, p. 17.

the power relations inherent to ways of reading and accounting for the domestic space of poorer communities. Indeed, her attention to the economics and politics of vision underpins the memoir's central demand not for a room of one's own but for a landscape. This view outwards forms part of Steedman's professed bifold defiance: a return of the gaze by which working-class households have been historically surveyed (from the outside in) and an insistence on the need for historians to evaluate how perspectives and viewpoints are determined by the material circumstances from which the subject is positioned. As Steedman comments:

> It matters then, whether one reshapes past time, re-uses the ordinary exigencies and crises of all childhoods whilst looking down from the curtainless windows of a terraced house like my mother did, or sees at that moment the long view stretching away from the big house in some richer and more detailed landscape.[103]

The idea of 'seeing things' in this text again plays on both senses of the phrase, as an awareness of the politics of vision is coupled with the idea of hyper-real or fantastical visions which exceed reality. In fact, the autobiographical protagonist throughout the pages of *Landscape* is either constantly seeing things or being prevented from fully seeing, as for example her recurring dream-like glimpses of a woman wearing the aptly named 'New Look' fashion, or her short-sightedness as a child that caused her to 'literally stop[...] seeing for a very long time'.[104] Moreover, she recalls at one point her sense that she and her sister believed themselves to be 'unnoticed, *unseen*', partly as a result of her parents' need to guard the family secret – the children's illegitimacy – from prying, censorious eyes.[105] An anxiety about being seen by others also underlies the self-conscious autobiographical framework of *Landscape*, which constantly reveals its deep uneasiness with the display of the self as any sort of object lesson.

Steedman's heightened self-reflexivity towards acts of perception and self-display is rooted in a sense that class exclusion is internalised from an early stage through social encounters which take place at home. Like *Reading in the Dark*, *Landscape* shows how it is within the domestic interior that the child can acquire a profound sense that the family is riven by secrets and a sense of social marginality. This is encapsulated in an early scene in which a representative of the State, in the form of a health worker (whose function alludes to the nineteenth-century sanitary visitor as well as

---

[103] Steedman, *Landscape*, p. 5.   [104] Steedman, *Landscape*, p. 44.
[105] Steedman, *Landscape*, p. 44.

the wicked fairy who lays a lifelong curse on a household), shames Steed-man's mother by telling her 'this house isn't fit for a baby'.[106] Significantly, the stigma and shame of poverty are jointly experienced by the young child and her mother as they 'both watched the dumpy retreating figure of the health visitor through the curtainless windows'.[107] The repeated use of 'curtainless' is a potent image that Steedman, who is well-versed in the social semiotics of nineteenth-century social exploration, deploys to signify the peered-into homes of the working class and the poor. It leads to the daughter's powerful promise: 'It is in this place, this bare, curtainless bedroom that lies my secret and shameful defiance.'[108]

As with Deane's *Reading in the Dark* and Winterson's *Why Be Happy*, *Landscape* reveals a fundamental sense that the impropriety of home is sensed by the young child. And in this text, the scholarship child also becomes a type of amateur detective who tries to piece the family puzzle together by interpreting various clues. A profound sense of illegitimacy in the family thus works like a type of Gothic curse: 'All family secrets isolate those who share them.'[109] The act of reading, as in so many of these grammar-school tales, thus involves a sense of isolation and self-preservation, in which the young girl pursues the world of fantastical storytelling:

> Out the back, outside the room where the child reads the book, there grew a dark red rose with an ecstatic smell. The South London back gardens pressed up against the open window like a sadness in the dusk, and I lay on my bed, and read, and imagined what it was they were doing downstairs.[110]

If Steedman assumes the role of the heroine of the fairy tale, the figure who achieves a form of social mobility and transformation through painful negotiations and transactions, then her mother is figured as the all-important double. For despite her mother's ambition and desire for mater-ial things and ideals, including 'a New Look skirt, a timbered country cottage, to marry a prince', her life seemed to have culminated in a reclusive retreat to the Streatham Hill interior: 'She'd moved everything down into the kitchen: a single bed, the television, the calor-gas heater. She said it was to save fuel. The rest of the house was dark and shrouded.'[111]

---

[106] Steedman, *Landscape*, p. 2. For an illuminating historical analysis of the role of the district or health visitor and its relations to working-class privacy (or assumed lack thereof), see Hewitt, 'District Visiting', pp. 121–41.

[107] Steedman, *Landscape*, p. 2.   [108] Steedman, *Landscape*, p. 2.

[109] Steedman, *Landscape*, p. 65.   [110] Steedman, *Landscape*, p. 54.

[111] Steedman, *Landscape*, pp. 9, 1.

There is finally no landscape view for this woman – 'only the fence and the kitchen wall of the house next door'.[112] In a further twist, as Steedman makes clear, it is the estranged rather than the devoted daughter who has come to visit after a prolonged absence of nine years: 'I was really a ghost who came to call'.[113] Indeed, as several critics have noted, no one castigates the mother in this text quite as effectively as the daughter, as she gives literary shape to the person she calls the 'figure of nightmares'.[114] Adhering to the classic fairy-tale structure, *Landscape*'s preface begins with the death of the 'good' mother and ends with her transformation into a 'witch' as she opens the door to her estranged daughter at their last meeting.[115]

This ending to the narrative, however, offers a further level of complexity. On this last visit before her mother's death, Steedman catches sight of a newly purchased Lowry reproduction on the wall. It is a detail which irritates and disturbs her by introducing an incongruous aesthetic element into the daughter's fairy-tale psychodrama: 'Why did she go out and buy that obvious representation of a landscape she wanted to escape, the figures moving noiselessly under the shadow of the mill?'[116] The comment and its underlying sentiment are significant and challenging. For Steedman's project throughout the book has involved refurbishing the classic working-class interior and infusing it with the symbolism and psychological depth usually associated with the bourgeois family saga. The Lowry reproduction, which the mother chooses for herself, epitomises a classic view of a working-class crowd centred upon traditional forms of urban industry (the factory) and a perceived lack of individuation. In this way, the decorative object of the mother's interior functions as her final act of resistance to the daughter's recuperative project – an act, moreover, that dialectically reproduces Steedman's own aesthetic of disruption and nonconformity to the stories and frames into which individuals are placed by others.

---

[112] Steedman, *Landscape*, p. 1.   [113] Steedman, *Landscape*, p. 142.

[114] Steedman, *Landscape*, p. 46.

[115] Steedman alludes directly to Anthony Browne's illustrated *Hansel and Gretel* (London: Walker, 2008); the stepmother and witch in this children's book bear uncanny visual similarities. See also Bruno Bettelheim's influential exploration of the 'splitting up of one person into two' of the fairy tale mother in *The Uses of Enchantment: The Meaning and Importance of Fairy Tales* (London: Penguin, 1991), pp. 66–73 (p. 67), and Marina Warner's analysis of the structural complexity of the mother/stepmother/mother-in-law and daughter relation in *From the Beast to the Blonde: On Fairy Tales and Their Tellers* (London: Vintage, 1995), pp. 218–40.

[116] Steedman, *Landscape*, p. 142.

iv Consanguinity in Lorna Sage's *Bad Blood* and Hilary Mantel's *Giving Up the Ghost*

The idea of maternal ambivalence, articulated through the discourse of Gothic and fairy tale, is also a distinctive feature of Lorna Sage's *Bad Blood: A Memoir*. The border in this text is again a geographical location (Sage grew up in the Welsh village of Hanmer near the English border) and a symbolic territory for the scholarship girl who passes the crucial Eleven Plus exam and eventually enters university. Revealingly, Sage casts herself as a type of female Dracula, a shape-shifting figure who is formed by her inhabitation of two worlds, sustained by books and the 'bad blood' that is said to run through the family.

Like Deane's protagonist in *Reading in the Dark*, Sage portrays her early self as defined by a rejection of realist description and possessed of a marked preference for deviant plots. 'Although I read indiscriminately', she writes, 'I edited out prosaic or realist stuff, I didn't want to meet *lifelike* characters ... Books didn't belong to a particular time or place of origin, their contents all mingled and transmigrated'.[117] Like other scholarship tales, Sage also depicts parents who are markedly silent, although in her case, they are obscured by the flamboyant personalities of her grandparents, with whom they lived at the Hanmer vicarage. 'Domestic life in the vicarage had a Gothic flavour', she notes with approval, and her representation of this home as deviant and eccentric, shabby and dilapidated, stands in stark relief to the account of the conformity and stagnation of mid-century Hanmer where everyone '[knew] what they were going to be from the beginning'.[118] Thus in an example of a type of Freudian 'family romance' (in which 'real' parents are supplanted by the child's aspirational alternatives), Sage relishes 'playing the vicarage child', aligning herself directly with her eccentric and anarchic grandfather:

> My real family didn't seem congenial to me at all but – a bit like school – interested in tidiness and obedience, and things I was no good at. My claims to specialness were books, the church and my fund of creepy stories – Grandpa's gifts, all associated with the dark spaces of the vicarage and the vestry, and with the familiar feeling of discontent and want, in which Grandma shared too.[119]

The young protagonist of the memoir vows to effectively dis-locate herself through deviancy: 'I had acquired from Grandpa (bad blood!) vanity,

[117] Lorna Sage, *Bad Blood: A Memoir* (London: Fourth Estate, 2001), p. 177.
[118] Sage, *Bad Blood*, pp. 9, 4.   [119] Sage, *Bad Blood*, pp. 88–89.

ambition and discontent along with literacy. I didn't know my place.'[120] The vicarage then appears to guard the young Sage from the stultifying social strictures of mid-century provincial Britain by rejecting the forces of modernisation and offering instead an insular retreat to the more timeless properties of myth, family feuds and old-fashioned decadence. Throughout *Bad Blood*, the vicarage serves as a symbolic site of origin that Sage envisages as an integral but dissolute element in her own sense of leading 'a double life'.[121]

Sage's early self-identification with Gothic forms is derailed to some extent as the family undertakes the socially mobile move to a newly built council house on the edges of Hanmer in the 1950s. The gloom and dust of the vicarage are exchanged for postwar modernist principles of functionality, transparency and uniformity: 'Bright lights and straight lines were signs of the times.'[122] Thus while the vicarage interior had provided a refuge for the private self, with places in which to read, hide and wallow in the resentment of others, the 1950s suburban semi is by contrast architecturally framed according to principles of transparency and light (deadly, of course, for the self-styled vampire-child who thrives on bad blood). Indeed, as Jane Alison has noted, modernist design, which strongly influenced the new mid-century home, can be read as the 'other' to the decadent, surreal house of the late-Victorian and early-twentieth century. 'With its fitted wardrobes, sliding doors, open-plan spaces, streamlined plumbing, raised living quarters, flat roofs', she argues, modernism 'attempted to iron out all the folds, pretend there were no in-between spaces, no dirt, no dust, no old furniture – no desire'.[123] Ironically, therefore, in an inversion of value that runs throughout the text – and in marked contrast to the spaces of autonomy and independence envisaged in Acorn and Woodward's early twentieth-century memoirs – here it is the bright white council house interior that presents a place of psychological horror and claustrophobia in contrast to the imaginative freedom and 'shadowy prestige' associated with Sage's grandfather and the unruly vicarage life.[124] For Sage, one of the most unsavoury aspects of the brand-new, clean spaces for the socially mobile people of Hanmer is

---

[120] Sage, *Bad Blood*, p. 130.   [121] Sage, *Bad Blood*, p. 17.
[122] Sage, *Bad Blood*, p. 97. The contrast between old, dilapidated, and thus apparently more signifying architectural forms and new, sterile council houses, frames the narrative of Sarah Waters' Gothic country house tale *The Little Stranger* (London: Virago, 2010).
[123] Jane Alison, 'The Surreal House', in Jane Alison (ed.), *The Surreal House* (New Haven: Yale University Press, 2010), p. 22.
[124] Sage, *Bad Blood*, p. 98.

precisely their modernist eschewal of historical traces. The new builds are deemed to preclude any type of privacy or individuality: 'Family life was the open-plan living-room, the family car. It was like a nightmare council house on wheels.'[125]

The exposure intrinsic to the bright, open-plan council house has the effect of forcing the autobiographical heroine outdoors, and Sage recalls her preference for wandering around outside rather than committing herself to the family in the generic, planned interior of the home. Her sense of separation turns her into an uncanny type of stranger within the home:

> the only interloper in that new nuclear family with the cot in the living-room. On dark afternoons I could see them there in the lamplight because, unlike the other houses, ours didn't have net curtains, an act of impropriety which showed from the start that we didn't know how to behave in our new life. Everything about our situation felt exposed, it was somehow safer outside.[126]

In contrast to Steedman's governing motif of the woman looking out of the curtainless window, Sage positions herself here as resolutely apart from the family, a Romantic wanderer in nature, 'on the outside looking in, through glass that's frosted by my breath'.[127] Thus the medium of fantasy – encapsulated by Sage's preference for Gothic plots and locations – is diametrically opposed in her mind to this 'impotent make-believe' of domesticity and nuclear family living.

> They always closed ranks and pretended that everything was solid, normal and natural. Here we have the family of the period: self-made and going places. Only when you look more closely can you see that this housewife is pathologically scared of food, hates home, is really a child dreaming of pretty things and treats; and this businessman will never accumulate capital, he's still a boy soldier, going over the top again and again.[128]

Like many of the other autobiographical narrators in this chapter (including Hoggart, Eagleton, Steedman, and Mantel), illness and bodily confinement ironically provide Sage's young self with the opportunity for privacy and thus facilitate the ever-significant act of reading. In *Bad Blood*, Sage's chronic sinusitis, which keeps her awake, results in a doctor ordering the family to allow her to read at night by leaving a light on: 'Dr McColl had won me space in the council house, a lighted box of my own.'[129]

---

[125] Sage, *Bad Blood*, p. 186. [126] Sage, *Bad Blood*, p. 102. [127] Sage, *Bad Blood*, p. 103.
[128] Sage, *Bad Blood*, pp. 273, 186. [129] Sage, *Bad Blood*, p. 110.

Thus like the young protagonist of *Reading in the Dark*, Sage's characteristic desire to break free of the burden of home and family is represented as
a desire for a narrative plot and the agency that will direct the self towards
autonomy. And again, as with Deane, it is reading Latin – 'the great dead
language . . . the tongue the dead spoke' – that signifies the ability 'to
detach yourself from here and now, abstract your understanding of words,
train your memory and live solitary in your head with only books for
company'.[130] Latin is representative, furthermore, of the language of the
grammar school (the learning by rote of Latin was one of the defining
principles of this schooling system). Indeed, language-learning itself, in so
many of these scholarship tales, is presented as deviance, in the sense of
taking a different course, as well as departing from norms of behaviour. As
Whitlock writes, 'badness here is the addiction to the book, to language
and to English literature . . . and the key to the world is always the book'.[131]
In this way, Sage's young self reads Bram Stoker's tale in her room as a way
of opposing suburban existence: 'I was sinning with an undead dandy
while innocents wallowed in oblivion. The night was mine and Dracula's.
How I yawned at the thought of common daylight's coffin.'[132]

As in Steedman's *Landscape*, the greatest threat to Sage's sense of
autonomy comes from within the household and is specifically located in
the person of the mother. Sage portrays her as the new archetype of the
unhappy, frustrated housewife, with a loathing of housework, who is
embarrassingly exposed in her brand-new council house 'full of light and
hard, washable surfaces'.[133] She is a domestic victim in two senses of the
phrase, for as Sage writes, 'although she so spectacularly lacked domestic
skills, she was nonetheless profoundly domesticated'.[134] Predictably, then,
Sage's attraction to the abject quality of the 'bad blood, excited blood' that
she sees herself as inheriting from her grandfather, places her in stark
opposition to the enforced conformism to the standards of the council
house interior that she associates with her mother. But while Sage's self-
identification is with male Gothic villains – her grandfather, Dracula, the
'bad wolf' – the narrative arc towards education and social transformation
is curtailed as Sage is forced to adopt the mantle of maternity herself. Sage's
unexpected pregnancy at sixteen thus seems like a plot twist, the final curse

[130] Sage, *Bad Blood*, p. 143.   [131] Whitlock, 'Disciplining the Child', pp. 48–49.
[132] Sage, *Bad Blood*, p. 219. For a discussion of the gendered nature of female 'bad blood', see Marie
Mulvey-Roberts, '*Dracula* and the Doctors: Bad Blood, Menstrual Taboo and the New Woman',
in William Hughes and Andrew Smith (eds.), *Bram Stoker: History, Psychoanalysis and the Gothic*
(Basingstoke: Macmillan, 1998), pp. 78–95.
[133] Sage, *Bad Blood*, p. 119.   [134] Sage, *Bad Blood*, p. 123.

of the pattern of bad blood designed to ensnare the heroine who had the temerity to think she might make her autonomous, self-sufficient escape. Indeed, the way in which Sage describes her pregnancy is precisely in terms of a loss of her own self-governance and the baring of the private interior space she had made her own: 'I'd been caught out, I would have to pay. I was in trouble, I'd have no secrets any longer, I'd be exposed as a fraud, my fate wasn't my own, my treacherous body had somehow delivered me into other people's hands.'[135]

Sage's sense of detachment, previously represented in the image of the girl looking into the windows of the house from the outside, is now given corporeal form. Her body seems to confirm her status as 'an outsider, harbouring an alien, an alien myself. Having such a secret was like having cancer – a disease which couldn't be mentioned except in shamed whispers'.[136] But becoming pregnant also seems to represent a peculiarly inflected return to the mother from whom she had wanted to escape. When told the news, Sage's mother's reaction is to ask '*What have you done to me?*', while the chapter ends on an unsettling, strange note: 'I've done it now', the teenager thinks to herself, 'I've made my mother pregnant' (italics in original).[137] This metaphorical impregnation of the mother can thus be read as a fantastical reversal of Nancy Chodorow's thesis concerning the passing on of the desire to reproduce from mother to daughter.[138] For in *Bad Blood*, it is precisely the ambivalence of mothering that is passed on from mother to daughter. Sage's memoir, then, may be best read in terms of what Claire Kahane has defined as a revealing feature of twentieth-century Female Gothic. That is, the heroine's adversarial relationship is no longer primarily in relation to the villainous male (often the father or brother) or the dead or displaced mother. Instead, she argues:

> in modern Gothic the spectral mother typically becomes an embodied actual figure. With that shift, the heroine is imprisoned not in a house but in the female body, which is itself the maternal legacy. The problematics of femininity is thus reduced to the problematics of the female body, perceived as antagonistic to the sense of self, as therefore freakish.[139]

The sentiment is reminiscent of the way in which Walkerdine expresses the need to sever ties with her 'ordinary' suburban life by turning against

---

[135] Sage, *Bad Blood*, p. 236.   [136] Sage, *Bad Blood*, p. 246.   [137] Sage, *Bad Blood*, p. 236.
[138] See Nancy Chodorow, *The Reproduction of Mothering: Psychoanalysis and the Sociology of Gender* (Berkeley: University of California Press, 1978).
[139] Claire Kahane, 'The Gothic Mirror', in Shirley Nelson Garner, Claire Kahane and Madelon Sprengnether (eds.), *The (M)other Tongue: Essays in Feminist Psychoanalytic Interpretation* (Ithaca: Cornell University Press. 1985), p. 343.

the maternal figure. Returning as an adult to her childhood home, an interwar semi in suburban Derby, Walkerdine comments that 'everything about it, its sense of safety, had felt for so long like a trap, the site and origin of an ordinariness both hated and desired. It was the place in which, if I were not careful and being so vigilant, I might turn into my mother'.[140] And yet for all its Gothic deviance, what is presented in *Bad Blood*'s dénouement is in many ways a conservative model – one that aligns the mother and the body as necessarily opposed to intellectual development, creativity and textuality. 'Turning into the mother' is posited as nothing less than a type of anti-intellectual horror story.

The body as a form of entrapment and estrangement – an obstacle to the scholarship girl's progress – fittingly becomes a key motif in Mantel's memoir *Giving Up the Ghost* (2003). From the opening pages, which deal with the bourgeois travails of buying a second home, the memoir rapidly shifts into a narrative concerned with the strangeness of houses and property as visions and ghosts – literal and metaphorical – take their place alongside the author as she looks back to the past. In the book's trajectory through manifestly haunted houses, the apparition of both benevolent and malign spirits again serves to represent the analytic child who, according to the paradigm set out in this chapter, is 'used to "seeing" things that aren't there'.[141] Yet unlike the ghosts of traditional haunted house literature, which are often rooted to a particular place, the spirits of Mantel's memoir move with the author and indeed finally come to serve as a trope for the narrating self.

Strikingly, as in the works by Deane and Eagleton, the domestic setting and uncanny quotidian proximity of the supernatural are aligned with an Irish Catholic aesthetic sensibility. For the young Mantel, growing up amid secrecy, disappearances and a submerged Catholic past, ghosts are not necessarily fearful presences, but a part of the domestic setting and a way of life in working-class mid-century Hadfield, a small town near Glossop in the north of England. Hadfield itself is, again, a type of border country, 'some no man's land', indeterminately located between the country and the city; a mill town which, by the mid-twentieth century, was rapidly changing as its central industry declined.[142] Mantel remembers it as a provincial place where new pebble-dash council houses were built for residents of Manchester displaced by the war, albeit to the

---

[140] Walkerdine, 'Dreams', p. 63.
[141] Hilary Mantel, *Giving Up the Ghost: A Memoir* (London: Fourth Estate, 2003), p. 1.
[142] Mantel, *Giving Up the Ghost*, p. 114.

exclusion of Catholic families. Irishness lurks as a type of guilty and unspoken secret in this community, one that bears residual connotations of poverty and shame. But this heritage is manifest in the text in an implicit faith in unexplained events and phenomena, and in the use of fragments of songs and tales that evoke an oral culture of storytelling. It is significant, then, that like *Reading in the Dark*, Mantel's story also begins with the apprehension of a ghost 'flickering on the staircase'.[143] As in the earlier tale, the narrative of the scholarship child is inaugurated by the perception of a phantasm, a border spirit that conveys the sense of belonging uncannily to the given world and another. Later, as a child lying in the back bedroom of her grandmother's house, Mantel recalls seeing 'shadows, objects that are unnameable, that float and are not solid, objects through which the wall behind them can be glimpsed' – a vision which sets up one of the book's structuring motifs concerning the tension between solidity and corporeality on the one hand, and forms that defy and cross boundaries on the other.[144]

Difficult family events rooted in a context of poverty and shame are translated into a spectral domestic idiom, in which the effect of secrecy is to render distortions a part of everyday life and guilt an ineluctable aspect of the young child's perception. Reminiscent of Steedman's *Landscape*, Mantel's depiction of her childhood is affected by family secrets that turn around issues of legitimacy as, early on, the father vanishes from the household (following the mother's shadowy affair) and is never seen by his children again. An internalised sense of social impropriety forces the family to hide themselves within the home, effecting not a sense of refuge, but its opposite, seething claustrophobia: 'We are talked about in the street. Some rules have been broken. A darkness closes about our house. The air becomes jaundiced and clotted, and hangs in gaseous clouds over the rooms.'[145] Home becomes a place of unexplained phenomena and self-estrangement and the analytical child is once more either 'seeing things' from within the interior, or located on the outside looking in. And again, like Steedman, the child's hypersensitivity to domestic tensions results in a pathological type of sensory deprivation. 'At eight, I give up hearing', she writes, with the consequence that 'words are a blur to me; a moth's wing, flitting about the lamp of meaning.'[146]

Like other scholarship narratives, secrecy is not simply a governing motif in *Giving Up the Ghost* but is woven into its very texture and form.

[143] Mantel, *Giving Up the Ghost*, p. 1. [144] Mantel, *Giving Up the Ghost*, p. 116.
[145] Mantel, *Giving Up the Ghost*, p. 86. [146] Mantel, *Giving Up the Ghost*, p. 103.

Mantel's prose style is deeply allusive and emblematises the notion that the self-chronicling autobiography is paradoxically the product of careful concealment. Thus in a line that could serve as an epigraph to many of the texts addressed in this chapter, Mantel acknowledges that 'once you have learned habits of secrecy, they aren't so easy to give up'.[147] The interior is once again a repository for secrets and a framing location which shapes how the child views the wider world. Windows have of course been commonly regarded as the 'eyes' of the house, and, like the mirror, have been a 'traditional metaphor of realist vision directed at the world'.[148] As with Steedman, however, Mantel complicates this simple equation of windows with mimetic 'truth-telling'. 'Good prose', she remarks, quoting George Orwell, may be 'like a window-pane', but she adds,

> window-panes undressed are a sign of poverty, aren't they? How about some nice net curtains, so I can look out but you can't see in? How about shutters, or a chaste Roman blind? Besides, window-pane prose is no guarantee of truthfulness. Some deceptive sights are seen through glass, and the best liars tell lies in plain words.[149]

In Mantel's memoir, the domestic interior becomes a powerful trope for the creative, recuperative methods of historical memory, but it also conveys indeterminacy rather than the certainty of an empirical record. Indeed, the interior as a site of recollection is governed by hesitancy and inscrutability, and the writing of the memoir itself is likened to

> blundering through your house with the lights fused, a hand flailing for points of reference. You locate the stolid wardrobe, and its door swings open at your touch, opening on the cavern of darkness within. Your hand touches glass, you think it is a mirror, but it is the window. There are obstacles to bump and trip you, but what is more disconcerting is a sudden empty space, where you can't find a handhold and you know that you are stranded in the dark.[150]

Elsewhere the metaphor of the room is used to indicate the way in which Mantel colours her past through synaesthetic patterning. Childhood memories become a type of expressive interior décor as the dark greens, creams and 'cloudy yellows' of her childhood are recast as red rooms of a vintage pigment which she labels 'oxblood' – 'a faded, rain-drenched crimson,

---

[147] Mantel, *Giving Up the Ghost*, p. 147
[148] Peter Brooks, *Body Work: Objects of Desire in Modern Narrative* (Cambridge: Harvard University Press, 1993), p. 89.
[149] Mantel, *Giving Up the Ghost*, p. 5.   [150] Mantel, *Giving Up the Ghost*, p. 161.

like stale and drying blood' that recalls the sculptor Louise Bourgeois' interior installations of childhood rooms in Gothic reds.[151]

The oxblood stain also makes clear the association that occurs throughout *Giving Up the Ghost* between the domestic interior, the body, and the notion of social mobility as a painful transformative process. For like Sage and Steedman's tales, Mantel's memoir contrasts the daughter's educational progress with that of her mother, a woman who was accidentally overlooked for the grammar school entrance exam because of a senseless 'clerical error' and who subsequently begins working in the mill at fourteen.[152] As the daughter who passes the fateful Eleven Plus (despite a family history which taught her that 'it just wasn't what you did, go to the grammar school. You accepted your place in life'), Mantel is determined not to follow her mother and, like Sage, she thrives on solitary reading: 'I wanted books like a vampire wants blood.'[153] Breaking with the family tradition of being excluded from a grammar school place (Mantel's grandfather, it turns out, had also passed the exam but could not afford the uniform), the girl's success in the Eleven Plus seems to summon up the ambivalent ghosts rolling under the stone shelves of the kitchen pantry, 'sucking their teeth in envy and malice'.[154]

Significantly, in the work of the female memoirists that I have considered, the fairy-tale themes of social transformation and metamorphosis are performed on and through the body. In these texts, in contrast to the accounts of the 'scholarship boy', the tale of personal transformation or social advancement is undertaken through an idiom of physical pain (which is in fact common to the fairy tale's portrayal of the shape-shifting bargain). Mantel, for example, like Steedman before her, is disturbed by the implicit violence of the transformation in the fairy tale, including the possibility of the glass slipper 'splintering, and cutting the curved, tender sole of the dancing foot'.[155] Thus in all three of the memoirs by women in this section, the vocation of writer is notably bound up with the body and specifically with maternity. For Steedman this takes the form of a 'refusal' of reproduction; for Sage it appears in the text as unplanned pregnancy; for Mantel it is her debilitating illness and subsequent diagnosis of infertility.

Thus whereas Sage's progress as a scholarship girl is interrupted by pregnancy, in *Giving Up the Ghost* the narrative of educational mobility is hijacked by Mantel's condition of long-undiagnosed endometriosis.

---

[151] Mantel, *Giving Up the Ghost*, p. 25. See Louise Bourgeois, 'Red Room (Parents)', (1974).
[152] Mantel, *Giving Up the Ghost*, p. 49.   [153] Mantel, *Giving Up the Ghost*, pp. 50, 114.
[154] Mantel, *Giving Up the Ghost*, p. 120.   [155] Mantel, *Giving Up the Ghost*, p. 50.

The motif of stepping through the looking glass into an unfamiliar world takes on painful literality as Mantel's tale of 'forming and re-forming in some other dimension' becomes a bodily, rather than imaginative, state.[156] From having been light and frail (which led her to be significantly 'cast as a ghost' in a production of Noël Coward's *Blithe Spirit*), Mantel is forced to play a different role through illness: 'I will be solid, set, grounded, grotesque: perpetually strange to myself, convoluted, mutated, and beyond the pale.'[157] The symptoms of the illness are portrayed as a malevolent force within her body: 'there was a pain behind my diaphragm, and from time to time something seemed to flip over and claw at me, as if I were a woman in a folk tale, pregnant with a demon'.[158] The etymology of 'endometriosis' (from the Greek 'endo' meaning 'within' and 'metra' meaning 'womb'), emphasises the internal nature of the disease, while its hiddenness, as a progressive scarring of the internal organs that commonly remains undiagnosed, explains Mantel's sense of otherworldliness:

> Those crippling spasms that had to be ignored, those deep aches with no name, those washes of nausea, were not evidence of a neurotic personality, or of my ambivalence about my gender, and they were not brought on by 'nerves' or by fear of failure in a man's world. They were evidence of a pathological process that would destroy the chance of my having a child and land me with chronic ill health.[159]

In Mantel's case, the narrative model of self-fulfilment and agency that the autobiographical form invites is resisted by the body itself. Indeed, she traces a shift from being the active agent of her self-narrated story to the dismal fate of being an object of medical scrutiny ('having my fertility confiscated and my insides arranged').[160] She notes how, lying in the doctor's surgery, she is forced to literally see inside herself in a manner which, ironically, produces a sense of utter estrangement: 'For the first and last time, I saw my womb, with two black strokes, like skilled calligraphy, marking it out: a neat diacritical mark in a language I would never learn to speak.'[161] Following a hysterectomy, she is left with a scar which crudely marks the suture between her body's interior and exterior realms.

Returning to the earliest recorded senses of the word 'interior', used in the fifteenth and sixteenth centuries to denote entrails and inner organs,

---

[156] Mantel, *Giving Up the Ghost*, p. 94.   [157] Mantel, *Giving Up the Ghost*, p. 54.
[158] Mantel, *Giving Up the Ghost*, p. 12.
[159] Mantel, *Giving Up the Ghost*, pp. 219–20. The condition is caused by the spread of endometrium cells which grow abnormally outside of the womb, causing an accumulation of internal scar tissue which webs and knots other organs inside the body.
[160] Mantel, *Giving Up the Ghost*, p. 179.   [161] Mantel, *Giving Up the Ghost*, p. 195.

Mantel's memoir itself turns into a progressively internalised narrative centring on her attempts to reclaim her body – and narrative of self – from the intrusions of disease, callous diagnosis, botched cures and invasive procedures. For according to her description, her body is a location from which things have been taken away, a place in which a type of changeling substitution has put paid to certain desires. Echoing Winterson, who uses the same metaphor to describe her experience of depression, Mantel figures herself as a form of evacuated haunted house in which she is a stranger to herself:

> Everything about me – my physiology, my psychology – feels constantly under assault: I am a shabby old building in an area of heavy shelling, which the inhabitants have vacated years ago. ... I am writing in order to take charge of the story of my childhood and my childlessness; and in order to locate myself, if not within a body, then in the narrow space between one letter and the next, between the lines where the ghosts of meaning are.[162]

The self as a haunted house, in Mantel's powerful invocation, is an expression of identity based precisely upon borders and a sense of doubling – the condition of being neither one thing nor the other. And yet, as Mantel's trope implies, this is a state that generates narrative and text, as she 'locates' herself, as she puts it, 'between one letter and the next' and 'between the lines', in defiance of others who seek to control the story.

Conclusion

This chapter has examined autobiographical works of writers looking back to mid-century childhoods through the lens of the uncanny – the unhomely – a peculiarly domestic trope which nevertheless lends itself to the idea of border crossings. I have thus sought to identify how representations of disturbed and unsettled domestic space, exemplified by the unhomely or haunted house, form a distinctive motif among a group of texts by writers who show a particular awareness of their status as first-generation university graduates.

Whereas narratives of nineteenth-century working-class autodidacticism frequently rendered the educational story as a passage of enlightenment (depicting the individual's movement from the 'darkness' of industrial life into the 'light' of literacy and autonomy), the twentieth-century grammar-school narrative resists this paradigm of illumination. Indeed, as Royle

---

[162] Mantel, *Giving Up the Ghost*, p. 216.

has noted, Freud's essay on the uncanny itself unravels binaries of darkness and light. For as Royle argues, Freud's text is marked by the underlying sense that 'it is not so much darkness itself (whatever that might be), but the process of ceasing to be dark, the process of revelation or bringing to light, that is uncanny'.[163] In much the same manner, these autobiographical works problematise the causal links between knowledge, enlightenment and revelation. Often resisting the memoir's traditional form of personal disclosure, these works are concerned precisely with the way in which reading, forms of education and social mobility result in an unsettling liminality. As Vidler comments, in relation to Freud's doubts about the effectiveness of the English translation of the German word 'unheimlich', 'the English word is perhaps more helpful than Freud was willing to admit: literally "beyond ken" – beyond knowledge – from "canny," meaning possessing knowledge or skill'.[164] These scholarship tales are arguably about both knowledge and that which remains unknown ('beyond ken'): family secrets, historical disturbances, the ghosts of the past.

The uncanny manifests itself through depictions of the strange, unsettled, or haunted spaces of the home across these autobiographical works as well as through the writers' portrayals of their sense of estrangement within the family home. It is an aesthetic that captures a sense of guilt and betrayal, for as Freud writes, referring to Schelling's definition of the uncanny: 'everything is *unheimlich* that ought to have remained secret and hidden but has come to light'.[165] The motif of unhomeliness further characterises the texts' presentation of subjectivity as being located and predicated on a type of border crossing and threshold, a process whereby the self is a part of two realms that are not easily assimilated. Finally, the uncanny also reveals itself through the inevitable preoccupation among these works with past selves. For life writing is fundamentally predicated on the idea of a return and a revisitation; the memoirist engages in direct and indirect ways with the uncanny act of creating a literary double – of becoming their own ghostwriter.

---

[163] Royle, *Uncanny*, p. 108.
[164] Vidler, *Architectural Uncanny*, p. 23. The word 'ken' is notably also a slang word – from the sixteenth century on – for a house, usually of a disreputable kind.
[165] Sigmund Freud, 'The "Uncanny"', in James Strachey (ed. and trans.), *The Standard Edition of the Complete Psychological Works of Sigmund Freud*, vol. XVII (London: Hogarth Press, 1955), p. 225.

CHAPTER 4

Estates

Social housing in twentieth- and twenty-first-century literature and culture

Introduction: The rise and fall of council housing

This final section provides a thematic return to many of the issues presented in Chapter 1. Taking the postwar housing estate as a distinctive residential location, my examination of fictional and non-fictional texts aims to unravel the meanings and politics of interiors in a housing setting that paradoxically has been culturally over inscribed and simultaneously overlooked.[1] From sociological surveys of housing estates to coming-of-age narratives of selfhood, my analysis posits the landscape of housing estates as a significant cultural setting and construct in twentieth- and twenty-first-century writing and film. I argue that depictions of interiors and housing take on unique and imaginative forms in the context of a domestic environment that has sometimes been negatively associated with homogeneity and social marginalisation.

The 'story' of British council housing is itself a compelling narrative. The controlled demolition of one of the towering Red Road Flats highrises in 2012 as part of the Glasgow Housing Association renewal project, for example, was widely recorded in the British media. For the images of shattering concrete provided a potent visual accompaniment to a particular way of narrating the fate of British council housing over the past century. In this account, the collapse into rubble of what were once the tallest buildings in Europe – which had acquired notoriety in the 1970s as a zone

---

[1] As Matthew Taunton notes, 'council estates appear all over London, but the rigorously applied and universally legible semiotic regime that prevents them from forming an ordinary part of the cityscape also reinforces the sense that their inhabitants are members of an indigent underclass'; *Fictions of the City*, p. 162. It is arguable, however, that the situation Taunton describes in the capital is rapidly changing, particularly in light of a severe housing shortage and rampant gentrification. According to James Meek, in the context of the current housing crisis, council homes 'are beginning to look like more attractive places to live. Too late for the less well-off; just in time for the hipsters. Rural peers now snap them up for their London pieds-à-terre. Wealthy parents buy them for their children. Buy-to-let investors cram them with students'; Meek, 'Where Will We Live?'.

and symbol of social exclusion – served as an effective metonym for the apparent failure of one of the central pillars of the welfare state: good housing for all.[2] This visual narrative thus emblematises an apparent story of decline, marking the failure of radical plans implemented in a succession of Housing Acts between 1914 and 1960 by dint of a plethora of social, political and design factors. As Joe Moran puts it: 'The demolition of the tower blocks serves as a kind of visible cautionary tale for those who might seek to provide planned solutions to everyday problems'.[3] For unlike the maligned Victorian inner-city tenements, which were the architectural by-product of decades of unregulated urbanisation and building speculation, housing estates and council housing were implemented by design – thus making the perceived failure of the project all the more noteworthy. In addition to this, the tower block and the suburban estate were also conceived as architectural emblems of postwar utopian ideals and high modern architecture, and were presented as such in many of the iconic housing documentaries of the interwar years.[4]

My book's preoccupation with the unstable affiliation between housing interiors and exteriors, as well as the relationship between housing types and the perceived 'character' of their inhabitants, has particular salience in the context of social housing. Plans for the building of council housing were, after all, explicitly concerned with the idea that model dwellings would in some sense produce model forms of citizenry and selfhood. If the degraded outgrowth of Victorian slums was imagined in the late nine-teenth century as having degenerative effects on its residents, it followed, according to the same way of thinking, that the model council dwelling would engender model citizens. As noted in Chapter 2, the postwar decades saw this idea embodied in a pervasive, government-driven dis-course about the home that advocated a retreat into the domestic sphere and championed the virtues of modern designs and 'model interiors' for healthy, family life.[5] As Ben Rogaly and Becky Taylor comment in relation to this period of reform, in line with national Labour party policies, 'the built environment was seen as the key to, not only removing the slums,

---

[2] The US documentary film *The Pruitt-Igoe Myth* (2011), for example, uses just this visual paradigm of the controlled explosion of high-rises to symbolise the decline and failure of a notorious housing project in St Louis, Missouri.

[3] Joe Moran, 'Housing, Memory and Everyday Life in Contemporary Britain', *Cultural Studies* 18:4 (2004), 616.

[4] See, for example, *Kensington Calling!*, dir. by Kensington Housing Trust, www.screenonline.org.uk/film/id/1185130/, and *Housing Problems*, dir. by Edgar Anstey and Arthur Elton, in *Land of Promise: The British Documentary Movement 1930–1950* (BFI, 2008).

[5] See Hornsey, *Spiv and the Architect*, pp. 201–04.

but also [to] eradicating the "slum mind" of those removed from crowded inner city areas'.[6] Or as two housing historians note, 'the spacious surroundings of Modern blocks of public housing signified, above all, the freeing of the lower classes from the darkness of the slums'.[7] The interdependence between architecture and selfhood, so often implicit in Victorian discourse, was now effectively enshrined in government policy.

In fact it was in relation to the domestic interior that twentieth-century council housing design came close to realising its ideals. While the prospect of living in newly built 'un-English' flats met with a great deal of resistance on the part of the residents of various slum clearance schemes in the 1920s and 1930s, many of these apartment spaces were considered to offer a vast improvement on Victorian terraces and back-to-backs. 'The inside of a building is as important as the outside', intones the narrator of one of the most famous British documentaries, *Housing Problems* (1935), as plans for the Quarry Hill Flats in Leeds city centre are exhibited as a remedy to the slum interiors so memorably portrayed in the film's opening sequences.[8] For structures such as the Quarry Hill Flats provided their tenants with modern living spaces that were clean, secure and dry, with the provision of running hot and cold water and inside toilets. As Alison Ravetz observes, 'the small-scale successes of council housing, as innumerable tenants' accounts confirm, were in the personal and domestic spheres, and nothing like as spectacular as its public failures could sometimes be – as in the episode of high-rise estates, for instance'.[9] In one of many ironies in the history of council housing in Britain, what would become some of the most maligned features of the project – for example, concrete, multi-storey tower blocks – were actually conceived for the comfort and well-being of the resident (for example, in the case

---

[6] Ben Rogaly and Becky Taylor, *Moving Histories of Class and Community: Identity, Place and Belonging in Contemporary England* (Basingstoke: Palgrave Macmillan, 2009), p. 44. Alison Ravetz is similarly clear about the relationship between model housing and model subjects in her pioneering study of council housing, *Model Estate: Planned Housing at Quarry Hill, Leeds* (London: Croom Helm, 1974).

[7] Miles Glendinning and Stefan Muthesius, *Tower Block: Modern Public Housing in England, Scotland, Wales and Northern Ireland* (New Haven: Yale University Press, 1994), p. 42.

[8] *Housing Problems* (BFI, 2008).

[9] Alison Ravetz, *Council Housing and Culture: The History of a Social Experiment* (London: Routledge, 2001), p. 4. In *Model Estate*, Ravetz records many of the Quarry Hill residents' marked approval towards, and affection for, their flats. See also Anne Power's comparative analysis of five European mass housing estates characterised by 'extreme decline'. She notes, 'once rehoused and settled, people could become strongly attached to their flats, and even when conditions outside were very poor, they showed a remarkable sense of identity with their home'; *Estates on the Edge: The Social Consequences of Mass Housing in Northern Europe* (Basingstoke: Macmillan Press, 1997), p. 293.

of the high-rises, the provision of maximum light and circulating air inside the dwelling).

The desire for private living had emerged as a popular demand among interwar and postwar generations. Referring to a 1943 Mass-Observation report, *People's Homes*, David Kynaston writes:

> Over and above 'all mod cons', what people wanted – and clearly, unambiguously wanted – was privacy in their homes. 'A garden that is overlooked, windows into which neighbours can see, balconies visible from the road or from houses opposite are all deplored,' the report noted.[10]

In the case of suburban estates – for example, the Chelmsley Wood estate in Solihull – the peripheral location on the outskirts of Birmingham was essential to the provision of homes that were spacious and offered self-contained garden plots. But this also had the effect of creating a residential landscape that seemed to militate against community and civic amenities. It could be argued that the drive towards the provision of privacy within the dwelling, and the separation of family households, were the very factors which led to many of the new estate tenants' feelings of isolation and discontent. The inner-city model, on the other hand, also had to tread a fine line between providing spatial privacy for tenants while not neglecting the importance of a sense of community with other residents and the surrounding city itself. Displaced residents, who had previously inhabited densely populated areas of working-class terraced housing, found themselves in some instances relocated to apartment buildings which provided all the inconveniences of living at close quarters with other people without any of the attendant benefits of 'community'. The 'deck access' tower block design, the basis of Manchester's doomed Hulme Crescents, for example, produced 'streets in the sky' that were arguably a major source of conflict rather than conviviality between neighbours.[11]

In this final chapter, I return to one of the contentions of the book: that the idea of the interior, and its relationship to the formation and expression of identity, is shaped by multiple external factors which include the relations of housing, gender and class. In the context of modern housing estates in particular, this chapter will trace how a range of creative and non-fictional texts attend to this tension between interiors and what surrounds them: from the stigmatisation of the locations of specific types of council

---

[10] Kynaston, *Austerity Britain*, p. 51.

[11] Ravetz argues that the 'deck access' layout produced 'peculiar horrors of interlocked dwellings, public walkways over domestic ceilings, and ground levels given to stores and parking space that were rapidly abandoned to wreckers'; *Council Housing*, p. 188.

housing to the resident's capacity for social mobility and their sense of social belonging. For ideas of privacy and inwardness, so often deemed to be ideal attributes for a secure sense of self, require careful negotiation in the context of lower-income mass housing. As will become clear, while dominant accounts of the home frequently associate ideas of inwardness and interiority with security and comfort, representations of life on particular modern housing estates highlight what can be another aspect of 'homely' seclusion: deep isolation. This phenomenon, in which the physical and social degradation of an environment may lead residents to retreat inwards, is at the root of Polly Toynbee's comment in relation to her experience of living for a fixed period on a dilapidated Clapham housing estate (for a report which adheres in many ways to what Seth Koven has identified as a long tradition of journalistic 'slumming'):

> The only place to be was inside the safe, familiar, private space of your own flat. That's how it felt; safe up here looking out, but with a desert down below to cross to get to the streets and bus stops of the outside world. Estates are curious places, locking the poor out of sight ... fatally turned inwards upon themselves instead of outwards to join the bustling world beyond.[12]

Class has been crucial to the conception of council housing, from its roots in the ideological imperative of providing decent housing for working-class families, to the way in which these residential environments are depicted in particular forms of cultural and media representation. Indeed, for some critics, it is class division itself that accounts for many of the mistakes associated with this housing experiment. According to this line of argument, the supposed failure of specific forms of council housing – the high-rise in particular – was rooted in the social discrepancy between the modern planners who drew up the prototypes and working-class people who had to live in them. The problem, as Peter Hall forcefully argues, was of 'design solutions laid down on people without regard to their preferences, ways of life, or plain idiosyncrasies; laid down, further, by architects who – as the media delighted to discover – themselves invariably lived in charming Victorian villas'.[13] Ravetz makes the point in stark terms:

> The whole operation was a culture transfer amounting to a cultural colonization: a vision forged by one section of society for application to another,

---

[12] Polly Toynbee, *Hard Work: Life in Low-Pay Britain* (London: Bloomsbury, 2003), p. 17. For a history of undercover reporters 'slumming' – from James Greenwood to George Orwell – see Seth Koven, *Slumming: Sexual and Social Politics in Victorian London* (Princeton, New Jersey: Princeton University Press, 2004).

[13] Peter Hall, *Cities of Tomorrow: An Intellectual History of Urban Planning and Design in the Twentieth Century*, 3rd edn. (Oxford: Blackwell, 2002), p. 246.

to whom it might be more, or less, acceptable and appropriate. . . . It asked nothing more of tenants than to live in the houses and to participate in estate life in ways approved by the middle-class reformers.[14]

Many postwar planners and architects had notably taken their inspiration from Le Corbusier, the Swiss-French forefather of the modern tower block who notoriously failed to actualise many of his vertical designs within his own lifetime. Le Corbusier famously attacked the idea of the 'cult of the home', proposing instead that the house should be stripped of its neo-Victorian sentimentalism, nostalgic artefacts and clutter in order to serve as an efficient and functional 'machine for living in'.[15] But as Hall points out, the most famous prototype for high-rise living designed by Le Corbusier – the *Unité d'Habitation* in Marseille – was in fact perfectly designed for a bourgeois clientele.[16] Indeed, as Hall wryly implies, the model tenant for urban high-density life was not a low-income family but a single, mobile, childless and affluent male, rather like Le Corbusier himself.

i Narrating the estate

Evoking stories, assumptions and stereotypes, housing estates function in popular culture and media as an important setting framed by class relations. Moreover, as with nineteenth-century urban tenements, a particular discourse has arisen in relation to council housing whereby the architectural structure and its occupants are closely identified, more often than not in negative terms. Council housing, as various writers have argued, is sometimes used as a generic term or journalistic short-hand for issues of crime, social exclusion and a welfare-dependent 'underclass'.[17] The offensive use of the term 'chav', for example, often plays precisely on this assumed relationship between place and antisocial behaviour.[18]

---

[14] Ravetz, *Council Housing*, p. 5.

[15] Le Corbusier, *Towards a New Architecture*, Frederick Etchells (trans.), (New York: Dover Publications, 1986), p. 95.

[16] Hall, *Cities of Tomorrow*, p. 247.

[17] For example, see Hanley, *Estates*, and Owen Jones, *Chavs: The Demonization of the Working Class* (London: Verso, 2012).

[18] Imogen Tyler addresses the 'slang vocabulary' that has emerged around the word 'chav', including its apparent derogatory use as an acronym of 'Council Housed and Violent' or 'Council House Associated Vermin'; '"Chav Mum Chav Scum": Class Disgust in Contemporary Britain', *Feminist Media Studies* 8:1 (2008), 21. The *OED* cites the origins of the word as related to the Romani word *čhavo* and the Angloromani word *chavvy*, meaning a 'male Romani child'.

The demonisation of council housing estates in some strands of media and cultural discourse functions as a prime example of what Loïc Wacquant calls 'territorial stigmatisation' or the 'blemish of place'.[19] According to Wacquant, the discourse of 'territorial infamy' can reinforce the conditions by which the state reproduces urban marginality and the exclusion of the poor from dominant social structures.[20] The word 'stigma', as Tom Slater and Ntsiki Anderson point out in their use of Wacquant's insights in their study of a working-class Bristol estate, derives etymologically from a Greek term meaning 'the practice of burning or cutting a mark into the flesh of criminals and slaves, so they would be forever identified as outcasts'.[21] This etymology is suggestive, for it makes clear that the effect of stigmatisation is not just symbolic; it has a real impact in material ways on particular forms of subjectivity. It also serves to highlight the relationship between place and the body, since the pernicious consequence of territorial stigmatisation is that a person belonging to a particular neighbourhood can themselves be perceived to bear the 'blemish' of the place. Again, conceptions or apparent assumptions concerning the figure of the 'chav' play precisely on this idea of the embodiment of place, in which the identification of accent, idiom, fashion, gait, hairstyle and choice of music and even food give rise to all kinds of amateur and discriminatory popular ethnographies.[22] Such figurations are not new since, as noted in Chapter 1, middle-class Victorians were notoriously preoccupied with the danger of place-inscribed bodies, such as that of the 'slum-dweller', breaching the limits of the neighbourhood boundaries and thus 'contaminating' bourgeois space. Such anxieties are of a slightly different order today, if only because current home ownership patterns and an unregulated rental market provide an almost insuperable barrier which can seal gentrified, affluent neighbourhoods from a more diverse socioeconomic population.[23]

---

[19] Loïc Wacquant, 'Territorial Stigmatization in the Age of Advanced Marginality', *Thesis Eleven* 91:1 (2007), 67.

[20] Wacquant, 'Territorial Stigmatization', 67.

[21] Tom Slater and Ntsiki Anderson, 'The Reputational Ghetto: Territorial Stigmatisation in St Paul's, Bristol', *Transactions of the Institute of British Geographers* 37:4 (2011), 542–43.

[22] See, for example, websites such as ilivehere.co.uk (formerly Chavtown.co.uk) as well as the entry 'chav' in the *Urban Dictionary*, www.urbandictionary.com/define.php?term=chav.

[23] Even those estates located within city centres, such as Little London in Leeds, can sometimes remain distinctly peripheral or cut off from the public and commercial spaces of the city through a combination of architectural features and a proximity to main roads and motorways. Recently, however, private land developers have begun to encroach into formerly stigmatised inner-city zones and to effectively expel the residents in the name of 'regeneration'. For an analysis and critique of

Any attempt to understand the cultural history of council housing also needs to take into account its origins as a form of tenure based on the principle of subsidised rent. The economic imperative underpinning the idea of housing choice (sometimes obscured in generalised discussions of 'home') is thus of crucial importance, particularly in a context in which the ownership of property has increasingly become a source of inherited wealth and social mobility. As Matthew Taunton puts it, today, 'home-ownership is not only a tenure, it is an ideological construct, and a major shibboleth'.[24] Given this, it is important to recall that the advancement of home ownership as a 'natural' good was a novel doctrine espoused by the Thatcher administration after 1979, although one that has now become hegemonic within neoliberal discourse. Indeed, the ideological conception of a 'housing ladder' resulted in the deliberate downgrading of the status value of council housing and renting in general as a form of tenure, thereby entrenching class division by way of space and housing type in a damaging, vicious cycle. The Right to Buy scheme, introduced in 1980, was a turning point in this respect; it gave council tenants the opportunity to purchase their council property at a discounted price but simultaneously led to a depletion of the stock of council housing and an entrenchment of the ideology of a 'property-owning democracy'.[25] But the Housing Act not only had a significant negative impact in terms of the availability (and quality) of the remaining council stocks; for as Peter Malpass notes, 'much more difficult to assess is the effect of other, unquantifiable, factors such as the constant rhetorical emphasis given to the virtues of home ownership by ministers, and the matching denigration of public renting'.[26]

Increasingly, within a neoliberal cultural and economic climate, home for many is not just a dwelling place but one that functions as a form of private investment, speculation and a source of inherited wealth. This shift

neoliberal strategies of contemporary urban gentrification, see Sarah Glynn, *Where the Other Half Lives: Lower Income Housing in a Neoliberal World* (London: Pluto Press, 2009).

[24] Taunton, *Fictions of the City*, p. 53.

[25] Margaret Thatcher used this phrase in her first leader's speech in Blackpool (1975). The Right to Buy legislation was embedded in the 1980 Housing Act, enabling tenants to purchase their council property at a significant discount. By 1988, 1 million council homes had been sold in this way. The long-term damaging effects, as widely noted by housing critics, were caused by the restrictions the Conservative government placed on how local authorities could use the income generated by the sale of council housing. Councils were required to use the funds from the sales of property to pay off the 'historic debt' of housing rather than invest in the building of new council homes; see Glynn, *Where the Other Half Lives*, pp. 100–02.

[26] Peter Malpass, *Housing and the Welfare State: The Development of Housing Policy in Britain* (Basingstoke: Palgrave Macmillan, 2005), p. 111.

in housing politics is revealed by the changing fortunes of council housing as a cipher in public discourse. Where in the first decades of the twentieth century it held a central place in a national narrative which presented such dwellings as the deserved reward for intolerable conditions and sacrifice borne by generations of working-class citizens, from the 1980s onwards, council housing has often been portrayed, with the significant exception of London, as the housing option of last choice, providing shelter for groups who are frequently economically vulnerable: the elderly poor, the disabled, the unemployed, immigrants, refugees, some single-parent households. Commenting on the way in which council housing became increasingly synonymous in public discourse with poverty and social exclusion, Rogaly and Taylor argue that 'unlike the post-war period when material deprivation was part of a wider national experience of austerity', this view was now 'at odds with the prevailing ethos of consumerism, success and individualism that characterized the 1980s and 1990s'.[27] In the early decades of the twenty-first century, against a context of austerity and an increase in the shortage of affordable accommodation, the fortunes of council housing, albeit in localised areas such as the South East, are clearly turning again to provide yet another twist in this housing tale.

Although council housing is a burgeoning topic in the media and social sciences, it is less frequently encountered as a subject of cultural significance.[28] In this respect, not much has changed since Ravetz argued that 'the study of council housing has so often been presented as the history of housing policy that its broader contributions to twentieth-century material culture and working-class life have not received as much attention as they deserve'.[29] As I will argue, however, housing estates form a ubiquitous part of the physical landscape, and this setting – in all its variations – needs to be considered in terms usually associated with literary place: narrative, plot, symbolism, subjectivity, viewpoint and aesthetics. My analysis will therefore be premised on the belief that the housing estate is a significant field of enquiry, concerned with large-scale drama and small intimacies in twentieth-century and contemporary life.

---

[27] Rogaly and Taylor, *Moving Histories*, p. 93.
[28] While Ravetz highlights the need to consider the 'culture' of the housing estate, Taunton's *Fictions of the City* provides a unique comparative examination of the narrative and aesthetic modes used to depict London and Parisian mass housing estates across a range of genres.
[29] Ravetz, *Council Housing*, p. 3.

ii Surveying the estate: Sociological accounts of council housing

> You can lose yourself in an area like this.
> –Ken Coates and Richard Silburn, *Poverty: The Forgotten*
> *Englishmen* (Nottingham: Spokesman, 1983), p. 122

In the mid-twentieth century, sociologists began to pay attention to forms of community in the type of working-class industrial districts that modern planning schemes were designed to replace.[30] One example is *Family and Kinship in East London* by Michael Young and Peter Willmott, a pioneering oral history of a shift in community that has become a classic in its field. Published in 1957, this study traced the movement of working-class Londoners from Victorian terraces in Bethnal Green to a newly built London County Council (LCC) housing estate in Dagenham, Essex (referred to by the pseudonym 'Greenleigh'). Through a series of interviews, the authors compared the respondents' memories of the East End with their lived experiences on the new estate, demonstrating how a 'highly articulated network of kinship relations' may be strongly linked to place.[31] In a striking passage, the new town of 'Greenleigh' is aptly presented through the opening doors of a commuter train. It is worth quoting at length:

> Less than twenty miles away from Bethnal Green, the automatic doors of the tube train open on to the new land of Greenleigh. On one side of the railway are cows at pasture. On the other, the new housing estate. Instead of the shops of Bethnal Green there is the shopping centre at the Parade; instead of the street barrows piled high with fruit, fish, and dresses, instead of the cries of the costermongers from Spitalfields to Old Ford, there are orderly self-service stores in the marble halls of the great combines. In place of the gaunt buildings rising above narrow streets of narrow houses, there are up-to-date semi-detached residences. Bethnal Green encases the history of three hundred years. Cottages built for the descendants of Huguenot refugees, with their wide weavers' windows and peeling plaster, stand next to Victorian red-brick on one side and massive blocs of Edwardian charity on the other. Greenleigh belongs firmly to the aesthetics of this mid-century. Built since the war to a single plan, it is all of one piece. Though the Council has mixed different types of houses, row upon row look practically identical, each beside a concrete road, each enclosed by a fence, each with its little

---

[30] According to Glendinning and Muthesius, one effect of this recognition was that 'dwellings in slums, or streets in slum districts, if not yet the slums as a whole, suddenly received a revaluation' (*Tower Block*, p. 103).
[31] Michael Young and Peter Willmott, *Family and Kinship in East London* (Berkeley: University of California Press, 1992), p. xiv.

patch of flower garden at front and larger patch of vegetable garden at back, each with expansive front windows covered over with net curtains; all built, owned, and guarded by a single responsible landlord.[32]

In this passage, the authors juxtapose the locale of the older working-class East End community with the strange, new suburban estate. The public, outdoor life of the market is contrasted with a new landscape comprised primarily of housing, while an older working-class culture defined by heterogeneity is set against a stolid model of residential sameness, in which things are 'all of one piece'. The tone is distinctly ambivalent, heralding the brave new world of Greenleigh, while implying that important forms of history and culture had been swept away by the zeal for better housing.

Such equivocation is appropriate in view of the fact that whereas some of Young and Willmott's respondents envisage the virgin estate of Greenleigh as a 'paradise' – the chosen land of a great 'exodus' – for others, it is a place of utter isolation: '"When I first came," said Mrs Sandeman, "I cried for weeks, it was so lonely. It was a shock to see such a steep hill going up to the shops."'[33] Mrs Sandeman's plaintive remark introduces one of Young and Willmott's recurrent themes in what is a notably female-centred sociology: that some of the most negative effects of the move to new estates were experienced by women. As well as loosening what had been presented earlier in the book as a central form of kinship in the older East End community – the relation between mother and daughter – this process of dislocation also increased women's isolation due to factors which centred on a lack of transport links which prevented not simply access to shops, but to the possibility of work outside the home. This incongruity, whereby a planned landscape of 'home' produced a deep sense of estrangement in its residents, is manifest through the terms the women used to describe the environment. As with the sense of dislocation reported by a female respondent in the quotation at the start of this section, Young and Willmott record Mrs Harper lamenting that the quietness will 'send people off their heads', and that 'it's like being in a box to die out here'; Mrs Ames, meanwhile, remarks that 'it's like a strange land in your own country'.[34] Such sentiments of profound disorientation are similarly voiced in Judy Attfield's interviews with women reminiscing about their experience of the 'New Town Blues' in the 'pioneer days' of the 1950s.[35]

---

[32] Young and Willmott, *Family*, p. 121.   [33] Young and Willmott, *Family*, pp. 127, 122.
[34] Young and Willmott, *Family*, pp. 132–33, 154.
[35] Judy Attfield, 'Inside Pram Town: A Case Study of Harlow House Interiors, 1951–61', in Attfield and Kirkham (eds.), *A View from the Interior*, p. 215.

One respondent, who had moved from Walthamstow to the apparent blankness of a new estate in Harlow, exclaims: 'When I used to look out of the window, I couldn't see a thing...I thought I was the only person on earth. ... I felt as if I'd been thrown right out of a nest, although I was 28 when I came here'.[36]

What Young and Willmott crucially identified was a profound social change taking place in this new landscape of housing, one in which the emphasis on the house and interior created a type of cultural narrowing. Neighbours were now 'strangers instead of kin', and for the residents of Greenleigh, 'their lives outside the family are no longer centered on people; their lives are centered on the house. This change from a people-centered to a house-centered existence is one of the fundamental changes resulting from the migration'.[37] In this 'house-centred' community, the homes are effectively the central figures in the landscape, and each separate household is distinguished by nothing more than house number: 'The small group which lives inside the same house hangs together, and where people are known as "from No. 22" or "37", their identity being traced to the house which is the fixed entity, each one of them affects the credit of the other.'[38] The idea of the house precluding or inhibiting human interaction is further implied in the authors' telling comment that exchanges between neighbours are carried out 'window-to-window, not face-to-face'.[39] Such distancing is ironically reinforced by the methodology of the study itself, since the writers retain a conspicuously detached distance from their female subjects, who are always addressed formally ('Mrs Sandeman', 'Mrs Harper'). It is as though the government-sanctioned ideology of privacy is reproduced through the very form (and formality) of the work in its reluctance to pry too far into the lives of its female ethnographic subjects.

By contrast, the maintenance of neutral distance is not the aim in the journalist Paul Harrison's later influential exploration of the reality of welfare state inner-city housing in Hackney, *Inside the Inner City: Life Under the Cutting Edge* (1983). The difference in focus and tone of this work marks an important shift in the fortunes of welfare housing, and its social and media perception, from *Family and Kinship*'s concern with the loneliness of housewives to Harrison's dramatic investigation of poverty and lawlessness on inner-city London housing estates in Thatcher's Britain. Borrowing heavily from the tropes and metaphors of colonial

[36] Attfield, 'Inside Pram Town', p. 218.   [37] Young and Willmott, *Family*, p. 154.
[38] Young and Willmott, *Family*, p. 163.   [39] Young and Willmott, *Family*, p. 163.

exploration deployed by late-Victorian reformers, the book's central aim, declared in the title, is to reveal the hidden interior: the 'inner city's inner city', or what Harrison calls a 'worm's-eye view of the welfare state'.[40]

The foreword to the revised edition of Harrison's work (by Michael Young of *Family and Kinship*, who hails the book in the 'great British tradition' of social exploration, from Mayhew to Orwell) announces that Harrison 'takes you behind the flaking façade to the people who are on the other side. He brings them alive'.[41] But despite the intention to access the reality of life for inner-city residents, Harrison's heavy-handed authorial voice, with its tendency towards sensationalist metaphors, dominates the survey in which the inner city is depicted as a 'bombardment chamber where the particles generated and accelerated by the cyclotron of a whole society are smashed to each other' or 'a universe apart, an alien world ... where all our sins are paid for'.[42] Recalling the tenor of Jack London's *The People of the Abyss* (1903), Harrison's adult informants are concealed by pseudonyms and sometimes disturbingly likened to species of animals. Like many of its Victorian predecessors, this late twentieth-century work of urban exploration, which professes to reveal economically (as well as figuratively) 'concealed households', performs its own process of obfuscation and exoticism.[43] Indeed, it ultimately produces a dramatic ethnography, which pities its subjects while simultaneously depriving them of any degree of agency; at one point, they are effectively dispatched as 'people with no future, drifting in time on the tiny raft of the present'.[44]

Harrison's book does, however, usefully draw attention to many of the causes of decline in Hackney housing estates during the years of welfare cuts. These included residents' lack of choice in relation to their place of habitation, the detrimental effects of high-density living, poorly designed public spaces open to criminality and vandalism, the problem of noise, the spiralling effects and vicious cycle of social residualisation and, again, the inhabitants' deep sense of isolation and social exclusion. Harrison also makes the argument – largely unacknowledged at the time – that housing conditions in Thatcher's Britain lay at the heart of a class divide that manifested itself in the form of a schism between owner-occupiers and renters (council tenants in particular).

---

[40] Harrison, *Inner City*, pp. 225, 11.
[41] Michael Young, 'Foreword' (1991)', in Harrison, *Inside the Inner City*, pp. 7–8.
[42] Harrison, *Inner City*, pp. 25, 21.   [43] Harrison, *Inner City*, p. 189.
[44] Harrison, *Inner City*, p. 201.

Harrison's work can usefully be contrasted with the oral historian Tony Parker's survey *The People of Providence* (1983). This text is strikingly different in tone, not least because Parker does not presume he needs to 'bring . . . alive' people living in poverty but insists instead that their voices should be heard and recorded. Indeed, *The People of Providence* is a subtly innovative work precisely for the way in which its portrait of life on the pseudonymous 'Providence' estate (in fact, the Brandon estate in Kennington, South London) is constructed through extended interviews that take place for the most part within each resident's own domestic space. Rather than the long-lens view or the voyeuristic fly-on-the-wall style, *The People of Providence* is distinguished by its striking tone of politesse. Parker is literally the invited guest in the various homes on the Brandon Estate, and he is treated by the respondents with reactions that range from curiosity and suspicion to hospitable friendliness.

There is in fact a sense in which Parker self-consciously stages the different interviews; as if introducing characters in a play, he begins the presentation of each dialogue with a descriptive passage, providing biographical information about the residents and describing the domestic setting. Parker's keen eye for the detail of an interior, often coupled in the italicised segments with an account of the interviewee's physical appearance, serves to connect the individual with their inner space. Reminiscent of Victorian social exploration, the detail of the interior works either to match its occupant or to highlight the discrepancy between 'character' and the traces of inhabited space. Formal and stylised in this way, Parker's interviews with the residents of the Brandon housing estate nonetheless reveal miniature life histories that are often quietly revealing and contrary to expectation. Like Mayhew's earlier domestic portrayals, secrets are revealed and appearances constantly deceive in Parker's tenant interviews.

Parker's choice of pseudonym – the 'Providence Estate' – encompasses two important aspects of this housing environment: the idea of welfare provision (the French for 'welfare state' is *État-Providence*) and the utopianism that underpinned its establishment. The false name also captures what is at times the irony of the notion of the housing estate as a providence for all; for while the estate appears as a form of 'paradise' for some, it is literally described as a type of 'hell' for others. Linda and Alan Norris, for example, residents of the 'Darwen' tower block, live in a large, airy, upper-floor flat with floor-to-ceiling windows – a space that exemplifies the model, well-planned council dwelling. The account Linda offers of their move to the estate, from rented rooms in Wandsworth ('furnished rabbit hutches'), to a fourteenth-floor room with a balcony, serves as an endorsement of council housing as a providential magical solution:

> I think when you've been unhappy and thought you've made a complete mess of your life, then suddenly somehow you get a second chance – well it's fantastic, like a miracle. . . . I do enjoy being up here, really enjoy it. I'm not a very religious person, so I say being up here is I'm sure it's the nearest to heaven I'll ever get.[45]

The idea of the council property providing a new lease of life and a blank slate is, in fact, a familiar trope in a number of postwar cultural texts. It occurs, for example, in Andrea Levy's novel *Never Far From Nowhere* (1996), which memorably depicts the family's move from an inner-city North London house ('just a notch above a slum') to the brightness and whiteness of a newly built Finsbury Park housing estate:

> On the first day we wandered round it – the fairy-tale kingdom of white concrete, radiant in the sun. Quiet with the sounds of birds and our footsteps echoing off the walls and corridors. It was like coming into the light after years underground. After years spent in a damp basement, where we could see the bottoms of people's legs as they went about their business on our busy road. Knees, ankles and feet in shoes all seen through railings – bars. But from our third-floor flat we could look down on people's heads and sometimes, when they were in the not too far distance, we could see them all.[46]

The representation of the arrival on the newly built estate as being emblematic of a radiant, new beginning also serves as an effective cinematic trope, notably in Lynne Ramsay's *Ratcatcher* (1999), set in Glasgow during one of the 'bin-men' strikes of the mid-1970s. In the film's final scene, the members of the family of the young male protagonist are depicted transporting their belongings and furniture through sunlit cornfields in a type of exodus from the dilapidated inner-city Glasgow schemes to the new housing estates being built on the edge of the countryside. Like the unfinished estates, the future for these individuals is presented as being replete with possibility.

Yet this presentation of the estate as a spatial utopia is, perhaps unsurprisingly, matched by an opposing view. The rhetorical duality of the estate as 'heaven' and 'hell' emerges throughout Parker's oral history, and the cumulative effect of interviews with residents reveals the extent to

---

[45] Tony Parker, *The People of Providence: A Housing Estate and Some of Its Inhabitants*, 2nd printing (London: Eland, 1996), pp. 21, 23.
[46] Andrea Levy, *Never Far From Nowhere* (London: Review, 1996), p. 3.

which subjectivity and particular circumstance fashion conflicting representations of the same place. The estate is thus presented as the object of
an almost kaleidoscopic set of views, constantly turning and shifting to
reveal new facets of this shared environment. Parker's study, in short,
highlights a very simple fact concerning housing (but one that has nevertheless not necessarily been heeded by designers and planners of mass
housing): that individuals have very different needs and preferences. One
person's private penthouse is another person's isolated cell. For Parker's
thirty-five-year-old respondent, Audrey Gold, for example, a depressed
cleaner living on the sixteenth floor of the 'Preston' tower, the Providence
estate 'is as near I could imagine as to what it must be like living in hell.
When I was a kid I used to read in books hell was down under the earth
somewhere; but it's not, it's up here in the sky'.[47] Another informant, a
part-time school cleaner living in the 'Vernon' block, has internalised the
'blemish of place' to the extent that she refuses to allow Parker to interview
her within the 'shaming' confines of her flat:

> I wouldn't want anyone to see where I live. Those places are just like being
> in prison, that's exactly what it's like: you've got a long long corridor down
> the middle inside, and all these front doors that all look the same. There are
> forty doors in the corridor where I live and every one looks exactly like all
> the others. Some days I go home and I'm not sure which number is
> mine. . . . Inside there are three levels. They're built like that you see, like
> an open pair of scissors.[48]

In this passage, the high-rise structure itself is depicted as having a
threatening and thus disciplinary effect on its residents ('like an open pair
of scissors'), one that produces a perceived sense of their socially marginalised status.

   Despite the fact that many of the respondents assert that the estate
cultivates a feeling of anonymity, the effect of Parker's compendium of
interviews is to counteract this claim. Indeed, the textual form and method
of *The People of Providence* can be read as a type of removal of the fourth
wall of the various buildings, revealing a collage of individuated and
idiosyncratic voices. As noted in Chapter 1, the Asmodean endeavour to
detach the rooftops and peer at the lives within remains, but the figure of
the social investigator as intrepid explorer and *raconteur* of the lives of
others has been drastically altered. For Parker's book lays particular
emphasis on the diversity of the tenants and their forms of residency; from

---

[47] Parker, *People of Providence*, p. 54.   [48] Parker, *People of Providence*, p. 285.

the couple who have leased their flat for more than twenty five years, to the single father squatting with his sons in a house scheduled for demolition, to the mother living on welfare and waiting for a transfer to better accommodation on the ladder of social housing. There is no monolithic council home in Parker's ethnography and, crucially, while there are correspondences and echoes among the parallel and stacked lives presented in his account, the end result is not one of sweeping uniformity. Using the vignette form – favoured by nineteenth-century social explorers, including Mayhew – Parker produces portraits that are complex, rich and open-ended. His translation of first-person oral histories into a dia-logic, collective text makes *The People of Providence* a striking example of a working-class oral history that takes council housing as a significant loca-tion in and of itself.

There is, however, a poignant aspect to the fact that it is only Parker, the outsider and oral historian, who has access to the residents as a community of voices. One tenant, a 'beleagured' alcoholic who describes herself as living in 'a state of siege, surrounded by life', puts her finger on precisely this irony:

> I suppose there must be thousands like me on the estate – it's just that we've no way of getting in touch with each other. Sometimes I feel like going outside there in the streets and walking up and down in the middle of the road with one of those loudspeakers and shouting out 'If there's anyone who feels like coming out and having a talk please come out because I feel like having a talk with someone too.' All these lives: how do you get in touch with them, how do you communicate? Perhaps I should do what you're doing, spread the word around and say I'm writing a book and asking people will they talk to me.[49]

According to this particular respondent, the only way in which you can access or visualise the estate community, ironically, is by being an outsider or by making the estate the ostensible object of an enquiry. To capture the community, in other words, is already to be outside of it – a conundrum that has long been at the heart of a particular strand of cultural inquiry.

A final example of a sociological study which considers the nature of housing estates as a site of historical and social interest is the journalist Lynsey Hanley's *Estates: An Intimate History* (2007). In this text, there is a marked shift from the stance of the professional sociologist or oral histor-ian, who takes the housing estate as a field of research, to Hanley's autobiographical account which is underpinned by a deep personal and

---

[49] Parker, *People of Providence*, pp. 329, 333.

political investment in the topic. For at the level of form and content, Hanley's account is premised on her experience of growing up on the vast Chelmsley Wood housing estate, built in the 1960s in Solihull on the fringes of Birmingham. This convergence of the personal and the political is significant because although the book takes mass housing as its focus, the analysis is always filtered through a subjective lens, thus providing at the level of form a correlation between ideas of individualism and collectivity which are central to the argument. Indeed, Hanley's distinctive use of the word 'intimate' in the book's title signals the fact that this is an emotional survey of housing. Such intimacy functions as a form of textual politics which challenges the external viewpoint of the traditional urban survey and its posited objectivity and reserve. The intersection of the autobiographical and analytical further serves to demonstrate Hanley's belief that subjectivity is forged through the material environment, and that the spaces individuals inhabit frame their interpretation of the world (what she calls a 'lifelong state of mind').[50] But equally, as a corollary to this, there is a sense in which Hanley brings subjectivity and raw affect to the issue of welfare housing, confessing: 'I can't think about council estates without having a pronounced emotional reaction to those very words. . . . There's something about them that makes me brim over with pain, and a sense of wrongness; even the bits that anyone else would think right'.[51]

Working at the juncture of personal and social history, Hanley aims to illustrate the layered and complex ways in which spatial configurations inscribe and preserve social inequality. The book's professed goal is to 'attempt to work out how much of the stubborn rigidity of the British class system is down to the fact that class is built into the physical landscape of the country' and to show 'that we are divided not only by income and occupation, but by the types of homes in which we live'.[52] Thus Hanley – perhaps at times too unequivocally – expresses the view that council housing estates have become zones of segregation, excluded from dominant and affluent spheres of public life in a way that leads to a spiralling effect of degradation and residualisation. The metaphors and tropes that she uses to portray these 'class ghettoes' invoke the housing estate as again a spatial and psychological 'prison': 'It's more a feeling of having been consigned, contained, delivered to a place, to serve a sentence that may never end.'[53] In a potent spatial dramatisation presented in the opening pages of the work, Hanley goes on to portray the feeling of social exclusion

---

[50] Hanley, *Estates*, p. 4   [51] Hanley, *Estates*, p. 6.   [52] Hanley, *Estates*, p. 18.
[53] Hanley, *Estates*, p. 6.

as an assault on the mind and the body. Thus she describes an occasion when she and her mother are caught by a 'whipping wall of wind' that literally prevents them from proceeding beyond the tower block to the school:

> A whirlpool of rubbish, by now containing my mum's glasses, sought an absent plughole. We were trapped inside it, assaulted by flying Panda Pops bottles and empty Quavers packets. ... It lasted until the monolith relented, after what had seemed like an hour but was probably no longer than ten minutes. The new glasses were snapped in two. We passed through in traumatized silence, with me leading my mum the rest of the way. I don't know how she found her way back home.[54]

The scene functions like those vignettes of the past in Carolyn Steedman's work which depict moments of class (self-) consciousness – episodes designed to show how the child is forced to witness the way in which the world treats her parents. Yet Hanley's moment of class epiphany does not bear any of the pathos of *Landscape*'s memorable encounter in which Steedman's father is given a dressing down by the gatekeeper of the bluebell woods; the detritus of estate life that are literally flung into the faces of the mother and daughter are reminders that this is a landscape apparently devoid of poetic or symbolic capital.[55] Moreover, in the context of Hanley's wider thesis that in contemporary Britain, you are where you live, the episode serves as a forceful induction to her portrayal of the effect that a degraded spatial landscape can have on the bodies, social prospects and psychological well-being of individuals.

Indeed, the autobiographical sections of the book frequently reveal the author's heightened bodily experience of the estate space; Hanley recalls her adolescent reaction to The Wood housing estate as a retreat into a defensive inwardness. Hanley's homescape is constantly shown to be something to which she is unable (and unwilling) to mould herself; as she so effectively puts it, she cannot wear her home 'like a happy skin'.[56] In this text, the self cannot settle into the receptacle of home emblematised by Benjamin's velvet compass case or Bachelard's shell. And yet Hanley goes on to describe the uneasy ways in which the estate nevertheless remains under her skin in adulthood, always prohibiting a linear narrative which might show her simply emerging chrysalis-like from an adolescence of low self-esteem to a wider world of cultural and educational fulfilment.

---

[54] Hanley, *Estates*, pp. 1–2.   [55] Steedman, *Landscape*, pp. 49–51.   [56] Hanley, *Estates*, p. 42.

Estates is ostensibly and self-reflexively articulated through the voice of the writer from the other side of the 'wall' (as Hanley terms it) in a manner which is important for the form and tone of the study. For Hanley consciously writes with the voice of the insider who is also an outsider, both empowered and anxious about her Janus-faced viewpoint. This type of informer status is manifest in passages in which she adopts the role of a native-turned-social-explorer as she returns to take a pedestrian tour of The Wood estate. This self-conscious walking tour, in which she deems it necessary to physically re-experience the space in order to understand it, also works to portray Hanley's preoccupation with the discrepancy between principles of town planning and the lived experience of those who inhabit a designed environment. Echoing respondents from the accounts of Young and Willmott as well as Parker, Hanley identifies how the sum effect of these designed and planned estates can be estrangement and the loss of a sense of self: 'You are sewn into rows of houses that are all inhabited, and yet you don't see anyone to whom you are not related for days at a time. You were put here and you don't know why. Your environment makes as little sense as your life.'[57] The rhetorical appropriation of the guise of the *flâneur* is ironically effective here. For whereas the urban milieu can keep the street stroller occupied for hours, Hanley is compelled – and at times stupefied – by the uniformity and unchanging landscape of this territory of 18,000 dwellings.

But if *flânerie* is redundant in this landscape, so too is the idea of rediscovering her roots. For Hanley sets out to tour the topography of her childhood – her place of origin – and yet is stumped by the fact that there is, at least in one sense, nothing to see at the core of this 'never-ending maze' and 'estate riddle'.[58] While in *Landscape for a Good Woman* Steedman rejects what she deems to be conventional descriptions of working-class industrial landscapes (exemplified for her by Lowry's factor-ies and Hoggart's Hunslet terraces), Hanley expresses envy for this type of older, more 'authentic' working-class environment: 'I find myself wishing I'd come from a real place, with proper, chimneyed houses instead of endless tragic boxes with people in them.'[59] The ruthless sole purposeness of The Wood, apparently devoid of civic, social or communal facilities, intrigues and baffles her on the walk:

> Five minutes later – five turns along short interlocking paths, and a hundred-odd homes, half a dozen terrace houses and a Battenburg-cake layer of one-

[57] Hanley, *Estates*, pp. 44–45.   [58] Hanley, *Estates*, pp. 23, 38.   [59] Hanley, *Estates*, p. 37.

bedroom flats on either side of the walkway, with a bollard at each end – I come to my first road. I look back at the domino contest I've just passed through and realize exactly what fascinates me about the estate I grew up on: it's all houses. That's what it is: houses everywhere, without a break. That's what it's there for. That's the only reason it's there.[60]

Hanley astutely questions how a sense of lifelessness should characterise a territory that is home to thousands of people. For it is part of her wider argument that housing lots of people in close residential proximity does not constitute a community. As Hanley points out, there is no reason for anyone who does not live on the estate to be there, thus reinforcing the steadfastness of an invisible, but efficacious, class barrier. And within the estate itself, households are separated from each other according to a suburban model where 'everyone is inside or out, but there is no one merely out and about'.[61] In a feature also noted in Young and Willmott's account of the new town of 'Greenleigh', the spatial landscape of The Wood provides forms of space and privacy at the cost of modes of economic advantage and community (including easy access to the city and its 'real' public spaces).

   In a culture in which the dominant ideology of home is coupled with a sense of individualism and propriety, Hanley's criticism of the fate of council housing in Britain is targeted precisely at the way in which collective housing failed to accommodate – and, in fact, worked hard in her view to obliterate – feelings of well-being and self-identity. 'In the early days, people would regularly get lost looking for their own houses', she remarks, 'such was the uniformity of the housing and the complexity of the design'.[62] Yet the question also arises as to what extent her negative portrayal of the estate in this walking tour is a product of her own methodology. To quote Raymond Williams' observation on George Orwell's ethnographic practice, 'as so often, the method depends ultimately on a point of view'.[63] For Hanley's 'insider' account stays, ironically, resolutely on the outside, which distinguishes it from Parker's attempt to people and individuate the monolithic estate through the dialogic form of interviews and detailed vignettes from within the tower block flats and maisonettes.[64] By contrast, Hanley's constructed landscape is a silent,

---

[60] Hanley, *Estates*, pp. 26–27.   [61] Hanley, *Estates*, p. 41.   [62] Hanley, *Estates*, p. 23.
[63] Raymond Williams, *Orwell* (London: Fontana, 1984), p. 23.
[64] See also Lisa McKenzie's *Getting By: Estates, Class and Culture in Austerity Britain* (Bristol, Policy Press, 2015); this text also works at the intersection of autobiographical and sociological forms, but is rooted in an ethnographic practice based on the author's 'insider' status as she conducts interviews with the residents of the St Ann's estate in Nottingham, where she has lived for over twenty years.

ghostly locale devoid of inhabitants or voices; in effect, it functions as a projection of her own internalised rejection of this setting and all that she deems it to represent.

In its presentation of identity, *Estates* seems to concede to the idea that welfare housing was the result of a group of male planners' ill-conceived and failed designs – that it created the conditions for limited forms of subjectivity and community from which the aspiring individual's only hope is to escape over the invisible, indomitable wall. This is in fact the evocative image with which she concludes her nuanced portrayal of partly overcoming these immaterial barriers to acquire forms of social capital made manifest through self-confidence and language: 'I began to knit together the strands of this other world to make a rope that would carry me over the final wall.'[65] The effect of the metaphor is to suggest that Hanley is either a type of fairy-tale princess, or possibly a prisoner-escapee, as she plots her exit. Her subsequent entrance into a world of popular and high-brow culture – from Ziggy Stardust to the *Observer on Sunday* – sparks the beginning of her sense of engagement with the wider world; in a nice variation on the house-as-shell paradigm, Hanley writes that 'the council-estate clam had opened up in the steamy hothouse of intellectual awakening'.[66]

Hanley's story of life on the other side of the 'wall' is informed – as narratives of escape, including the scholarship boy/girl paradigm, so frequently are – by the painful knowledge that what she now knows about the space of her childhood has been acquired by leaving it behind. But this trajectory is underpinned by individualist assumptions: 'Unlike many of those ordinary girls, I had the secret knowledge, so curiously opaque and inaccessible on estates like ours, that life could be free and good.'[67] This raises an important tension: for while on the one hand Hanley is adamant that housing in Britain is constructed along class lines, and that where you live informs for the most part what you can achieve, on the other, she claims that in her case at least, there existed some kind of essential self that not even the moribund estate could engulf. She comments:

> It was the anonymity and conformity of the estate as a whole that threatened to consume me. It felt as though the identikit homes produced identikit people. I'm ashamed to reduce people like this, for I know that every one of them has a story far more fascinating than the flat face of their house would ever reveal. But there, somehow, I never felt free to be the person I knew I was inside.[68]

[65] Hanley, *Estates*, p. 159.   [66] Hanley, *Estates*, p. 161.   [67] Hanley, *Estates*, p. 18.
[68] Hanley, *Estates*, p. 34.

By using tropes of interiority and exteriority ('I never felt free to be the person I knew was inside'), Hanley reveals a telling inconsistency in her argument: subjectivity cannot be simply produced by the surrounding environment since she presents herself as having a core sense of self that survives the concrete estate maze. Indeed, it could be said that by equating the outward facade of the home with the residents, Hanley's account comes close to reiterating the emphases of many of the Victorian social explorers. Her narrative provides a crucial template of one individual's escape, but it emerges at the expense of what she knows – but does not show – to be other people's similarly complex accounts.

iii   Not at home: Gender, space and housing estates in contemporary fiction

I have addressed the ways housing estates have been represented through different forms of sociological account, from Young and Willmott's study of a new town to Hanley's intimate survey of the landscape of her adolescence. From tropes evoking pioneer narratives to metaphors of heaven and hell, paradise and prison, the mundane housing estate has produced multifarious and emotionally charged images in non-fictional representation. In the remainder of this chapter, I will consider how the estate has functioned as a setting and formative environment for character development and narrative plot in novels and films.

As a spatial setting, the estate has often served as a backdrop for the type of coming-of-age story of the young boy in films such as *Kes* (1969), *Ratcatcher* (1999), *Sweet Sixteen* (2002) and *The Selfish Giant* (2013) as well as novels including Glenn Patterson's *Burning Your Own* (1988) and Stephen Kelman's *Pigeon English* (2011). While such cultural depictions present the space of the housing estate as fraught with hardship, danger and sometimes tragedy, they also construct it as a place that facilitates a young boy's active exploration of the environment. Indeed, it could be said that things happen on estates for young boys in fiction and film; they are dramatic spaces for adventure and plot development in which young male protagonists actively move in and out of a landscape of flats and houses and the often abandoned spaces in between.

Many literary narratives of female experience on mass housing estates, by contrast, are characterised by a defining sense of physical immobility, usually in the form of the protagonist's confinement to the domestic sphere, resulting in a paralysing sense of isolation and inwardness. This sense of spatial seclusion, coupled with intense self-surveillance, was memorably captured by Young and Willmott's female respondents who testified to a sense of solitude, 'looking at ourselves all day'.[69] And it is this feeling of enforced self-contemplation, far removed from any notion of positive affirmation, which functions as the structuring device for Janice Galloway's *The Trick Is to Keep Breathing* (1989) and Livi Michael's *Under a Thin Moon* (1992), two novels that take as their subject the experience of women living in urban high-rises. In Galloway's text, the protagonist, Joy, suffering from depression, bulimia and the pain of a broken relationship, spends her time in a flat on a derelict estate, finding ways of waiting, coping and surviving. Highly stylised and experimental in form, the novel presents an interior monologue, replete with ellipses, hesitations and unorthodox pagination, thereby projecting an internal world riven by a sense of disruption and dislocation. The notably deviant form of the book, in terms of its stylistic innovations, marks a visual enactment of this inward turn upon the self. The faltering, broken style produces a visceral sense of the claustrophobic parameters of Joy's life, in which the narrator's interior ruminations and obsessions seem to rebound against the four walls of the box-like council flat in a self-perpetuating process that effects little outlet or progression.

A similar textual effect is produced in Michael's first novel *Under a Thin Moon*, which interweaves the lives of four women living in a tower block in north Manchester. The place-bound nature of the women's lives is under-scored by the novel's emphasis on interior/exterior dichotomies. From the start, there is a contrast between the women's isolation and consequent limited opportunities for social engagement, and the sheer scale of the towering blocks they inhabit, their forced proximity to other people and the view from their high-rise windows which stretches out across the city. Likewise, the bleak and monotone appearance of the apartments and wider estate – the 'greyish scum of the bath', the drab apartment décor and the uniform 'airforce blue and cream' colour scheme enforced across the entire block – is at odds with the spectrum of colour glimpsed through the apartment windows.[70] If the view from a higher point has historically denoted power, command and the possession of property, for the woman in the tower block, such as the single mother Wanda, the effect is one of ambivalence:

> She cannot get over the view. It is evening already, and a thousand windows facing west reflect the sunset like a fiery ball. There are glittering ribbons of

---

[69] Young and Willmott, *Family*, p. 149.
[70] Livi Michael, *Under a Thin Moon* (London: Martin Secker & Warburg, 1992), p. 1.

light from the main roads into the city . . . It is like a free show for her and
Coral. Out there, she feels, is life, excitement. Things are happening.

Look Coral she says. The whole of the great big shining world out there,
just for us.[71]

For Laurie, another female resident, the view out over the estate presents a
similar duality – a scene of desolation accompanied by the glimpse of
something transcendent:

[The estate] spread out before her like the crumbling remains of a picnic,
cooling towers, factory chimneys, warehouses, scrapyards, tower blocks and
terraced houses stacked tightly together, block after block, but now at
evening it takes her by surprise in its magnificence, like the silent God
she half believes in.[72]

The fact that the women spend a lot of time at the window looking out
reinforces the way in which life in the tower block is predicated on a form
of private life that precludes social interaction. This is underlined by the
narrative form of the novel, which alternates between the four first-person
perspectives of the women, thus bringing the voices together while keeping
them steadfastly apart. In this way, the paradoxical circumstance of what is
in effect a collective of isolated women is manifest at the level of style:

So here they all are in this crumbling heap of concrete, plasterboard and
cement. The walls are so thin they are aware of all the small private
details of one another's lives, and in many ways their lives run on similar
lines, yet they are all encased in small apartments so that each is
absolutely alone.[73]

The tower block and narrative structure are thus closely interrelated
since, in both, the women lie close to each other and yet exist in atomised,
self-contained units. This effect is reinforced by the absence of chapter
headings, which allows for a seamless continuation of the separate voices of
the four women, compounded by Michael's use of recurring symbols and
tropes (including the dominant 'feminine' image of the moon in the title
of the novel) which threads together their common anxieties and longings
in a network of symbolic allusion.

As in Galloway's *The Trick*, domestic seclusion within the high-rise in
Under a Thin Moon results in portrayals of female selfhood that are
marked by debilitating forms of inwardness. Michael herself notes in an
interview that 'one of the results of extreme isolation is a form of extreme

---

[71] Michael, *Under a Thin Moon*, pp. 2–3.   [72] Michael, *Under a Thin Moon*, p. 15.
[73] Michael, *Under a Thin Moon*, p. 29.

self-consciousness'.[74] In this sense, as also noted by Hanley, the undistinguished features of the surrounding estate seem to contribute to the individual's feeling of anonymity:

> The buildings around her loom enormous, their darkened shapes and blind black eyes press in on her. She is very tired. All the buildings begin to look alike. . . . Street after street is the same to Wanda because none of them has any meaning. There is nothing for her to recognize in them. . . . Without a sense of place it is hard to remember yourself. You could be anyone at all.[75]

One strategy that Michael's character Wanda employs in order to give herself a more 'solid' sense of identity is to engage in a recurring daydream in which she imagines herself as the subject of a documentary film, fantasising about being tracked by a camera lens that would turn her into an object 'worthy' of surveillance. This pattern of seeking compensation for a lack of identity by assuming a type of exterior view of oneself is enacted in different ways by many of the female characters in this novel. It is a projection that derives from a system of class and gender relations based precisely on a hierarchy of observation.

The Trick Is to Keep Breathing and *Under a Thin Moon* use highly stylised, experimental prose forms to convey the material and psychological despondency of working-class women living on mass housing estates. Both novels also place emphasis on the development of a sense of female subjectivity through forms of interior monologue, thereby using an established literary mode to express the subject's inner life. However, what becomes at times the almost solipsistic nature of the prose, together with the rejection of narrative and plot development, risks veering towards the sense that nothing happens and nothing will ever change for these characters. As a consequence, the women are effectively barred from transformative action, with the exception, in Michael's novel, of the young girl Coral who, according to a somewhat traditional formula, sees authorhood and the penning of the story of her life as a symbolic means of achieving autonomy. Additionally, the stylised form runs the danger of collapsing the distinctive subjectivities and diversity of experience of these women into something that is, ironically, homogeneous and recursive.

By way of contrast with representations of high-rise living that have ascribed its isolating effects solely to women, James Kelman's fiction serves to highlight the complexity of gender and class in the context of mass

---

[74] Michael, quoted in Pat Wheeler and Sharon Monteith, 'Interview with Livi Michael', *Critical Survey* 12:3 (2000), 100.
[75] Michael, *Under a Thin Moon*, p. 11.

housing. In Kelman's short stories set in Glasgow tenement blocks during the period of deindustrialisation in the 1980s and the severe unemployment that went with it, the male protagonists share many of the traits and anxieties of Michael and Galloway's female characters, including crippling isolation, helplessness and depression. Indeed, the situation for Kelman's protagonists – men who are confined to the home through unemployment – disrupts traditional alignments of the domestic interior with femininity and the world of work as a masculine sphere. As a result, many of Kelman's male protagonists find themselves disoriented by the so-called increasingly 'feminised' postindustrial workplace, constituted by 'flexible' and insecure labour conditions.[76] Within the home, they are also shown to struggle with their sense of status and belonging, particularly in relation to their female partners who are often the household breadwinners.

Like many of the female characters that appear in Galloway and Michael's stories, thoughts of suicide form a disconcertingly familiar subtext to many of Kelman's male interior monologues located in the home. Indeed, the short stories that are set within the domestic space of council flats or schemes are strikingly more bleak in tone than those that take place in the public (and masculine) settings of betting shops, pubs and snooker halls. The unemployed men in these stories anxiously – and, at times, reluctantly – undertake the unpaid domestic work of cooking, cleaning, child care and decorating. Thus the domestic interior in these stories is a site of particular ambivalence; while it shelters these men who are often shown to be vulnerably exposed in the outside world (Kelman's male characters are often car-less and even coat-less in an inhospitable urban environment), the home also serves as a disturbing reminder of their unemployed status and, in a wider sense, a loss of identity.

In 'Forgetting to Mention Allende' (1987), an unemployed father looks after his young toddler daughter at home while his wife is at work as a supermarket cashier. The short story is filled with the minutiae and rhythms of Tommy's necessarily domestic life: overheating the milk, worries about the noise from the flat next door interfering with the nap, getting his toddler to nursery on time, clearing away the breakfast things. But at the gates of the nursery, Tommy is palpably relieved as he briefly has the opportunity to talk with another man, a grandfather who is also minding the children: 'I was telling my lassie, makes a change to see a

---

[76] See, for example, Sara Willott and Christine Griffin, '"Wham Bam, am I a Man?": Unemployed Men Talk About Masculinities', *Feminism & Psychology* 7:1 (1997), 107–28.

friendly face. All these women and that eh!'[77] Such gendered ambivalence towards home also characterises Ronnie in 'Greyhound for Breakfast' (1987), who wanders aimlessly around the neighbourhood with his newly purchased racer dog. The animal displays a vitality that the owner seems to sorely lack: 'Sleek. That way it gave a genuine impression of energy, real energy – power and strength, and speed of course.'[78] Crossing women with toddlers and pushchairs in the park, Ronnie rambles on, taking refuge in conversations with other men, delaying the return home and the anticipation of his wife's disapproval of his recent purchase:

> He just wasnt ready to go home yet, not yet, not quite; . . . He still needed to think things out. Where to keep the dog for instance. The boy's room Could he keep it there? Would Babs accept it? Would she fuck. She would just fucking, she would just laugh at him.[79]

As he approaches a derelict pier – a veritable path to nowhere – with his incongruous racer dog, Ronnie's overwhelming sense of desolation and shame prevent him from being able to go home. For home is precisely the place in which he is confronted by an internalised sense of inadequacy and lack of belonging:

> It was because he felt like a, well, because he felt like he'd fucking let them down, he'd let them down, it was because he felt like he'd let them all down, the whole lot, the lassies and Babs and the boy.[80]

Throughout Kelman's stories, council housing is depicted as little more than basic, physical shelter – a frugal form of containment for unemployed men which ill-equips them for even the possibility of social and economic reintegration in the public sphere. This darkly ironic portrayal of social housing as social handicap is again depicted to devastating effect in Kelman's masterpiece of the short story genre, 'by the burn' (1991). Playing on the material and figurative connotations of the waste ground surrounding the tenement block (that the council has failed to pave over), the male protagonist, on his way to a crucial job interview, finds himself literally anchored down by the physical environment:

> Fucking boggin mud man a swamp, an actual swamp, it was fucking a joke. He pulled his foot clear but the boot was still lodged there like it was quicksand and it was going to get sucked off and vanish down into it forever.[81]

---

[77] James Kelman, 'Forgetting to Mention Allende', in *Busted Scotch* (New York: W. W. Norton & Company, 1997), p. 134.
[78] Kelman, 'Greyhound for Breakfast', in *Busted Scotch*, p. 160.
[79] Kelman, 'Greyhound for Breakfast', p. 165.   [80] Kelman, 'Greyhound for Breakfast', p. 172.
[81] Kelman, 'by the burn', in *Busted Scotch*, p. 258.

The ordeal leads him to consider turning back to the flat ('He felt like going away home again, back to the fire, cup of tea and put the feet up'), but the return home in this case would be a form of self-disempowerment.[82] Literally stuck in the mud, unable to steer a clear course towards the job interview, he reflects:

> He needed a car. Every cunt needed a car. That was what happened when you stayed out in the schemes, it was fine till you wanted to go someplace, once you did you were in fucking trouble.[83]

Likewise, in 'A Walk in the Park' (1991), another short story in which individuals are ostensibly forced outdoors because of where they live, a couple pursue a necessarily public form of courtship. As they amble around, the male protagonist displays proficiency at reading the spatial semiotics of class and private life:

> They crossed the road into the park, past the line of red sandstone villas – Victorian, four bedrooms maybe plus lounge, dining room, kitchen and bathroom; with probably an extension built out the back garden – maybe even with the attic kitted out into a wee annex bedroom and play area for the kids. . . . One of his wife's aunties lived in a big house. Not a great big house but big enough, big enough to get a bit of privacy. Wee rooms to go and sit in, empty rooms, ones that had fireplaces and standard lamps, you could sit there and read a book, on your own, really good; the sort of place you dreamed about owning, plenty room, not tripping over one another; . . . plus the privacy, that much space you could go away and be by yourself, you could be alone, you could just sit and think, work things out.[84]

The interior monologues of Kelman's protagonists serve as an attempt to carve out room for themselves in language as a compensation for their lack of personal space in run-down housing blocks. These streams of consciousness, traditionally associated with the expression of 'pure' interiority, become the place in which the characters find the means to 'be alone . . . just sit and think, work things out'. Like the anxious, harried protagonists of James Joyce's *Ulysses*, who eke out an existence in the mean spaces of the

---

[82] Kelman, 'by the burn', p. 259.

[83] Kelman, 'by the burn', p. 260. In her study on the literature of the urban peripheries, Mary M. McGlynn draws attention to the fact that many of the protagonists in the texts she examines – including Kelman's novels – are unable to drive. She contends that while this constitutes a practical problem for the characters, it more broadly suggests their 'literal lack of control of modernity's technology and a powerlessness to navigate through the national space'; *Narratives of Class in New Irish and Scottish Literature: From Joyce to Kelman, Doyle, Galloway, and McNamee* (Basingstoke: Palgrave Macmillan, 2008), pp. 1–2.

[84] Kelman, 'A Walk in the Park', in *Busted Scotch*, pp. 190–91.

city, many of the characters of Kelman's short stories find a rather spartan refuge in language and inner rumination. The interior monologue thus simultaneously articulates subjectivity, but also projects the sense in which these speakers are cut off – barred in various ways – from wider social engagement and public lives.

iv Making space I: High-rises and agency in Andrea Arnold's *Fish Tank*

In the previous section, I addressed the ways in which literary texts provide influential representations of the experience of deep isolation felt by individuals living in social housing environments. There is a danger, however, that taken together, these works serve only to replicate in cultural form the idea of council housing settings as a type of world apart. Yet like all forms of residence, social housing is a historical space which is always undergoing change. In fact, the bleak landscape of council housing, which is dominant in literature and film of the 1980s, has to some extent been supplemented by cultural representations that explore the originality and creative potential of these residential environments; examples include Simon Terrell's photographic Balfron Project (2010), Clio Barnard's experimental documentary of Bradford's Buttershaw estate as a radical stage set in *The Arbor* (2011), and the depiction in the sci-fi comedy film *Attack the Block* (2011) of a London council estate as an opportune setting for an alien invasion.

It is with this shift in mind that I turn now to a contemporary film and a novel: Andrea Arnold's *Fish Tank* (2009) and Monica Ali's novel *Brick Lane* (2003). Through extended close readings of these works, I will argue that both texts demonstrate a concern with issues of gender and class while making innovative use of the aesthetic and narrative possibilities afforded by the space of the council estate. In this way, the texts are important additions that complicate a cultural repertoire that risks portraying mass housing environments as merely psychic and narrative dead ends. Against an interpretative model that sees space as having a determining power over the subject, these recent texts deal with the possibility of representing complex versions of selfhood and agency in mass housing environments; significantly, both works present female protagonists using the space in which they reside in ways which are strategic, creative and potentially liberating.

Fish Tank, written and directed by the British filmmaker Arnold, was filmed on the now demolished Mardyke Estate on the London–Essex borders and to a certain extent shares Hanley's bleak view of the stultifying and abusive effects of this environment on a vulnerable young woman (in this case, fifteen-year-old Mia). But the depiction of this modern day 'problem estate' – originally built for workers at the Ford Dagenham plant in the 1960s – is notably different in its tone and presentation from the work of other female writers, such as Galloway, Michael and indeed Hanley herself. This is perhaps due to the use of the visual medium, for while the housing estate has often been deemed unaesthetic – synonymous in effect with towering, grey buildings – the visual impact of high-rise flats has been strikingly rendered in film. In fact, housing estates have often served as arresting and dramatic backdrops in British cinema – from Stanley Kubrick's *A Clockwork Orange* (1971) filmed on the Thamesmead South Housing Estate, to Anthony Minghella's *Breaking and Entering* (2006) which highlighted the architectural modernist form of the North London Alexandra Road estate.

Arnold had already demonstrated in her cinematic debut *Red Road* (2006) that high-rise blocks could present a suggestive backdrop and *mise-en-scène* to potent and devastating psychological effect. But in *Fish Tank*, she turns away from the lurid and almost threatening vision of *Red Road*'s tower blocks to portray a different kind of space. For the estate in *Fish Tank* is shown to be replete with stimuli for its protagonist Mia, from the glittering night-time views from the upper-floor windows, to the cacophonous sounds of music and voices which provide an aural setting for this coming-of-age story based around urban music and street dance.[85] Indeed, the Mardyke estate is often captured in the film against starkly contrasting backdrops of blue skies, thunderstorms and brilliant sunsets. Through Arnold's lens, it becomes a vibrant setting for drama, a place where the young female protagonist is given a stage for movement, forms of action and a degree of change. If interiority is generally thought of as portraying a quiet stillness – exemplified by the motif in European painting since the seventeenth century of a woman reading, working or gazing out of the window – Mia by contrast is often situated against a background of intensive noise, from the onrush of the A13 traffic surrounding the estate, to the clatter of voices rebounding through the tower block's deck-access walkways. The estate may be poor and rowdy then, but it is

---

[85] While the noise issue, endemic to concrete structures and exacerbated by the architectural layout of decked walkways and internal corridors, emerged as a distinctive problem in high-rise housing, Taunton, for example, astutely notes the way in which films have made creative use of the 'sonic qualities' of apartment blocks for marked aesthetic and storytelling effect (*Fictions of the City*, pp. 44–45).

Figure 5   – Katie Jarvis as Mia in *Fish Tank* (Artificial Eye, 2009). Photo credit Limelight
Communication/RGA.

never merely a scene of bland conformity and homogeneity. For Arnold
directs sequences in what seems like a nostalgic vision of the height of
summer, offsetting the tower blocks against a blue sky, and always highlighting the shared – although not necessarily communal – spaces of mass
housing.[86]

Turning away from the voyeuristic, stalker-like gaze which characterised
Red Road (literalised through the frames in which the blocks are surveilled
through the filter of CCTV security cameras), Arnold presents the events
in *Fish Tank* from the viewpoint of her teenage protagonist. The hand-
held camera often paces closely behind and alongside her, almost as an ally,
presenting an intimate portrayal of the subjectivity of someone who is
socially marginalised in many ways. Yet there is a skilful avoidance of too
much narrative exposition, as the viewer follows Mia's stride and witnesses
extended scenes containing little dialogue. In part, this technique stays true
to this reluctant heroine's resistance to forms of exposure or self-revelation;
body language and movement are her dominant means of expression and
self-defence.[87] The viewer shares in Mia's aural soundscape: the sound of
her amplified breath opens the film and music constitutes a crucial element
throughout. Mia's self-taught routines are themselves based around sweeping movements that seem to reach out for, and lay claim to, space. Most

[86] Arnold's engagingly positive view of the film's Essex location is expressed in the press book: 'I drove
out from east London along the A13 and loved it straight away. The madness of the A13, the steaming
factories and the open spaces, the wilderness, the empty car parks where Ford used to be. I love too
this part of the Thames, where it widens out to meet the sea. It's where Elizabeth spoke to the troops
before they went out to fight the Spanish. It just all felt good'; Artificial Eye Film Company, *Fish
Tank* press book, www.artificial-eye.com/database/cinema/fishtank/pdf/pressbook.pdf.
[87] Anne Power interprets forms of 'strident behaviour' among young people on run-down estates as an
'attempt at asserting independence in a situation of dependence where there was little prospect of
real independence and autonomy'; *Estates on the Edge*, p. 298.

importantly, however, Mia dances, for the most part, alone and for herself. In a manner that echoes Wanda's fantasy of being the object of a video camera's gaze in Michael's *Under a Thin Moon*, Mia records herself on a borrowed camcorder dancing. Her decision is both functional (she is compiling her own audition tape) but also indicates an important assumption of agency. Effectively disrupting the gender binary of the gaze, she performs a masculine type of street dance for what is effectively a self-reflective female gaze (this disruption is later rendered explicit when she refuses to 'perform' – or take her clothes off – at what turns out to be an audition for a strip club). The viewer is thus encouraged to see the world of the estate through Mia's eyes, and when the camera draws back to frame this amateur dancer's silhouette backlit against one of the wide high-rise windows, the effect is one of intimacy with, rather than distance or estrangement from, this marked figure of social exclusion.

Fish Tank takes the viewer into the interior of Mia's home, showing how domestic space is framed and shaped by the external landscape of the estate and foregrounding the dynamics of family life which a writer like Hanley, by contrast, keeps carefully held back from the central narrative. The flat housing the single mother, Mia and her sister is bright, airy and decorated in a conventionally feminine style; seashells hang from the door, and the soft furnishings are in pinks and purples. That is not to say that *Fish Tank*'s exposition of interiority offers any comforting image of the home as a refuge of hermetic security. In fact, Mia's home is characterised by an all-too-open threshold which renders her and her sister vulnerable on several levels. This is made especially clear through the film's treatment of the young girls' sexuality in that both are shown, in this respect, to be simultaneously naïve and over exposed. Ironically, in what appears as a bounded, isolated landscape, a lack of boundaries is portrayed ambivalently throughout the film, and the important point is made that the close proximity of bodies does not equal, and indeed might prevent, the formation of safe, intimate bonds between people.

Through its open deck-access walkways, where fights occur and neighbours shout abuse, the *Fish Tank* estate reinforces Mia's lack of personal security and privacy, and she is subjected on several occasions to violent attacks by groups of girls as well as men. Her resistance to the environment takes the form of pacing the estate, finding refuge in the neighbouring wasteland, and sitting, drinking, or dancing in a disused apartment in the high-rise block. The latter replicates a symbolic moment in many coming-of-age narratives, as the abandoned flat provides her with a room of her own, indeed a room with a view, whose sweeping horizons symbolise yearning and longing for escape. Thus in a suggestive reversal of expectations, it turns out that the room in which Mia is most 'free' or at ease has the box-like dimensions of a fish tank (replicating in miniature the block structure of the tower block itself). The sound of underwater bubbles that accompany her breathing as she dances in this setting confirms the use of visual and aural motifs of water and fluidity as ciphers of self-expression and escape that occur throughout the film.

Like the estate itself, Mia's life is simultaneously bounded and precariously open and is defined by a lack of guardianship – either in the form of parental care or protection by the state (in one scene, she makes a swift exit away from a social worker who visits the home). The blurring of boundaries between proximity, intimacy and intrusion are highlighted by Mia's relationship with an attractive outsider who becomes an integral part of her development and betrayal. Thus her mother's charismatic boyfriend Connor is quickly established within the household by his charm, self-ease and ready cash handouts for the two young girls. Connor initially appears to be a stabilising and protective figure in the eyes of all three women. Indeed, he works as a security guard at a hardware store and has cause to complain about Mia's habit of helping herself to his 'stuff' ('Mia' literally means 'mine'), a proclivity that unwittingly highlights her own lack of – and thus lack of respect for – interpersonal boundaries. This theme of unregulated borders is compounded and takes on criminal implications when Connor moves from the role of mentor and benevolent father-substitute to having sex with Mia (who is legally a minor).

There is a real ambivalence in the fact that the donor figure in Mia's quest to discover herself, and to find her own place, is Connor, whose role is partly also that of a spatial catalyst offering Mia a new view of the world beyond the island estate. For among the chief attractions this outsider figure has to offer is his car and the mobility that it promises (this is particularly interesting to Mia who is repeatedly seen piggy backing on others). Mia's ability to travel is limited by her socio economic status and her gender, a point underscored by Massey's assertion that 'the limitation of women's mobility, in terms both of identity and space, has been in some cultural contexts a crucial means of subordination'.[88] Thus in a memorable sequence, Connor takes the family out in the car for a drive, and the reactions of the girls and the mother make it clear that leaving the estate is in itself a rare event. The 'day trip' scenes in *Fish Tank* – reminiscent of the Bolton Abbey sequence in David Storey's British New Wave film *This*

[88] Massey, *Space*, p. 179.

Sporting Life (1963) – are significant for the way in which they capture the banality of the outing (a drive along a motorway lined with pylons; a drink in a pub car park) with moments of transcendent delight as Connor catches a fish bare-handed from a river in the Essex countryside.[89]

Spatial dislocation is also key to the climactic sequence in which Mia decides to track Connor down (after he bids a hasty retreat following their illicit sexual encounter) and finds her way to his home on foot. There is a telling quality to the way in which the dark secret that Connor is hiding from those around him is presented as an almost visual anticlimax as she finds herself outside his home: a neat semi-detached house on a cul-de-sac in a private newly built estate. Mia walks around its blank walls before climbing over the alley door and breaking in through a window. It is notable that whereas Connor could walk straight into her flat and family life, Mia has to exert physical effort in order to gain illicit entrance to his private space. The representation of Mia as a housebreaker makes clear that, in social terms, she is an interloper within this environment of private domesticity, and the only way she can gain access to the suburban interior is through forced entry.[90] Once inside, however, as it slowly becomes clear that Connor's 'secret life' is paradoxically that of suburban husband and father, Mia urinates on the living room floor in an act that signifies the desecration of the normative family interior and one which simultaneously reveals her child-likeness, her capacity for antisocial behaviour, and a desire to mark her territory through the body.

The film concludes with an image of Mia driving away from the estate with her traveller friend Billy, who has managed to fix a car together from scrap yard parts. This might be interpreted in terms of the narrative resolution posited in Hanley's autobiographical story, in which case leaving the estate would be the only possible resolution for the young female adolescent. But Mia's progression is portrayed not as a form of social mobility, but simply as an act of geographical movement. In her departure, Mia rejects a range of social forms – the family unit, the neighbourhood and welfare support – by seizing just the 'mobility' part of the upward mobility story. Without any sense that she is on the rise, Mia's rejection of

[89] For an analysis of the cinematic trope whereby urban protagonists 'escape' for the day into a romanticised rural landscape in social realist films of the 1960s, see Andrew Higson's 'Space, Place, Spectacle: Landscape and Townscape in the "Kitchen Sink" Film', in Andrew Higson (ed.), *Dissolving Views: Key Writings on British Cinema* (London: Cassell, 1996), pp. 145–47.

[90] The act of 'breaking and entering', signifying the young protagonist's forced entry into spaces from which they are excluded, also provides a notable motif in Pat Barker's novel *Union Street* (1982) and Anthony Minghella's film *Breaking and Entering* (2007).

the spatial parameters of the estate is the only defiance she has left to offer. The ambiguity of the ending is emphasised by her younger sister's departing words – 'Say hello to the world for me!' – a cry that reinforces the sense that life for Mia can only begin with a giant leap over the clear but constraining walls of the fish tank, after which she simply disappears from view.

v   Making space II: The woman in the tower block in Monica Ali's *Brick Lane*

In Hanley's *Estates* and Arnold's *Fish Tank*, the female coming-of-age story is based on the protagonist's physical departure from the oppressive environment of the mass housing estate. The discovery of a sense of vocation or escape is shown to be possible only by effecting a breach from an environment that inhibits self-development. As I will show, Monica Ali's bestselling novel *Brick Lane* (2003) also posits the idea that the lived environment of social housing negatively affects female agency and autonomy. However, Ali's novel also introduces a protagonist who makes the apparently impersonal environment of the housing estate 'her own' and uses it to achieve that elusive quality of the twenty-first century: a place in the world.

Ali's quasi-realist fairy tale follows the story of a young immigrant, Nazneen, who arrives from rural Bangladesh to the fictional Dogwood estate in Tower Hamlets in the mid-1980s after an arranged marriage, through to her experiences (including a pivotal love affair) on the same housing estate sixteen years later. Eschewing social realism for the narrative shape of the nineteenth-century *Bildungsroman*, the text nonetheless reveals the fraught living conditions of the Bangladeshi community that settled in Tower Hamlets in the 1970s (mainly from the Sylhet region of north eastern Bangladesh). Unlike Indian and Pakistani immigrants, many of whom entered into home ownership, the Bangladeshi community mainly settled into the less desirable, but more widely available, social housing in East London.[91] Ali's novel depicts this landscape as stunted by social neglect, racial tension and inner-city isolation: 'every type of cheap hope for cheap housing lived side by side in a monument to false economy. The low-rises crouched like wounded monsters along concrete banks. . . .

---

[91] Hamnett, *Unequal City*, pp. 121–23. See also Stuart Cameron and Andrew Field's analysis of 'exclusion *through* housing' experienced by particular sectors of the Bangladeshi community in Britain; 'Community, Ethnicity and Neighbourhood', *Housing Studies* 15:6 (2000), 827–43 (829).

A desolate building, gouged-out eyes in place of windows, announced "Tenants' Association: Hall for Hire".[92]

As in many of the texts addressed above, the portrayal of this concrete residential landscape constantly juxtaposes its architectural brutality with the vulnerability of the people it shelters. From her window post, Nazneen views the flats as 'piles of people loaded one on top of the other, a vast dump of people rotting away under a mean strip of sky, too small to reflect all those souls'.[93] The material of these tenement buildings – the dull red brick of the novel's title – serves to emphasise the quality of an environment in which the inhabitants are unable to see themselves 'reflected' in the surrounding architecture. 'What can you tell to a pile of bricks?' Nazneen muses, as she looks out on the Dogwood estate.[94] Yet one of the most effective features in *Brick Lane* pertains to the way in which life does seep out from under the brickwork – for example, in Ali's rendering in sensory detail the practices of a flexible, low-wage economy, where the smell of food cooking is pervasive throughout the estate day and night to fit the domestic rhythms of shift work. In this way, the solid, implacable council blocks perform a striking contrast with the estate's resident population who are immersed in shifting modes of labour and global movement.

If mass housing estates have been associated with forms of social realism (particularly in film), it is Ali's renovation of nineteenth-century novelistic structures that becomes central to her representation of female self-development. The immigrant Bangladeshi experience is thus rehoused, as it were, in the European novel of education, with its capacity to develop in textured and leisured detail the narrative quest for knowledge, self-awareness and embourgeoisement.[95] Strikingly, Ali's novel uses the unassuming interior of the council flat as a space for the exploration of Nazneen's sense of self, and this is the location within which the formative action takes place (a setting which, for the most part, relegates the city to the role of backdrop). The narrative style, comprised of extended, detailed passages and epistolary sections, complements this story of deep interiority and private spaces. Thus in contrast to the stark, confessional but often dead-ended narrative tones of *Under a Thin Moon* and *The Trick Is to Keep Breathing*, Ali uses an engaging mode of free indirect discourse which

---

[92] Monica Ali, *Brick Lane* (New York: Scribner, 2003), pp. 393–94.   [93] Ali, *Brick Lane*, p. 303.
[94] Ali, *Brick Lane*, p. 66.
[95] For a discussion of this novel as a postcolonial *Bildungsroman*, see Alistair Cormack, 'Migration and the Politics of Narrative Form: Realism and the Postcolonial Subject in *Brick Lane*', *Contemporary Literature* 47:4 (2006), 695–721.

traces the contours of Nazneen's world while progressively rendering her consciousness through a consistent use of narrative point of view and focalisation.

Indeed, focalisation is an apt term to represent the way in which the reader follows the visual compass of Nazneen, who is framed from the start of the story as a woman who watches. Nazneen is thus often figured within the conventions of what Isobel Armstrong has called prose fiction's 'over-determined "window moment"' – whereby the window serves to demarcate boundaries of self and the outside world.[96] But while the iconography of the woman gazing out of the window has functioned as an scene of longing, whereby the exterior landscape or view is posited as a thing of desire, this image in *Brick Lane* marks the female protagonist's sense of estrangement. For Nazneen, the estate appears like a remote island and the tower block her vista upon this alien world. This is, of course, a contemporary rendering of a familiar mythic and fairy-tale setting, but the tower is now a run-down housing block in Tower Hamlets and the princess is a migrant homeworker stitching together sequined tops.

The domestic seclusion that Ali portrays in the early part of the novel reinforces the idea, as Mary M. McGlynn notes, that 'housing estates are part of the maintenance of the division of space into public and private spheres that has, within [the twentieth century], been pivotal in containing women within the home'.[97] This segregation is further reinforced by ethnic, class and religious factors, specifically Nazneen's confinement within domestic space in accordance with the norms of Islamic purdah.[98] In addition, the architectural setting of the home on the estate serves as another obstacle to Nazneen's communication either with people or the city itself. For the estate is built in such a way as to make the blocks visible

---

[96] Isobel Armstrong, *Victorian Glassworlds: Glass Culture and the Imagination, 1830–1880* (Oxford: Oxford University Press, 2008), p. 124. Tracing the motif of the open window in art, Sabine Rewald examines how in Romantic painting, the 'juxtaposition of the close familiarity of a room and the uncertain, often idealized vision of what lies beyond was immediately recognized as a metaphor for unfulfilled longing'; *Rooms with a View: The Open Window in the 19th Century* (New York: Metropolitan Museum of Art, 2011), p. 3. In Victorian art and literature, however, the trope of the 'woman at the window' more unambiguously tends to serve as a representation of women's confinement within domestic space.

[97] McGlynn, *Narratives of Class*, pp. 148–49.

[98] In her comparative study of female textile workers, Naila Kabeer notes that 'purdah literally means "veil" or "curtain"', and she emphasises how religion, culture and the postindustrial outsourcing of low-waged labour to the home are central to an understanding of London Bangladeshi seamstresses in the late twentieth century; *The Power to Choose: Bangladeshi Women and Labour Market Decisions in London and Dhaka* (London: Verso, 2000), p. 34. Carried out within domestic space, Kabeer adds that 'it was the "veiled" character of homework which explained its appeal to some of the homeworkers and their families' (p. 285).

but inaccessible to each other, with the effect that the people Nazneen can see, such as her tattooed neighbour, are in fact the ones she is least likely to encounter physically. In this regard, as Richard Sennett suggests, the paradox of high-density buildings and the dilemma of 'dead public space' is that public visibility may encourage inhabitants to maintain their own privacy more ruthlessly. 'Human beings need to have some distance from intimate observation by others in order to feel sociable', he argues. 'Increase intimate contact and you decrease sociability'.[99] In fact, it is precisely because the flats in *Brick Lane* are visible to each other that the interiors are carefully guarded from view: 'Most of the flats, which enclosed three sides of a square, had net curtains, and the life behind was all shapes and shadows.'[100]

Nazneen's relationship to her interior space is meticulously rendered in the novel in a manner which signifies her own development towards agency and autonomy. Early on, she is described as a figure who surveys not only outwards, as the 'woman at the window', but one who also directs her scrutinising gaze inwards towards the unfamiliar interior of her new home. As a recently arrived immigrant bride, the domestic interior confronts her as an alien space (another example of an unfamiliar terrain that requires a form of translation). Here, Nazneen describes the décor of the living room in memorable detail:

> There were three rugs: red and orange, green and purple, brown and blue. The carpet was yellow with a green leaf design. One hundred percent nylon and, Chanu said, very hard-wearing. The sofa and chairs were the color of dried cow dung, which was a practical color. They had little sheaths of plastic on the headrests to protect them from Chanu's hair oil. There was a lot of furniture, more than Nazneen had seen in one room before. Even if you took all the furniture in the compound, from every auntie and uncle's ghar, it would not match up to this one room. There was a low table with a glass top and orange plastic legs, three little wooden tables that stacked together, the big table they used for the evening meal, a bookcase, a corner cupboard, a rack for newspapers, a trolley filled with files and folders, the sofa and armchairs, two footstools, six dining chairs, and a showcase. The walls were papered in yellow with brown squares and circles lining neatly up and down. . . . There were plates on the wall, attached by hooks and wires, which were not for eating from but only for display. Some were rimmed in gold paint. 'Gold leaf,' Chanu called it. His certificates were framed and mixed with the plates. She had everything here. All these beautiful things.[101]

[99] Richard Sennett, *The Fall of Public Man* (London: Penguin, 2002), p. 15.
[100] Ali, *Brick Lane*, p. 6.   [101] Ali, *Brick Lane*, p. 9.

Chanu's crammed room bears some of the features of what Michael McMillan identifies as a distinctive 'front room' aesthetic typical of many postwar migrant households in Britain.[102] Focusing on first-generation West Indian front rooms in particular, McMillan analyses this kind of interior as one which expressed social mobility, aspiration, status and respectability: 'Its maintenance and social function followed codes of *good grooming* and conduct that had their roots in the colonial fusion of religion, hygiene and the Protestant Work Ethic'.[103] In *Brick Lane*, this combination of aspiration and no-nonsense practicality is evident in Chanu's 'gold leaf' rimmed plates and antimacassars. Chanu's stockpiled parlour articulates his strong sense of class distinction, specifically his desire to differentiate himself from the stereotype of the overcrowded Bangladeshi family household ('It's a Tower Hamlets official statistic: three point five Bangladeshis to one room', he reminds Nazneen).[104] But as the novel progresses, Chanu's accumulation of objects comes to resemble less a well-ordered parlour than a junk room. The growing heap of useless furniture becomes a visual manifestation of Chanu's life story of postponement and unrealised ambition. In an ironic echo of Robinson Crusoe, Chanu attempts to fortify himself against the outside world – its racism, rejection and poor rewards – by replenishing and enumerating his possessions. But as Nazneen observes, the more he crams into the room, the less he seems able to orient himself; he possesses *things* but still lacks any sense of rootedness or belonging. His confident, modern daughters – who have a more canny understanding of contemporary markers of status – will later berate him for having missed the chance of buying the council flat outright.

If the high-density estate seems an incongruous setting for the kind of traditional romance tale that *Brick Lane* undoubtedly is in parts, Ali uses it to play precisely on the contrast between the homogeneity of the housing on the one hand and the intimate exposition of the protagonist Nazneen on the other. Thus Nazneen, the 'invisible' immigrant woman, has to assert herself over the course of the novel against a spatial setting that reinforces conformity and neglect. For in a manner that echoes Parker's

---

[102] Michael McMillan, 'The "West Indian" Front Room: Migrant Aesthetics in the Home', in Aynsley and Grant (eds.), *Imagined Interiors*, pp. 256–57.

[103] McMillan, 'Front Room', pp. 256–57. A similar description of a council flat 'migrant front room' is given in Andrea Levy's *Every Light in the House Burnin'* (London: Review, 1995): 'Our front room was packed with furniture. Every bit of wall space had something pressed against it. There was a green three-piece suite with a long settee that could double up as a bed should we have any guests—which we never did. A bookcase with volumes of the *Encyclopaedia Britannica* placed untouched, practically where the extremely convincing salesman had left them' (p. 30).

[104] Ali, *Brick Lane*, p. 34.

Providence tenants, she notes how the doors of the individual apartments along her corridors are 'all the same. Peeling red paint showing splinters of pale wood, a rectangular panel of glass with wire mesh suspended inside, gold-rimmed key-holes, stern black knockers'.[105] Such alienation is compounded by the sense of invisibility and erasure that the domestic interior creates: 'She looked and she saw that she was trapped inside this body, inside this room, inside this flat, inside this concrete slab of entombed humanity. They had nothing to do with her.'[106] In the cluttered and over-stuffed parody of a bourgeois interior created by her quixotic husband Chanu, she is merely part of someone else's backdrop, one of the key objects constituting the display of home: 'Life made its pattern around and beneath and through her.'[107]

In one of several false trails that Ali lays in the text, *Brick Lane* appears at first to suggest that it will be through her heroine's transgression of public and private boundaries – specifically through Nazneen's explorations of the cityscape – that she might find some form of autonomy or freedom. But among the City's skyscrapers or 'white stone Palaces' that represent financial and symbolic capital, Nazneen finds herself, in Hall's phrase, 'in but not of the city'.[108] Despite the estate's inner-city setting, Nazneen is prevented from entering the commercial centre by the traffic and by her own sense of being marked out by her gender, ethnicity and appearance. So while Nazneen gradually gains more confidence in her interactions in public space, Ali interestingly chooses to make the council flat interior the crucial site for the heroine's transformation and independence.

This narrative shift is produced in part by the novel's expanded view of the domestic interior as a social space of exchange and dynamic networks. Thus the council flat in this novel is revealed as a product of historical and contemporary conditions, and the site of political and social relationships that extend beyond the individual family. The housing blocks, in other words, have a history and are part of the contemporary social fabric, specifically in relation to the extended networks of the Bangladeshi community. In this way, *Brick Lane* shows the estate to be not just a boxed world of alienated individuals but a space in which a different – or translated – version of community exists in quotidian forms. Through the sounds of running taps and shifting furniture that constantly interrupt the not-so-hermetic space of the apartment, Nazneen begins to understand the residential environment as a social sphere of 'unknown intimates':

---

[105] Ali, *Brick Lane*, p. 37.   [106] Ali, *Brick Lane*, p. 56.   [107] Ali, *Brick Lane*, p. 26.
[108] Hall, *Cities of Tomorrow*, p. 425.

All day and into the evening she was aware of the life around, like a dim light left on in the corner of the room. They used to disturb her, these activities, sealed and boxed and unnerving. When she had come she had learned first about loneliness, then about privacy, and finally she learned a new kind of community.[109]

Thus the outwardly grim blocks in *Brick Lane* serve as the basis for a narrative not simply of individual aspiration but of social forms, in a way that accords with Sharon Marcus' delineation of the 'trajectory of the apartment-house narrative, which transforms facades, walls, and doors from barriers that keep secrets into transmitters of sounds and stories'.[110] In this way, the novel optimistically hints at the promise of change as the lives of the newer inhabitants of London take innovative forms and configurations. This sense of metamorphosis is appropriately encapsulated by a passage describing graffiti sprayed onto one of the walls of the estate, which, seen through Nazneen's eyes, 'had kaleidoscoped to a dense pattern of silver and green and peacock blue, wounded here and there with vermilion, the color of mehindi on a bride's feet'.[111]

Crucially, Ali transforms Nazneen's domestic interior from an impersonal place of exile into a site for paid labour. Nazneen's piecework, or what Chanu likes to see as the 'old and honorable craft of tailoring', is thus meaningful on a number of levels; it links Nazneen to the fairy tale as well as to the figure of the seamstress in Victorian social reports and fiction, in that the trope of clothing offers the possibility of personal transformation and a degree of social mobility.[112] Likewise, Chanu's reference to 'honourable' work proves ironic since the piecework functions as a narrative device, bringing Karim, the middleman who becomes Nazneen's lover, into the story but equally providing a historical connection to the long-established colonial relations of textile manufacturing stretching from Dhaka to London. Thus when this *Bildungsroman* ends not in marriage but in a sisterly business alliance between Razia and Nazneen (who set up the aptly named 'Fusion Fashions'), *Brick Lane* proposes a double-edged inversion of traditional narratives. Karim really does end up as the 'middleman' since not only is his offer of marriage rejected by Nazneen at the end of the novel, he also functions as a stepping-stone on Nazneen's path towards economic and emotional self-sufficiency and partnership with Razia. Ali's move is thus a bold one, in which economic emancipation

---

[109] Ali, *Brick Lane*, p. 145.   [110] Marcus, *Apartment Stories*, p. 34.   [111] Ali, *Brick Lane*, p. 229.
[112] Ali, *Brick Lane*, p. 168.

and capitalist ownership of the business stand in stark contrast to the anticipated climax of marital dependency.[113]

Moreover, by depicting the council flat as a place of outsourced work, Ali's novel again appears to question the rigidity of the estate boundaries, posited in Hanley's *Estates* and Arnold's *Fish Tank*, and the implication that change and development can only occur through a form of escape. In fact, the depiction of the blocks in *Brick Lane* seem closer to Rogaly and Taylor's interpretation of the space of housing estates as marked by 'lines and divisions – social as well as spatial – [that] are blurred, shifting and profoundly relational'.[114] In their more optimistic view, residents in mass housing gain forms of agency through their 'own spatial practices in sometimes subverting the space and its meaning'.[115] Rogaly and Taylor's work also points to the importance of recognising 'the historic and central role of women in working class households in terms of their part in creating and sustaining social networks . . . in relation to the feminization of the labour market . . . and in the context of challenges to "traditional" working class masculinities'.[116] This is played out in *Brick Lane* as the private space of the flat and the community of women within the estate become crucial resources for the heroine. For apart from anything else, the domestic setting shields Nazneen from the type of overt racism, discrimination and humiliation that Chanu experiences through his various jobs as council worker and cab driver.[117] Thus in what is perhaps the ultimate irony, it is the mostly home-bound Nazneen rather than the socially invisible Chanu, who reaps the rewards of the *Bildungsroman* plot.

Yet while it could be argued that Ali rejects traditional romance structures, she nevertheless uses the novelistic form to spin another type of social fairy tale. For the portrayal of homeworking in the novel, which appears to offer Nazneen not just a degree of financial independence but erotic possibilities too, is perhaps among the most romanticised of the fictions the novel has to offer.[118] Nazneen in the end need not leave the

---

[113] In this way, Ali's novel conforms to the narrative of 'migrant agency' as 'bourgeois individualism', which John Kirk detects in a text such as Meera Syal's *Anita and Me* (London: Harper Perennial 2004); *Twentieth-Century Writing and the British Working Class* (Cardiff: University of Wales Press, 2003), p. 182.

[114] Rogaly and Taylor, *Moving Histories*, p. 6.   [115] Rogaly and Taylor, *Moving Histories*, p. 59.

[116] Rogaly and Taylor, *Moving Histories*, p. 78.

[117] For a discussion of race in constructions of the 'public' and 'private', see Gillian Rose, *Feminism and Geography: The Limits of Geographical Knowledge* (Minneapolis: University of Minnesota Press, 1993), pp. 125–27.

[118] For an analysis of structures of capitalism, patriarchy and homework, see Massey, 'A Woman's Place?', in *Space*, pp. 191–211.

housing estate in order to achieve her 'place in the world', but as she expands from outsourced home labour into small entrepreneurship with Razia, she completes a move from the black economy to entry into the capitalist economy. She thus becomes a member of the entrepreneurial manufacturing class, who is also able to redraw for herself a version of home and hearth backed by self-belief and sorority. In this sense, then, the book remains an old-fashioned fairy tale at heart, one in which the home-based worker of Mayhew's accounts has been transformed into a self-sufficient single mother and owner of the means of production.

Conclusion: Red Road revisited

The flattening of Glasgow's Red Road high-rise blocks with 275 kilos of explosives was presented at the start of this chapter as a visual metaphor for the perceived failure and fate of British council housing over the past century. But these controlled explosions of domestic residences also present another important element in the story of council housing. For media reports which chronicled the demolitions also made reference to the fact that there were many among the crowds who had gathered to watch as former residents; these people felt a deep nostalgia for the buildings that had functioned as home, community and neighbourhood over several decades. Indeed, tenants of the media-reviled blocks have increasingly begun to contribute their own 'folk memories' of particular estates, thereby adding a significant dimension to the story of social housing. Likewise, novels such as Alison Irvine's *This Road Is Red* (2012) and community projects such as the multimedia exhibition *Red Road: Past, Present, Future*, and the associated website containing residents' histories and photographs, are examples of a wider turn towards a more progressive reassessment of the histories – or, in what is a telling anthropomorphic term, the 'biographies' – of housing estates.[119] Irvine's novel, based on oral interviews conducted with previous inhabitants of the flats which she rendered into fictional form, interweaves personal stories under the framework of a collective structure – much like the Red Road blocks themselves. The narrative tone throughout the novel is poetic and sensitive to the nuances of the space it describes, highlighting many of the positive aspects of decades of life at Red Road and expressive of a strong and complex sense of community. The blocks are effectively humanised through Irvine's narrative as the impassive concrete towers become the locus for human

---

[119] The website can be found at www.redroadflats.org.uk.

stories of birth, death, survival and new beginnings. The imbrication of physical bodies and architecture in this novel is a compelling motif, as it is in so much fictional and non-fictional writing on housing.

Beginning with a description of the erection in 1964 of steel frames that would become the skeleton for the Red Road complex, Irvine adopts the masculine imagery and 'pioneer' narrative style characteristic of the housing documentaries of the 1930s:

> The man sees Arran on the clearest day yet. Its blue-grey bulk at the far side of the sky. The Clyde and the shipyards. Grit and glitter. It's shipyard steel they're building with. Sand and gold on the Campsie Fells. The men stop work to look and take bunnets off and wipe foreheads. . . . Red Road. Houses for thousands.[120]

Yet even so, *This Road Is Red* articulates an ambivalent stance towards the estate it surveys. The towers are portrayed as imposing, bulky forms, 'blank and massive', which loom over the heads of the protagonists.[121] They are a form of protective shelter for the residents (swaying, but not falling, during the Hurricane Low Q storm of 1968) and yet always tinged with incipient threat: asbestos lines the ceilings and walls, and falling objects – as well as the bodies of 'jumpers' – plunge intermittently from the buildings over the course of the narrative.

Crucially, however, the novel shows how the towers have witnessed the effects of globalisation and change. From their construction in the mid-1960s to their successive demolition, the Red Road Flats have housed the lives of a population in flux – from Glaswegian slum evacuees, to children born and raised within the walls, to those seeking refuge from war-torn countries. Indeed, some of the most moving sections of *This Road Is Red* are those that trace the varied trajectories of individual asylum seekers who take shelter in the empty flats, arriving with nothing to put on the accommodating shelves or well-fitted wardrobes. Through the eyes of Khadra, for example, a Somalian asylum seeker, young children are depicted as attempting to 'capture' the buildings as part of a community project, using home made pinhole cameras made from shoeboxes and tin cans:

> Khadra remembered standing with the same woman in the dark room on the twenty-seventh floor of the YMCA and developing her own pinhole photographs, seeing the skewed, silent images her camera had created. She remembered, too, watching Red Road appear on the silent walls and

---

[120] Alison Irvine, *This Road Is Red* (Edinburgh: Luath, 2011), pp. 12–13.
[121] Irvine, *This Road Is Red*, p. 54.

ceiling of another dark room and gasping at the fine magic of the Camera
Obscura; ... It was a delicate art and one that had given her solace in the
dark years of her asylum.[122]

This image invokes the possible reappropriation of narratives of this space
through the subjective viewpoints of its latest tenants, for whom, in
Britain, claims to a rooted history and architectural tradition are all but
luxuries. The refugees' home made use of the Camera Obscura – that
quintessential nineteenth-century mode of representing the world – strikes
a poignant note, highlighting the way in which representational forms are
adopted, transformed and reinterpreted to present new subjectivities,
modes of perception and possible stories of place and identity.

Thus while the dominant ideology or discourse about home ownership
manages to make social housing seem residual at best, although more often
in fact peripheral, the narratives and stories centred on, or projected
against, mass housing estates are in fact key to any consideration of
twentieth- and early twenty-first-century British society. As Peter
Stallybrass and Allon White note, with enduring relevance, what is 'socially
peripheral is so frequently symbolically central'.[123] Writing about their
research into a number of white working-class Norwich housing estates,
Rogaly and Taylor make the more broadly significant point that

> rather than being a bounded and isolated outpost of deprivation on the
> edge of a provincial city, the Norwich estates were intimately tied to
> the deep structural changes of the twentieth century. There was not a life
> revealed to us that had not been affected by the expansions and contractions
> of the state, by the shifts from the mid-1970s towards a neo-liberal deregu-
> lation of the labour market and consequent re-regulation of workplace
> relations, nor by profound changes in experiences of class, gender relations
> and cultural expectations.[124]

Recent works which creatively reimagine the landscape of the estate – such
as Irvine's *Red Road* – serve to disrupt the set of images that have
frequently been recycled to characterise the story of council housing and
mass housing developments: from the 'dark blot' of the slums, to the clean
lines of postwar housing estates, to the 'sink' estate. These accounts that
take into consideration the subjectivity and viewpoints of particular individuals in specific circumstances result in portraits of mass housing estates
that, against the dominant narrative, reveal images of heterogeneity,
ambivalence and difference.

---

[122] Irvine, *This Road Is Red*, p. 277.   [123] Stallybrass and White, *Politics*, p. 5.
[124] Rogaly and Taylor, *Moving Histories*, p. 3.

Conclusion
Housing questions

From the nineteenth century, debates and narratives about housing have provided a context as well as a metaphor for understanding class relations and social division. Indeed, many recent invocations of a 'housing crisis' suggest a cyclical return to conditions of inequity that the welfare state was supposed to guard against. As the chief executive of the Joseph Rowntree Foundation, Julia Unwin, recently noted:

> At the turn of the 20th century, the free market had provided squalid slums. We undoubtedly face the re-creation of slums, the enrichment of bad landlords, the risk of people being destitute. Beveridge had soup kitchens. We have food banks. We've got something that does take us back full circle, a deep divide in way of life between people who are reasonably well off and those who are poor. There's always been a difference, but the distinction seems to be more stark now.[1]

In this instance, the slum functions discursively, as it has previously, as a byword for the widening chasm between rich and poor – one that recalls Benjamin Disraeli's image of 'two nations' who are as remote from each other 'as if they were dwellers in different zones, or inhabitants of different planets'.[2] Yet it is debatable whether the current crisis really is simply a question of a 'return' to Victorian conditions of inequity expressed through housing. For as this book has demonstrated in various ways, for many people living in Britain, the problem of insecure and destitute housing conditions has never gone away. For the tenants of Victorian slum housing, for those affected by the various displacements and housing shortages during and after the Second World War, for the inhabitants of ill-maintained or badly designed housing estates, there has always been a housing crisis. Indeed, it may be that this rhetorical turn simply signals the

[1] Julia Unwin, quoted in Meek, 'Where Will We Live?'
[2] Benjamin Disraeli, *Sybil; Or, The Two Nations* (London: Henry Colburn, 1845), p. 149.

moment when the political issue of dwelling has, so to speak, hit home for the metropolitan middle classes. As another commenter notes:

> The cliché is that Britain has a housing crisis. It doesn't: rather it has a whole series of different housing crises. In Northern Ireland huge swaths of homeowners remain in negative equity after the credit crunch. In Liverpool the problem isn't of expensive housing, but of residents in Anfield and Granby fighting to maintain some say in what happens to their neighbourhoods. And in London the problem is that it is now almost impossible for anyone coming to the city to buy here, or increasingly to rent somewhere decent, either.[3]

But if the housing crisis itself is more multiple and localised than the phrase implies, it is nevertheless clear that its repeated invocation has prompted widespread public reflection on dwellings as affective, symbolic and emotional spaces. For even though the right to adequate 'housing' is enshrined in the Universal Declaration of Human Rights, recent debates have touched upon the wider question of homes as spaces which should afford dignity, privacy and the choice to live with (or away from) people, even in contexts of economic hardship and poverty.[4]

This issue was recently brought to the fore by the introduction of the 'Bedroom Tax' in Britain (which the Coalition Government attempted to rename, in another deceptive domestic metaphor, as the 'Removal of Spare Room Subsidy'). As a matter of policy, from 2013, council and housing association tenants' Housing Benefit Entitlement was substantially cut if they occupied a property with one or more spare bedrooms. The so-called bedroom tax thus has pernicious economic and ideological effects; penalising those who have the least amount of money to spend on their homes, it also ensures that the class semiotics of living space – functional and rigidly quantified for the poor, capacious and richly symbolic for the wealthy – endures.[5]

But over and against the reinvoked discourse of 'crisis', there is also evidence of a more optimistic and progressive rethinking of forms of dwelling in the new millennium, as evinced, for example, by a surge of innovative and ecological co-housing schemes. There may also be the

---

[3] Aditya Chakrabortty, www.theguardian.com/society/2014/nov/19/new-era-estate-scandal-london-families-international-speculators.

[4] See Article 25 of the Universal Declaration of Human Rights, www.un.org/en/documents/udhr/.

[5] See, for example, Michael Rosen's personal response to the tax in relation to the function of the 'spare room' in the context of family bereavement; 'Bedroom Tax Plans Are a Levy on the Grief of the Poor', *Guardian*, 14 January 2014, www.theguardian.com/commentisfree/2014/jan/14/bedroom-tax-death-leveller.

beginnings of a key cultural shift which has forced a timely re-evaluation not only of the history of council housing but of its material benefits too. This was strikingly illustrated in the case of the sale of the New Era housing estate in Hoxton, London, and the residents' successful protest against their threatened eviction (in order that the flats could be re-let at full-market value).[6] It was not just the victory that was significant – nor the distinctive gendered nature of the commentary surrounding this collective protest – but the noticeable shift in the portrayal of social housing. Throughout the campaign and its media reportage, the fortuitously named New Era estate was actively defended as a site of history and community, qualities which had, at another time and in a different political context, been seen as precisely absent from this housing environment. The collective achievement of the protestors, and the fact that social housing was defended in the interests of a common good, may mark an emergent valorisation of a resource defined in terms of the 'social' – a term which one critic has called '*the* keyword in the discourse of many contemporary opponents of neo-liberalism [and] transnational resistances to capitalist globalization'.[7]

My book has argued that housing and interiors are defined by the idea of the social, a term which urges a move away from a focus on the domestic interior as primarily the locus for thinking about the individual and an object-filled private life. Emphasising by turn the sociality of the interior sphere, and the affective and oddly intimate ways in which shared structures of homes of all kinds are inscribed in social commentary and literature, this book has shown that there are no easy distinctions to be made between interiors and exteriors, or insiders and outsiders. My analysis of the relations between forms of housing and identity has been rooted in an awareness that architectural forms in Britain – tenements, suburban semis, tower blocks – produce their own semiotic codes which often pre-emptively narrate a particular kind of story even before the interior, or occupant, is glimpsed. Although the notion that class is inscribed into the landscape, or that you are where you live, is powerfully articulated through

---

[6] The campaign against the eviction plans was led by Lindsey Garrett and a group of female residents (repeatedly characterised as 'single mothers' in media reports) against not a single landlord but rather Westbrook, an asset management investment firm based in New York in a twenty-first century, globalised version of absentee landlordism. The campaign led to investors eventually transferring ownership of the estate to a London-based affordable housing group committed to providing low-cost rented homes.

[7] Richard Johnson, see 'Socialism', in Tony Bennett, Lawrence Grossberg and Meaghan Morris (eds.), *New Keywords: A Revised Vocabulary of Culture and Society* (Oxford: Blackwell, 2005), p. 326.

a variety of popular, cultural and political rhetoric and images, many of the texts surveyed in this book show that this ideology needs to be treated with caution. For while interiors and housing may well be underpinned by longstanding and persuasive mythologies, attention to the intricacy of people's engagements with specific dwelling places can undermine theories of the determinist role of place. Such refocusing helps to destabilise the liberal (and neoliberal) idea that the domestic interior is simply and necessarily a product of choice and, by extension, expressive of the self.

So while much writing on domestic space produces narratives of correspondence that are structured by an aesthetics of symmetry and reflection, I have shown that there is good reason to think more closely about dislocation, paradox and strangeness. For considering these disjunctures and mismatches between people and places is a way of resisting the ideology of the home as a mimetic or 'reflective' space from which individual or social character may be read. Indeed, as has been made clear in this book, such disconnection is common in examples such as the marked contrast between exterior descriptions of houses and the people who reside within; evidence of privacy and homeliness in the Victorian slums; empty high-rise flats that provide a liberating space for self-expression; and ghosts that appear in urban terraces rather than Victorian country houses. Thus my readings have actively sought out dissonance and irregularity, not only because this provides an alternative to Bachelard's lyrical evocations to *'felicitous space* ... the space we love ... eulogized space', but also because it says something fundamental about housing, interiors and identity: that individuals are not entirely determined by their circumstances and that rooms and interiors may speak volumes about the 'individuality' of their occupant, or may be an entirely redundant messenger.[8] Indeed, I have argued that like the interior itself, subjectivity or identity can be meaningfully traced through the social forms, narratives and structures that articulate, in idiosyncratic and personal ways, our relational lives.

In an extension of this aim to unsettle dominant or normalised ways of reading representations of people in places, this book has moved more marginalised cultural spaces to the centre of debates about home, property and identity. By focusing on domestic spaces that are not part of the traditional panoply of cultural dwelling places – the apparently inexorable British country house, the Gothic mansion, the suburban home, the dwelling places of celebrated writers and artists – this study has portrayed

[8] Bachelard, *Poetics*, p. xxxv.

the different, complex and opaque ways in which housing and lives are underpinned by stories of class and refracted by the specificities of gendered experience. The focus on predominantly working-class domestic spaces and histories also serves to redress a common tendency to draw generalisations about class and gender from middle-class settings and values. But as I have also suggested, there is no monolithic working-class interior, or sense of interiority, that can serve to displace the persistent model of bourgeois interiority. For the 'other' interiors of the slum, boarding-house, postwar home and council estate offer a variety of heterogeneous tales of shelter and lack of hospitality, belonging and estrangement, solidarity and loneliness, haunted spaces and blank canvases. Evidently, then, the mythical, apocryphal and oft-invoked idea of 'home', to which all belong and aspire and within which all find their place, is an illusion that renders far less illumination or revelation than its frequent evocation promises. In its stead, it would be more productive to recognise that there is an intricate net of housing types and housing tales that are inherited, altered and refurbished, and that always yield significant social insights into the culture of our times.

Bibliography

Primary material

Acorn, George, *One of the Multitude* (New York: Dodd, Mead & Company, 1912)

Ali, Monica, *Brick Lane* (New York: Scribner, 2003)

Beames, Thomas, *The Rookeries of London: Past, Present, and Prospective* (London: Thomas Bosworth, 1852)

Booth, Charles, *Life and Labour of the People in London*, 2nd edn. (London: Macmillan & Co., 1902), First Series, vol. II

   Life and Labour of the People in London, 2nd edn. (London: Macmillan & Co., 1902), Third Series, vol. I

Browne, Anthony, *Hansel and Gretel* (London: Walker, 2008)

Deane, Seamus, *Reading in the Dark* (London: Vintage, 1997)

Dickens, Charles, 'The Boarding House', in Michael Slater (ed.), *Sketches by Boz and Other Early Papers, 1833–39* (Columbus: Ohio State University Press, 1994)

Disraeli, Benjamin, *Sybil; Or, The Two Nations* (London: Henry Colburn, 1845)

Eagleton, Terry, *The Gatekeeper: A Memoir* (London: Penguin, 2003)

Eliot, George, *The Mill on the Floss* (London: Penguin, 1985)

Eliot, T. S., *Collected Poems, 1909–1962* (London: Faber & Faber, 1974)

Evaristo, Bernardine, *Lara*, new edn. (Tarset: Bloodaxe, 2009)

Friswell, James Hain, *Houses With the Fronts Off* (London: James Blackwood, 1854)

Galloway, Janice, *The Trick Is to Keep Breathing* (Mclean Dalkey Archive Press, 1995)

Gavin, Hector, *Sanitary Ramblings: Being Sketches and Illustrations of Bethnal Green* (London: John Churchill, 1848)

Godwin, George, *London Shadows: A Glance at the 'Homes' of the Thousands* (London: George Routledge & Co., 1854)

   Town Swamps and Social Bridges (London: Routledge, Warnes & Routledge, 1859)

Goldman, Willy, *East End My Cradle: Portrait of an Environment* (London: Faber & Faber, 2011)

Greenwood, James, 'A Night in a Workhouse', in Peter Keating (ed.), *Into Unknown England 1866–1913: Selections from the Social Explorers* (London: Fontana, 1976), pp. 33–54

Hamilton, Patrick, *Twenty Thousand Streets Under the Sky* (London: Vintage, 2004)

The Slaves of Solitude (New York: NYRB Classics, 2007)

Hanley, Lynsey, *Estates: An Intimate History* (London: Granta, 2008)

Hill, Octavia, *Homes of the London Poor* (New York: State Charities Aid Association, 1875)

Hoggart, Richard, *The Uses of Literacy: Aspects of Working-Class Life with Special Reference to Publications and Entertainments* (London: Penguin, 1991)

Irvine, Alison, *This Road Is Red* (Edinburgh: Luath, 2011)

Joyce, James, *Dubliners* (New York: Penguin Classics, 1993)

Kelman, James, *Busted Scotch* (New York: W. W. Norton & Company, 1997)

Kuhn, Annette, *Family Secrets: Acts of Memory and Imagination*, new edn. (London: Verso, 2002)

Law, John [Margaret Harkness], *In Darkest London, Captain Lobe* (London: Bellamy Library, 1891)

Levy, Andrea, *Every Light in the House Burnin'* (London: Review, 1995)

Never Far From Nowhere (London: Review, 1996)

Small Island (London: Review, 2004)

London, Jack, *The People of the Abyss* (London: Macmillan & Co., 1903)

Macaulay, Rose, 'Miss Anstruther's Letters', in Anne Boston (ed.), *Wave Me Goodbye: Stories of the Second World War* (London: Penguin, 1989), pp. 65–73

Mantel, Hilary, *Giving Up the Ghost: A Memoir* (London: Fourth Estate, 2003)

Mayhew, Henry, *London Characters and the Humorous Side of London Life* (London: Stanley Rivers & Co., 1871)

'Home is Home, Be It Never So Homely', in Viscount Ingestre (ed.), *Meliora, or Better Times to Come* (London: Frank Cass, 1971), pp. 258–80

The Morning Chronicle Survey of Labour and the Poor: The Metropolitan Districts, vols. I–VI (Horsham: Caliban Books, 1981)

London Labour and the London Poor (London: Penguin, 1985)

Mearns, Andrew, *The Bitter Cry of Outcast London: An Enquiry into the Condition of the Abject Poor* (London: James Clarke & Co., 1883)

Michael, Livi, *Under a Thin Moon* (London: Martin Secker & Warburg, 1992)

Moore, Brian, *The Lonely Passion of Judith Hearne* (New York: NYRB Classics, 2010)

Naipaul, V. S., *The Mimic Men* (New York: Vintage International, 2001)

O'Mara, Pat, *The Autobiography of a Liverpool Irish Slummy* (London: Martin Hopkinson, 1934)

Orwell, George, *The Road to Wigan Pier* (San Diego: Harcourt, 1958)

Parker, Tony, *The People of Providence: A Housing Estate and Some of Its Inhabitants* (London: Eland, 1996)

Sage, Lorna, *Bad Blood* (London: Fourth Estate, 2000)

Selvon, Sam, *The Lonely Londoners* (Harlow: Longman, 1985)

Sims, George, *How the Poor Live; and, Horrible London* (London: Chatto & Windus, 1889)

The Sketch, 'The "Modern Art" Boarding House: Kensington "Frescoed"', 12 February 1930, p. 280

Soyinka, Wole, 'Telephone Conversation', in Gerald Moore and Ulli Beier (eds.), *The Penguin Book of Modern African Poetry*, 3rd edn. (Harmondsworth: Penguin, 1984)

Steedman, Carolyn, *Landscape for a Good Woman: A Story of Two Lives* (London: Virago, 1986)

Syal, Meera, *Anita and Me* (London: Harper Perennial, 2004)

Vaux, James Hardy, *Memoirs of James Hardy Vaux*, 2nd edn. (London: Hunt & Clarke, 1827)

Walkerdine, Valerie, 'Dreams from an Ordinary Childhood', in Liz Heron (ed.), *Truth, Dare or Promise*, pp. 63–77

Waters, Sarah, *The Night Watch* (London: Virago, 2006)
The Paying Guests (London: Virago, 2014)

Whiteread, Rachel, 'House' (1993–94)

Williams, Raymond, *Border Country* (Cardigan: Parthian Press, 2006)

Winterson, Jeanette, *Why Be Happy When You Could Be Normal?* (London: Vintage, 2012)

Woodward, Kathleen, *Jipping Street: Childhood in a London Slum* (New York: Harper & Brothers, 1928)

Woolf, Virginia, *A Room of One's Own* (London: Penguin, 1945)
'Old Bloomsbury', in Jeanne Schulkind (ed.), *Moments of Being* (London: Grafton, 1978), pp. 159–79

Secondary material

Alexander, Sally, 'Room of One's Own: 1920s Feminist Utopias', *Women: A Cultural Review* 11:3 (2000), 273–88

Alison, Jane, 'The Surreal House', in Jane Alison (ed.), *The Surreal House* (New Haven: Yale University Press, 2010), pp. 14–33

Armstrong, Isobel, *Victorian Glassworlds: Glass Culture and the Imagination, 1830–1880* (Oxford: Oxford University Press, 2008)

Artificial Eye Film Company, *Fish Tank* press book, www.artificial-eye.com/database/cinema/fishtank/pdf/pressbook.pdf

Attfield, Judy, 'Inside Pram Town: A Case Study of Harlow House Interiors, 1951–61', in Judy Attfield and Pat Kirkham (eds.), *A View from the Interior: Women & Design*, 2nd edn. (London: Kirkham, 1995), pp. 215–38

Aynsley, Jeremy, and Charlotte Grant (eds.), *Imagined Interiors: Representing the Domestic Interior Since the Renaissance* (London: V&A, 2006)

Bachelard, Gaston, *The Poetics of Space*, Maria Jolas (trans.), (Boston: Beacon, 1994)

Back, Les, *New Ethnicities and Urban Culture: Racisms and Multiculture in Young Lives* (London: Routledge, 1996)

Ball, John Clement, 'Immigration and Postwar London Literature', in Lawrence Manley (ed.), *The Cambridge Companion to the Literature of London* (Cambridge: Cambridge University Press, 2011), pp. 222–40

Behlmer, George K., *Friends of the Family: The English Home and Its Guardians, 1850–1940* (Stanford: Stanford University Press, 1998)

Benjamin, Walter, *Charles Baudelaire: A Lyric Poet in the Era of High Capitalism*, Harry Zohn (trans.), (London: Verso, 1983)

'I [The Interior, The Trace]', in Rolf Tiedemann (ed.), *The Arcades Project*, Howard Eiland and Kevin McLaughlin (trans.), (Cambridge: Belknap, 2002), pp. 212–27

Bettelheim, Bruno, *The Uses of Enchantment: The Meaning and Importance of Fairy Tales* (London: Penguin, 1991)

Boone, Troy, *Youth of Darkest England: Working-Class Children at the Heart of the Victorian Empire* (New York: Routledge, 2005)

Borzello, Frances, *At Home: The Domestic Interior in Art* (New York: Thames & Hudson, 2006)

Botting, Fred, *Gothic* (London: Routledge, 1996)

Bourdieu, Pierre, *Distinction: A Social Critique of the Judgement of Taste*, Richard Nice (trans.), (London: Routledge & Kegan Paul, 1984)

'Social Space and Symbolic Power', *Sociological Theory* 7:1 (1989), 14–25

Brewster, Scott, 'Building, Dwelling, Moving: Seamus Heaney, Tom Paulin and the Reverse Aesthetic', in Gerry Smyth and Jo Croft (eds.), *Our House*, pp. 141–59

Briganti, Chiara, and Kathy Mezei, 'Reading the House: A Literary Perspective', *Signs* 27:3 (2002), 837–46

The Domestic Space Reader (Toronto: University of Toronto Press, 2012)

Brooks, Peter, *Body Work: Objects of Desire in Modern Narrative* (Cambridge: Harvard University Press, 1993)

Brophy, Sarah, 'Entangled Genealogies: White Femininity on the Threshold of Change in Andrea Levy's Small Island', *Contemporary Women's Writing* 4:2 (2010), 100–13

Brown, Julia Prewitt, *The Bourgeois Interior: How the Middle Class Imagines Itself in Literature and Film* (Charlottesville: University of Virginia Press, 2008)

Brown, Richard, and Gregory Castle, '"The Instinct of the Celibate": Boarding and Borderlines in "The Boarding House"', in Vicki Mahaffey (ed.), *Collaborative Dubliners: Joyce in Dialogue* (Syracuse: Syracuse University Press, 2012), pp. 144–63

Bryden, Inga, and Janet Floyd (eds.), *Domestic Space: Reading the Nineteenth-Century Interior* (Manchester: Manchester University Press, 1999)

Burnett, John (ed.), *Useful Toil: Autobiographies of Working People from the 1820s to the 1920s* (London: Allen Lane, 1974)

A Social History of Housing: 1815–1970 (London: Methuen, 1980)

Cameron, Stuart, and Andrew Field, 'Community, Ethnicity and Neighbourhood', *Housing Studies* 15:6 (2000), 827–43

Chodorow, Nancy, *The Reproduction of Mothering: Psychoanalysis and the Sociology of Gender* (Berkeley: University of California Press, 1978)

Chu, Ben, *The Independent*, 9 February 2014, www.independent.co.uk/property/house-and-home/property/britain-is-suffering-from-a-housing-crisis–who-is-to-blame-and-how-can-we-fix-it-9113329.html

Cleere, Eileen, 'Victorian Dust-Traps', in William A. Cohen and Ryan Johnson (eds.), *Filth*, pp. 133–54

Coates, Ken, and Richard Silburn, *Poverty: The Forgotten Englishmen* (Nottingham: Spokesman, 1983)

Cohen, Deborah, *Household Gods: The British and Their Possessions* (New Haven: Yale University Press, 2006)

Cohen, Monica, *Professional Domesticity in the Victorian Novel: Women, Work and Home* (Cambridge: Cambridge University Press, 1998)

Cohen, William A., and Ryan Johnson (eds.), *Filth: Dirt, Disgust, and Modern Life* (Minneapolis: University of Minnesota Press, 2005)

Collins, Patricia Hill, *Black Feminist Thought: Knowledge, Consciousness, and the Politics of Empowerment*, 2nd edn. (New York: Routledge, 2000)

Corbin, Alain, *The Foul and the Fragrant: Odor and the French Social Imagination* (Leamington Spa: Berg, 1986)

Corbusier, Le, *Towards a New Architecture*, Frederick Etchells (trans.), (New York: Dover Publications, 1986)

Cormack, Alistair, 'Migration and the Politics of Narrative Form: Realism and the Postcolonial Subject in Brick Lane', *Contemporary Literature* 47:4 (2006), 695–721

Corner, John, 'An Interview with Richard Hoggart: Studying Culture: Reflections and Assessments', in Richard Hoggart, *The Uses of Literacy*, pp. 379–99

Davidoff, Leonore, 'The Separation of Home and Work? Landladies and Lodgers in Nineteenth- and Twentieth-Century England', in Sandra Burman (ed.), *Fit Work for Women* (New York: St Martin's Press, 1979), pp. 64–97

Davidoff, Leonore, and Catherine Hall, *Family Fortunes: Men and Women of the English Middle Class, 1780–1850* (Chicago: University of Chicago Press, 1987)

Dawe, Gerald, 'The Revenges of the Heart: Belfast and the Poetics of Space', in Nicholas Allen and Aaron Kelly (eds.), *The Cities of Belfast* (Dublin: Four Courts Press, 2003), pp. 199–210

Deane, Seamus, 'Why Bogside?', *The Honest Ulsterman* 27 (1971), 1–8

  Strange Country: Modernity and Nationhood in Irish Writing Since 1790 (Oxford: Oxford University Press, 1997)

  'Dead Ends: Joyce's Finest Moments', in Derek Attridge and Marjorie Howes (eds.), *Semicolonial Joyce* (Cambridge: Cambridge University Press, 2000), pp. 21–36

Domosh, Mona, and Joni Seager, *Putting Women in Place: Feminist Geographers Make Sense of the World* (New York: Guilford Press, 2001)

Donald, Moira, 'Tranquil Havens? Critiquing the Idea of Home as the Middle-Class Sanctuary', in Inga Bryden and Janet Floyd (eds.), *Domestic Space*, pp. 103–20

Eagleton, Terry, *Heathcliff and the Great Hunger: Studies in Irish Culture* (London: Verso, 1995)

  'The Bogside Bard', *New Statesman*, 30 August 1996, p. 46

Fitzpatrick, Maurice, *The Boys of St Columb's* (Dublin: Liffey Press, 2010)

Fraser, Nick, 'A Kind of Life Sentence', *Guardian*, 28 October 1996, p. 9

Freud, Sigmund, 'The "Uncanny"', in James Strachey et al. (eds. and trans.), *The Standard Edition of the Complete Psychological Works of Sigmund Freud*, vol. XVII (London: Hogarth, 1955), pp. 217–52

Fuss, Diana, *The Sense of an Interior: Four Writers and the Rooms That Shaped Them* (New York: Routledge, 2004)

Gagnier, Regenia, *Subjectivities: A History of Self-Representation in Britain, 1832–1920* (New York: Oxford University Press, 1991)

Gamble, Sarah, 'North-East Gothic: Surveying Gender in Pat Barker's Fiction', *Gothic Studies* 9:2 (2007), 71–82

Gibson, Sarah, 'Accommodating Strangers: British Hospitality and the Asylum Hotel Debate', *Journal for Cultural Research* 7:4 (2003), 367–86

Giles, Judy, *The Parlour and the Suburb: Domestic Identities, Class, Femininity and Modernity* (New York: Berg, 2004)

Girard, René, *Deceit, Desire, and the Novel: Self and Other in Literary Structure*, Yvonne Freccero (trans.), (Baltimore: Johns Hopkins Press, 1965)

Glass, Ruth, *Newcomers: The West Indians in London* (London: Centre for Urban Studies, 1960)

Glendinning, Miles, and Stefan Muthesius, *Tower Block: Modern Public Housing in England, Scotland, Wales and Northern Ireland* (New Haven: Yale University Press, 1994)

Glynn, Sarah, *Where the Other Half Lives: Lower Income Housing in a Neoliberal World* (London: Pluto Press, 2009)

Goldman, Ronald (ed.), *Breakthrough: Autobiographical Accounts of the Education of Some Socially Disadvantaged Children* (Oxon: Routledge, 2012)

Gordon, Mary, 'Afterword', in Brian Moore, *The Lonely Passion of Judith Hearne* (New York: NYRB Classics, 2010), pp. 225–30

Grant, Charlotte, 'Reading the House of Fiction: From Object to Interior, 1720–1920', *Home Cultures* 2:3 (2005), 233–50

Hall, Peter, *Cities of Tomorrow: An Intellectual History of Urban Planning and Design in the Twentieth Century*, 3rd edn. (Oxford: Blackwell, 2002)

Hall, Stuart, 'The Rediscovery of "Ideology": Return of the Repressed in Media Studies', in Michael Gurevitch, Tony Bennett, James Curran and Janet Woollacott (eds.), *Culture, Society and the Media* (London: Methuen, 1982), pp. 56–90

'Reconstruction Work: Images of Post-War Black Settlement', in Ben Highmore (ed.), *The Everyday Life Reader* (London: Routledge, 2002), pp. 251–61

Hamlett, Jane, *Material Relations: Domestic Interiors and Middle-Class Families in England, 1850–1910* (Manchester: Manchester University Press, 2010)

Hamnett, Chris, *Unequal City: London in the Global Arena* (London: Routledge, 2003)

Harrison, Paul, *Inside the Inner City: Life Under the Cutting Edge*, rev. ed. (London: Penguin, 1992)

Harte, Liam, 'History Lessons: Postcolonialism and Seamus Deane's Reading in the Dark', *Irish University Review* 30:1 (2000), 149–62

The Literature of the Irish in Britain: Autobiography and Memoir, 1725–2001 (Basingstoke: Palgrave Macmillan, 2009)

Haslam, Richard, 'Gothic: A Rhetorical Hermeneutics Approach', *Irish Journal of Gothic and Horror Studies* 2 (2007), http://irishgothichorrorjournal .homestead.com/IrishGothicHaslam.html

Heron, Liz (ed.), *Truth, Dare or Promise: Girls Growing Up in the 50s* (London: Virago, 1985)

Hewitt, Martin, 'District Visiting and the Constitution of Domestic Space in the Mid-Nineteenth Century', in Inga Bryden and Janet Floyd (eds.), *Domestic Space*, pp. 121–41

Higson, Andrew, 'Space, Place, Spectacle: Landscape and Townscape in the "Kitchen Sink" Film', in Andrew Higson (ed.), *Dissolving Views: Key Writings on British Cinema* (London: Cassell, 1996), pp. 133–56

hooks, bell, *Where We Stand: Class Matters* (New York: Routledge, 2000)

Hornsey, Richard, *The Spiv and the Architect: Unruly Life in Postwar London* (Minneapolis: University of Minnesota Press, 2010)

Jameson, Fredric, *The Political Unconscious: Narrative as a Socially Symbolic Act* (London: Routledge, 1996)

Johnson, Richard, 'Socialism', in Tony Bennett, Lawrence Grossberg and Meaghan Morris (eds.), *New Keywords: A Revised Vocabulary of Culture and Society* (Oxford: Blackwell, 2005), pp. 324–6

Jones, Owen, *Chavs: The Demonization of the Working Class* (London: Verso, 2011)

Joshi, Priti, 'The Dual Work of "Wastes" in Chadwick's *Sanitary Report*', University of California, Santa Cruz, http://omf.ucsc.edu/london-1865/ victorian-city/sanitary-report.html

Kabeer, Naila, *The Power to Choose: Bangladeshi Women and Labour Market Decisions in London and Dhaka* (London: Verso, 2000)

Kahane, Claire, 'The Gothic Mirror', in Shirley Nelson Garner, Claire Kahane and Madelon Sprengnether (eds.), *The (M)other Tongue: Essays in Feminist Psychoanalytic Interpretation* (Ithaca: Cornell University Press, 1985), pp. 334–51

Kay, Alison C., 'A Little Enterprise of Her Own: Lodging-House Keeping and the Accommodation Business in Nineteenth-Century London', *London Journal* 28:2 (2003), 41–53

Kelley, Victoria, *Soap and Water: Cleanliness, Dirt and the Working Classes in Victorian and Edwardian Britain* (London: I.B. Tauris, 2010)

King, Peter, 'The Room to Panic: An Example of Film Criticism and Housing Research', *Housing, Theory and Society* 21:1 (2004), 27–35

Kirk, John, *Twentieth-Century Writing and the British Working Class* (Cardiff: University of Wales Press, 2003)

Kirkland, Richard, 'Reading the Rookery: The Social Meaning of an Irish Slum in Nineteenth-Century London', *New Hibernia Review* 16:1 (2012), 16–30

Koven, Seth, *Slumming: Sexual and Social Politics in Victorian London* (Princeton, New Jersey: Princeton University Press, 2004)

Kynaston, David, *Austerity Britain, 1945–51* (London: Bloomsbury, 2007)

Lejeune, Philippe, 'The Autobiographical Contract', in Tzvetan Todorov (ed.), *French Literary Theory Today*, R. Carter (trans.), (Cambridge: Cambridge University Press, 1982), pp. 192–222

Light, Alison, *Forever England: Femininity, Literature, and Conservatism Between the Wars* (London: Routledge, 1991)

Livesey, Ruth, 'Reading for Character: Women Social Reformers and Narratives of the Urban Poor in Late Victorian and Edwardian London', *Journal of Victorian Culture* 9 (2004), 43–67

Lodge, David, 'Introduction', in Hamilton, *The Slaves of Solitude*, pp. vii–xviii

Luthra, Mohan, *Britain's Black Population: Social Change, Public Policy and Agenda*, 3rd edn. (Aldershot: Arena, 1997)

Maleuvre, Didier, *Museum Memories: History, Technology, Art* (Stanford: Stanford University Press, 1999)

Malpass, Peter, *Housing and the Welfare State: The Development of Housing Policy in Britain* (Basingstoke: Palgrave Macmillan, 2005)

Marcus, Sharon, *Apartment Stories: City and Home in Nineteenth-Century Paris and London* (Berkeley: University of California Press, 1999)

Marcus, Steven, 'Reading the Illegible', in H. J. Dyos and Michael Wolff (eds.), *The Victorian City: Images and Reality*, vol. I (London: Routledge Kegan & Paul, 1973), pp. 257–76

Marx, Karl, *Economic and Philosophical Manuscripts*, in Karl Marx, *Early Writings*, Rodney Livingstone and Gregor Benton (trans.), (London: Penguin, 1992)

Massey, Doreen, *Space, Place, and Gender* (Minneapolis: University of Minnesota Press, 1994)

McClintock, Anne, *Imperial Leather: Race, Gender and Sexuality in the Colonial Contest* (New York: Routledge, 1995)

McCuskey, Brian, 'Not at Home: Servants, Scholars, and the Uncanny', *PMLA* 121:2 (2006), 421–36

McGlynn, Mary M., *Narratives of Class in New Irish and Scottish Literature: From Joyce to Kelman, Doyle, Galloway, and McNamee* (Basingstoke: Palgrave Macmillan, 2008)

McKenzie, Lisa, *Getting By: Estates, Class and Culture in Austerity Britain* (Bristol, Policy Press, 2015)

McMillan, Michael, 'The "West Indian" Front Room: Migrant Aesthetics in the Home', in Jeremy Aynsley and Charlotte Grant (eds.), *Imagined Interiors*, pp. 256–57

'The "West Indian" Front Room: Reflections on a Diasporic Phenomenon', *Small Axe* 28 (2009), 135–56

Meek, James, 'Where Will We Live?', *London Review of Books* 36:1 (2014), www.lrb.co.uk/v36/no1/james-meek/where-will-we-live

Mengham, Rod, '"Anthropology at Home": Domestic Interiors in British Film and Fiction of the 1930s and 1940s', in Jeremy Aynsley and Charlotte Grant (eds.), *Imagined Interiors*, pp. 244–45

Minton, Anna, *Ground Control: Fear and Happiness in the Twenty-First-Century City* (London: Penguin, 2009)

Moran, Joe, 'Housing, Memory and Everyday Life in Contemporary Britain', *Cultural Studies* 18:4 (2004), 607–27

Moretti, Franco, *The Way of the World: The Bildungsroman in European Culture*, new ed. (London: Verso, 2000)

Mort, Frank, 'Scandalous Events: Metropolitan Culture and Moral Change in Post-Second World War London', *Representations* 93:1 (2006), 106–37

Mulvey-Roberts, Marie, 'Dracula and the Doctors: Bad Blood, Menstrual Taboo and the New Woman', in William Hughes and Andrew Smith (eds.), *Bram Stoker: History, Psychoanalysis and the Gothic* (Basingstoke: Macmillan, 1998), pp. 78–95

Owens, Alastair, Nigel Jeffries, Karen Wehner and Rupert Featherby, 'Fragments of the Modern City: Material Culture and the Rhythms of Everyday Life in Victorian London', *Journal of Victorian Culture* 15:2 (2010), 212–25

Panayi, Panikos (ed.), *The Impact of Immigration: A Documentary History of the Effects and Experiences of Immigrants in Britain Since 1945* (Manchester: Manchester University Press, 1999)

Patterson, Nicholas, 'An Interview with Seamus Deane', *The Boston Phoenix*, 8 June 1998, http://weeklywire.com/ww/06–08-98/boston_books_1.html

Patterson, Sheila, *Dark Strangers: A Sociological Study of the Absorption of a Recent West Indian Migrant Group in Brixton, South London* (London: Tavistock, 1963)

Poovey, Mary, *Making a Social Body: British Cultural Formation, 1830–1864* (Chicago: University of Chicago Press, 1995)

Power, Anne, *Estates on the Edge: The Social Consequences of Mass Housing in Northern Europe* (Basingstoke: Macmillan Press, 1997)

Procter, James, *Dwelling Places: Postwar Black British Writing* (Manchester: Manchester University Press, 2003)

Ramdin, Ron, *The Making of the Black Working Class in Britain* (Aldershot: Gower, 1987)

Ravetz, Alison, *Model Estate: Planned Housing at Quarry Hill, Leeds* (London: Croom Helm, 1974)

'A View from the Interior', in Judy Attfield and Pat Kirkham (eds.), *A View from the Interior*, pp. 187–205

Council Housing and Culture: The History of a Social Experiment (London: Routledge, 2001)

Rewald, Sabine, *Rooms With a View: The Open Window in the 19th Century* (New York: Metropolitan Museum of Art, 2011)

Rice, Charles, 'Rethinking Histories of the Interior', *The Journal of Architecture* 9 (2004), 275–87

Roddy, Sarah, Julie-Marie Strange and Bertrand Taithe, 'Henry Mayhew at 200 – The "Other" Victorian Bicentenary', *Journal of Victorian Culture* 19:4 (2014), 481–96

Rogaly, Ben, and Becky Taylor, *Moving Histories of Class and Community: Identity, Place and Belonging in Contemporary England* (Basingstoke: Palgrave Macmillan, 2009)

Rose, Gillian, *Feminism & Geography: The Limits of Geographical Knowledge* (Minneapolis: University of Minnesota Press, 1993)

Rose, Jonathan, *The Intellectual Life of the British Working Classes*, 2nd edn. (New Haven: Yale University Press, 2010)

Rosello, Mireille, *Postcolonial Hospitality: The Immigrant as Guest* (Stanford: Stanford University Press, 2001)

Rosen, Michael, 'Bedroom Tax Plans Are a Levy on the Grief of the Poor', *Guardian*, 14 January 2014, www.theguardian.com/commentisfree/2014/jan/14/bedroom-tax-death-leveller

Rosner, Victoria, *Modernism and the Architecture of Private Life* (New York: Columbia University Press, 2008)

Ross, Andrew, 'Irish Secrets and Lies', *Salon*, 11 April 1997, www.unz.org/Pub/Salon-1997apr-00017

Royle, Nicholas, *The Uncanny: An Introduction* (Manchester: Manchester University Press, 2002)

Rumens, Carol, 'Reading Deane', *Fortnight*, July/August 1997, pp. 28–30

Sedgwick, Eve Kosofsky, *Between Men: English Literature and Male Homosocial Desire* (New York: Columbia University Press, 1985)

Tendencies (London: Routledge, 1994)

Seed, John, 'Did the Subaltern Speak? Mayhew and the Coster-Girl', *Journal of Victorian Culture* 19:4 (2014), 536–49

Sennett, Richard, *The Fall of Public Man* (London: Penguin, 2002)

Slater, Tom, and Ntsiki Anderson, 'The Reputational Ghetto: Territorial Stigmatisation in St Paul's, Bristol', *Transactions of the Institute of British Geographers* 37:4 (2011), 530–46

Smyth, Gerry, and Jo Croft (eds.), *Our House: The Representation of Domestic Space in Modern Culture* (Amsterdam: Rodopi, 2006)

Smyth, Gerry, *Space and the Irish Cultural Imagination* (Basingstoke: Palgrave Macmillan, 2001)

Stallybrass, Peter, and Allon White, *The Politics and Poetics of Transgression* (New York: Cornell University Press, 1986)

Steedman, Carolyn, 'Introduction', in Kathleen Woodward, *Jipping Street* (London: Virago, 1983), vi–xvi

'What a Rag Rug Means', in Inga Bryden and Janet Floyd (eds.), *Domestic Space*, pp. 18–39

'Mayhew: On Reading, About Writing', *Journal of Victorian Culture* 19:4 (2014), 550–61

Stein, Mark, *Black British Literature: Novels of Transformation* (Columbus: Ohio University Press, 2004)

Stewart, Susan, *On Longing: Narratives of the Miniature, the Gigantic, the Souvenir, the Collection*, new ed. (Durham: Duke University Press, 1993)

Taunton, Matthew, *Fictions of the City: Class, Culture and Mass Housing in London and Paris* (Basingstoke: Palgrave Macmillan, 2009)

Toynbee, Polly, *Hard Work: Life in Low-Pay Britain* (London: Bloomsbury, 2003)

Tristam, Philippa, *Living Space in Fact and Fiction* (London: Routledge, 1989)

Trotter, David, 'The New Historicism and the Psychopathology of Everyday Modern Life', in William A. Cohen and Ryan Johnson (eds.), *Filth*, pp. 30–48

Turner, John F. C., 'Housing as a Verb', in John F. C. Turner and Robert Fichter (eds.), *Freedom to Build: Dweller Control of the Housing Process* (New York: Collier Macmillan, 1972), pp. 148–75

Tyler, Imogen, '"Chav Mum Chav Scum": Class Disgust in Contemporary Britain', in *Feminist Media Studies* 8:1 (2008), 17–34

Ulin, Julieann Veronica, 'Fluid Boarders and Naughty Girls: Music, Domesticity, and Nation in Joyce's Boarding Houses', *James Joyce Quarterly* 44:2 (2007), 263–89

Vickery, Amanda, *Behind Closed Doors: At Home in Georgian England* (Yale: Yale University Press, 2009)

Vidler, Anthony, *The Architectural Uncanny: Essays in the Modern Unhomely* (Massachusetts: Massachusetts Institute of Technology Press, 1992)

Vincent, David, *Bread, Knowledge & Freedom: A Study of Nineteenth-Century Working Class Autobiography* (London: Methuen, 1981)

Wacquant, Loïc, 'Territorial Stigmatization in the Age of Advanced Marginality', *Thesis Eleven* 91:1 (2007), 66–77

Walkerdine, Valerie, 'Dreams from an Ordinary Childhood', in Liz Heron (ed.), *Truth, Dare*, pp. 63–77

Walkerdine, Valerie, Helen Lucey and June Melody, *Growing Up Girl: Psycho-Social Explorations of Gender and Class* (Basingstoke: Palgrave, 2001)

Walkowitz, Judith, *City of Dreadful Delight: Narratives of Sexual Danger in Late-Victorian Britain* (Chicago: University of Chicago Press, 1992)

Walton, John K., *The Blackpool Landlady: A Social History* (Manchester: Manchester University Press, 1978)

'The Blackpool Landlady Revisited', *Manchester Region History Review* 8 (1994), 23–31

Walton, John K., and Alastair Wilcox, *Low Life and Moral Improvement in Mid-Victorian England: Liverpool Through the Journalism of Hugh Shimmin* (Leicester: Leicester University Press, 1991)

Warner, Marina, *From the Beast to the Blonde: On Fairy Tales and Their Tellers* (London: Vintage, 1995)

Waters, Sarah, 'Romance Among the Ruins', *Guardian*, 28 January 2006, www.theguardian.com/books/2006/jan/28/fiction.sarahwaters

Watt, Ian, *The Rise of the Novel: Studies in Defoe, Richardson and Fielding* (London: Pimlico, 2000)

Webster, Wendy, *Imagining Home: Gender, 'Race', and National Identity* (London: Routledge, 1998)

Wheeler, Pat, and Sharon Monteith, 'Interview with Livi Michael', *Critical Survey* 12:3 (2000), 94–107

Whitlock, Gillian, 'Disciplining the Child: Recent British Academic Memoir', *a/b: Auto/Biography Studies* 19 (2004), 46–58

Williams, Raymond, *The Country and the City* (Oxford: Oxford University Press, 1973)

Culture & Society: 1780–1950 (New York: Columbia University Press, 1983)
Orwell (London: Fontana, 1984)
Willott, Sara, and Christine Griffin, '"Wham Bam, am I a Man?": Unemployed Men Talk About Masculinities', *Feminism & Psychology* 7:1 (1997), 107–28
Wills, Clair, *Improprieties: Politics and Sexuality in Northern Irish Poetry* (Oxford: Clarendon Press, 1993)
  'Rocking the Cradle? – Women Studies and the Family in Twentieth-Century Ireland', *Bullán* 1:2 (1994), 97–106
Wilson, Elizabeth, 'The Rhetoric of Urban Space', *New Left Review* 209 (1995), 146–60
Wilson, Nicola, 'Reproducing the Home in Robert Tressell's The Ragged Trousered Philanthropists and D. H. Lawrence's Sons and Lovers', *Home Cultures* 2:3 (2005), 299–314
  Home in Working-Class British Writing (Farnham: Ashgate, 2015)
Young, Michael, and Peter Willmott, *Family and Kinship in East London* (Berkeley: University of California Press, 1992)
Ziegler, Philip, *London at War, 1939–45* (New York: Alfred A. Knopf)

Film

The Arbor, dir. by Clio Barnard (Verve Pictures, 2011) [on DVD]
A Taste of Honey, dir. by Tony Richardson (BFI, 2002) [on DVD]
Breaking and Entering, dir. by Anthony Minghella (Weinstein Company, 2007) [on DVD]
Fish Tank, dir. by Andrea Arnold (Artificial Eye, 2009) [on DVD]
Housing Problems, dir. by Edgar Anstey and Arthur Elton, in *Land of Promise: The British Documentary Movement 1930–1950* (BFI, 2008) [on DVD]
Kensington Calling!, dir. by Kensington Housing Trust (1930), www.screenonline.org.uk/film/id/1185130/ [online]
Kes, dir. by Ken Loach (Twentieth Century Fox, 2003) [on DVD]
The Pruitt-Igoe Myth, dir. by Chad Freidrichs (First Run Features, 2011) [on DVD]
Ratcatcher, dir. by Lynne Ramsay (Twentieth Century Fox, 2003) [on DVD]
Red Road, dir. by Andrea Arnold (Verve Pictures, 2007) [on DVD]
The Selfish Giant, dir. by Clio Barnard (Artificial Eye, 2014) [on DVD]
This Sporting Life, dir. by Lindsay Anderson (Network, 2008) [on DVD]

Cited websites

www.writinglives.org/
www.artangel.org.uk/projects/1993/house
www.redroadflats.org.uk
www.un.org/en/documents/udhr/

Index